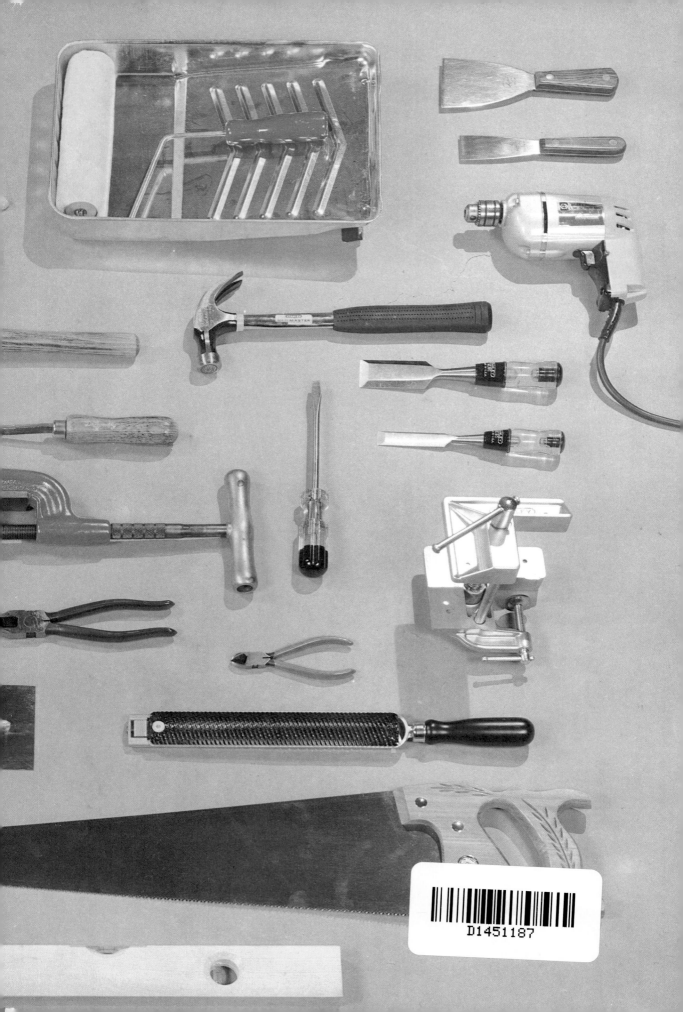

THE
PRACTICAL
HANDYMAN'S
ENCYCLOPEDIA

THE
[PRACTICAL]
HANDYMAN'S
ENCYCLOPEDIA

THE COMPLETE

ILLUSTRATED

[DO IT YOURSELF]

LIBRARY FOR HOME & OUTDOORS

VOLUME SEVEN

 Greystone Press, 100 Sixth Ave., N. Y. 10013, N. Y.

CONTENTS FOR VOLUME SEVEN

	Page
HOW TO PLAN A FOUNDATION	1156
PLANNING AND POURING A SLAB	1160
BASIC HOUSE FRAMING	1164
HEATING FUELS	1170
CONVERTING HEATING FUELS	1174
FUEL SYSTEMS	1176
SERVICING FURNACES	1182
FURNACE ALTERATIONS	1192
OUTDOOR FOLD-AWAY FURNITURE	1194
TWO-TIER END TABLE	1210
FURNITURE WITH METAL LEGS	1214
BUDGET FURNITURE	1220
TEA WAGON	1226
BOY'S ROOM FURNITURE	1228
GIRL'S ROOM FURNITURE	1230
FUSES AND CIRCUIT BREAKERS	1232
BUILDING A GABLE	1240
TABLE TENNIS BASE AND TOP	1254
MODEL TRAIN TABLE	1256
BUILD YOUR OWN GARAGE	1260
BASIC GARDENING PRINCIPLES	1270
SPRING FLOWER BEDS	1276
SUMMER FLOWER BEDS	1280
AQUATIC GARDEN	1284
CUT-FLOWER GARDEN	1288
PLANTING BORDERS	1292
BOX FLOWERS	1298
PLANTING FOR SHADE	1302
NATURAL PLANTING	1304
URBAN FLOWER GARDENS	1306
SEASIDE GARDENS	1312
15 POPULAR FLOWER VARIETIES	1315

Formwork should never be haphazard. Footing forms are being installed for a house addition, above.

How to Plan for a Foundation

SINCE THE HOUSE must forevermore rest on the foundation it is most obvious that this type of project deserves considerable care. The best way to choose an appropriate foundation is to copy the methods and materials used by professionals in your particular area. Climate and soil conditions are not the same throughout the country. In areas of extreme weather conditions, heavy foundations must be set below the frost line. In milder areas and especially where basements are not used, a foundation wall can set 12 in. to 18 in. below grade. This can be a perimeter wall with concrete piers set

between them to support interior loads.

Good idea, in addition to seeing what professional builders are doing, is to check with the local building inspector. He will know what is best for you to do so you can start right with preliminary planning.

Excavation is also very important. The foundation must carry the entire weight of the structure without settling so the soil on which it rests must be stable. If it isn't, then special techniques are in order. Building on soil which is mostly fill, for example, will call for a broader foundation and possibly piers to be sunk down to solid ground. However, and it is worth repeat-

Batter boards do not have to be fancy, but they should be rigid enough to stand up for a while.

Foundation wall, above, was formed with integral ledges for brick veneering and a block facing.

When house is built over a crawl space, the loads between are supported on concrete piers, above.

Future concrete porch floor will be tied to the foundation through these set-in-place steel rods.

ing, local building techniques and local codes will provide the most applicable and most intelligent instructions you can find for your area.

And while you are doing this checking be sure to get sufficient information concerning setbacks. You don't want to form up for a foundation a couple of feet closer to property lines than the law will allow. This applies to additions and to out-buildings as well as to complete structures.

Batter boards, stakes and lines are used to establish the shape and dimensions of any foundation before you even begin to think about formwork. Best bet is to establish a base line from which you can proceed. Easiest method is to take a side of the structure which is parallel to a lot line (or a side of an addition which is parallel to the house) and to set up a line

to establish this. Measure in from each end of the lot or from each corner of the existing structure and then stretch a line between temporary stakes. This should give you enough of a start so you can set up batter boards (see sketch) at each corner.

There are several methods you can use to get corners square. With one method you mark off particular dimensions, as shown in the drawing, along batter board lines and then measure across these two points. When the three sides of the right triangle you are creating measure as indicated, the corner will be 90 degrees. Another way is to actually make an oversize right triangle (using the same dimensions) and use it like you would a square. In the long run this may be your best bet, since you'll be able to use it at all corners,

Crawl space vent, left, above, is provided for in the original formwork constructed for pour.

This split level house has concrete slab, block walls for remainder of foundation up to frame

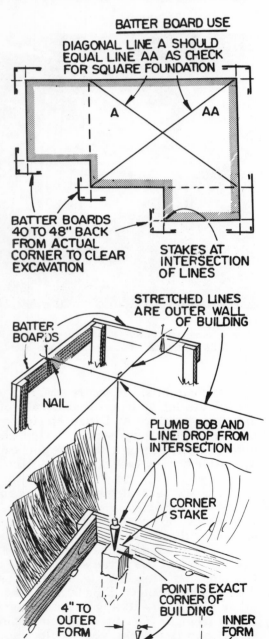

BATTER BOARD USE

DIAGONAL LINE A SHOULD EQUAL LINE AA AS CHECK FOR SQUARE FOUNDATION

A   AA

BATTER BOARDS 40 TO 48" BACK FROM ACTUAL CORNER TO CLEAR EXCAVATION

STAKES AT INTERSECTION OF LINES

STRETCHED LINES ARE OUTER WALL OF BUILDING

BATTER BOARDS

NAIL

PLUMB BOB AND LINE DROP FROM INTERSECTION

CORNER STAKE

4" TO OUTER FORM

POINT IS EXACT CORNER OF BUILDING

INNER FORM

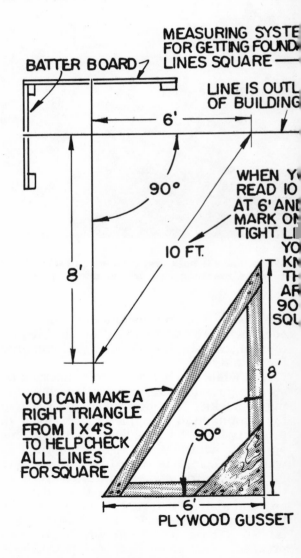

MEASURING SYSTE FOR GETTING FOUND LINES SQUARE

BATTER BOARD

LINE IS OUTL OF BUILDING

6'

90°

10 FT.

8'

WHEN Y READ 10 AT 6' AND MARK ON TIGHT LI YO KN TH AR 90 SQU

YOU CAN MAKE A RIGHT TRIANGLE FROM 1 X 4'S TO HELP CHECK ALL LINES FOR SQUARE

90°

8'

6'

PLYWOOD GUSSET

Vent through concrete block wall is provided by eliminating one block. Note steel rods stay.

intersections and projections. It will also prove useful later when you start to frame the building.

Lines stretched between batter boards cross exactly at corners of the building. Once these basic lines are established, drive nails into the batter boards or saw small notches so the lines can be replaced correctly should it be necessary to remove them. A plumb bob dropped from the batter board lines' intersections indicate the corner at grade. Here, a stake is driven and a nail placed to indicate exact locations. As shown in the drawing, formwork for foundations or wall footings are started outside this corner.

Forms for footings can be quite simple, but the soil which will support the pour must be firm and level. With average soil conditions the footing width should be about twice the thickness of the foundation wall it will support. Its thickness— or depth—should at least equal the wall thickness.

The biggest mistake you can make is to rush the form construction. You may consider it a nuisance and a bore but, if you do feel this way, just remind yourself that everything else you do will, literally, rest on this preliminary work. Actually, the formwork for a concrete pour is the important element. Once this is accomplished, the pouring itself will seem like a minor procedure.

How much formwork you will have to do depends on the project. A high, poured concrete wall has tremendous weight and formwork must be adequately braced. Follow the instruction shown in the sketches and, when in doubt, use more bracing rather than less. You won't be wasting anything since form sheathing and studding can eventually be used elsewhere in the structure.

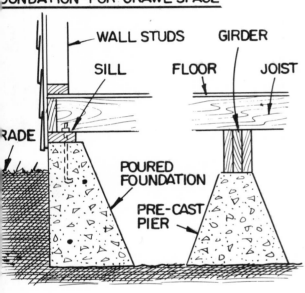

FOUNDATION FOR CRAWL SPACE

WALL STUDS · GIRDER · SILL · FLOOR · JOIST · GRADE · POURED FOUNDATION · PRE-CAST PIER

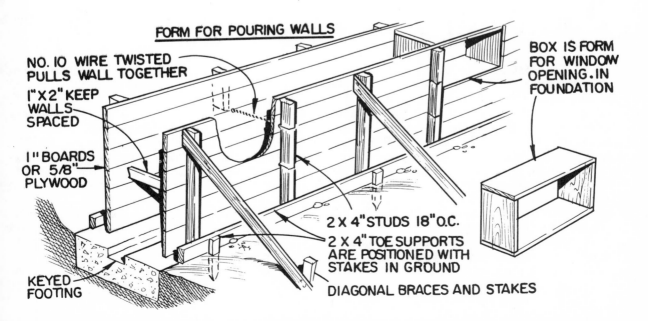

FORM FOR POURING WALLS

NO. 10 WIRE TWISTED PULLS WALL TOGETHER

1" X 2" KEEP WALLS SPACED

1" BOARDS OR 5/8" PLYWOOD

KEYED FOOTING

BOX IS FORM FOR WINDOW OPENING. IN FOUNDATION

2 X 4" STUDS 18" O.C.

2 X 4" TOE SUPPORTS ARE POSITIONED WITH STAKES IN GROUND

DIAGONAL BRACES AND STAKES

Plan carefully. It would be rather awkward to install a conduit or pipe after the slab is set.

Planning and Pouring a Slab

ALL OF THE IDEAS expressed concerning adequate preliminary planning for a foundation or footing apply as well to concrete slab construction. Check local codes, spy on professional builders in your area, and be sure you stay inside setback regulations. Size of footings—whether they are poured separately or integrally with the slab—height above grade, depth below grade, width and steel reinforcement requirements will all be spelled out for you by local regulations.

A concrete slab, especially if existing grades do not impose severe restrictions, can be a simple means of providing for an addition and, of course, it is the ideal answer for a garage, carport or a special little workshop.

Many modern homes are built entirely on a slab, some with hot water pipes embedded in the concrete to provide for radiant heating. This points up one very important fact. The addition must be carefully planned so that all plumbing, etc., can be installed before the concrete is poured.

All of the information concerning layout of the project as outlined in the section on foundations apply to staking out the slab.

The amount of formwork necessary depends on the site. If the slab must be

As in foundation work, the job layout starts with the erection of simple but sturdy batter boards.

Anchor bolts, gas lines, etc. should all be in place and inspected before concrete is poured.

If job calls for doubled plates you can easily drill for second set. Bolts must be long enough.

Forming is simple but solid. Don't spare bracing because "wall" is low—this is heavy stuff.

LAYING OUT SLAB ADDITION TO EXISTING BUILDING

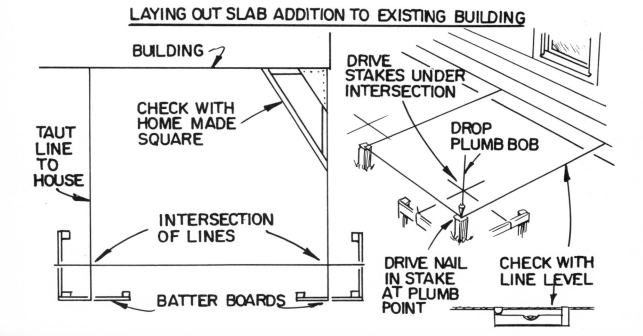

BUILDING

CHECK WITH HOME MADE SQUARE

TAUT LINE TO HOUSE

INTERSECTION OF LINES

BATTER BOARDS

DRIVE STAKES UNDER INTERSECTION

DROP PLUMB BOB

DRIVE NAIL IN STAKE AT PLUMB POINT

CHECK WITH LINE LEVEL

When the slab is set, uprights can now be put in place. Posts and studs can be toenailed in.

Plates on footings can be set in wet concrete—interior wall plates are bolted down to dry slab.

Plan carefully so that anchor bolts do not interfere with studs; if they do—notch stud to fit.

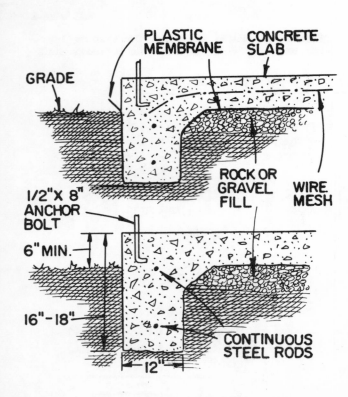

GRADE

PLASTIC MEMBRANE   CONCRETE SLAB

ROCK OR GRAVEL FILL   WIRE MESH

1/2" X 8" ANCHOR BOLT

6" MIN.

16"-18"

CONTINUOUS STEEL RODS

12"

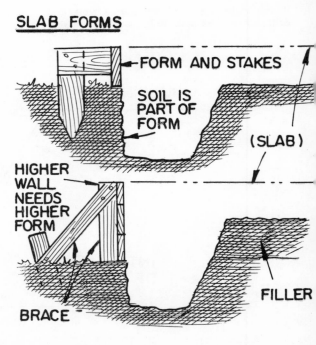

SLAB FORMS

FORM AND STAKES

SOIL IS PART OF FORM

(SLAB)

HIGHER WALL NEEDS HIGHER FORM

BRACE

FILLER

raised well above grade, it will call for what amounts to a foundation wall, and enough fill to bring the slab up to the correct height. In this case it is probably best to consider the footing as a separate project and to tackle the slab itself after the footing and filling are complete. Since this will be fresh fill, be sure that it is adequately tamped to provide a firm base for the slab.

Ideally, and especially where the ground is level, the top surface of the slab should be planned for about 6 inches above grade. Forming can be quite simple since you can trench the ground itself to provide forms for the footing and little, if any, fill will be needed.

Most often, a slab which will be level or below existing grade is not a good idea. There is too much opportunity here for excess water to run under or over the slab. However, below grade slabs are accomplished but adequate provision must be made to provide for waterproofing the project and to guard against floating it away.

The bottom of the footing trench should be firm and level; the sides, smooth and vertical. The angle between the underside of the slab and the break into the trench should not be sharp. It should slope into the trench, or it can be rounded off.

FOOTING AND SLAB
(SUCH AS FOR GARAGE)

SIDING
WALL STUDS
ANCHOR BOLT
SILL
1/2" STEEL RODS
GRADE
WIRE MESH
FOOTING
FILL
GRAVEL
4" DRAIN TILE
PLASTIC MEMBRANE
STEP CAN BE CAST INTO FOOTING FOR SLAB SUPPORT

Place steel after formwork is complete. Usually this will consist of two lines of ½-in. steel running continuously around the project. This doesn't mean the steel must be one piece; only that different pieces should be adequately overlapped. Since you can't hang the steel from a skyhook, drive short pieces of steel into the ground in the trench and tie the reinforcement to these so they will be suspended in the concrete when you pour. The support steel driven into the ground does not have to be removed, but be sure they are low enough to be at least two inches under the surface of the slab.

If the new slab is going to project from an existing foundation, you can tie the two together by drilling holes in the foundation (with a star drill or carbide-tipped bit) and locking in some long bolts in expansion sleeves. Or you can use an epoxy cement to bond in some short lengths of reinforcement steel.

Usually, anchor bolts are set in the pour for attachment of sills and you should have these ready and their locations determined beforehand.

When pouring begins, direct the concrete into the footings first, using a shovel to move it around and the end of a 2x4 to tamp it *lightly*. Don't overdo this or you will be pushing all of the large aggregate to the bottom. You can do some tapping on the outside of the forms with a hammer. This will help to settle the concrete and will provide a smooth texture on the visible face of the footing, assuming that some of it will be above grade.

Be especially careful around any plumbing fixture which have already been installed or around any gas lines or conduits. Work the concrete around such items so that they will be encased, but be sure you don't disturb how they are set.

As the footing trenches fill you can start to spread out over the slab area. A good-sized slab is a job for at least two men even if you use a ready-mix truck. Chances are the truck chute won't reach all areas of the slab so some concrete will have to be dumped from a wheelbarrow. One man dumping and another raking makes a fairly efficient setup. Raking should be done so the pour is just a bit higher than actually needed. This so you won't have to follow the strikeboard procedure with shovelfuls of concrete to fill in low areas.

Insert anchor bolts before the concrete sets. Do this with a twisting motion as you press them in so the concrete will settle around them. Actually, if the sills have already been cut to length and the anchor bolt holes have been drilled, sills can be floated on the wet concrete. •

TYPICAL FRAME WALL AND BRACING

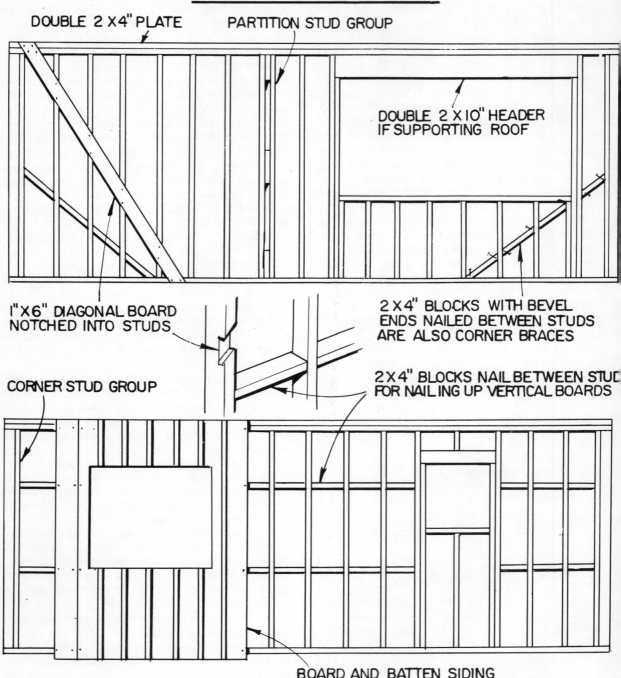

DOUBLE 2 X 4" PLATE

PARTITION STUD GROUP

DOUBLE 2 X 10" HEADER IF SUPPORTING ROOF

I" X 6" DIAGONAL BOARD NOTCHED INTO STUDS

2 X 4" BLOCKS WITH BEVEL ENDS NAILED BETWEEN STUDS ARE ALSO CORNER BRACES

CORNER STUD GROUP

2 X 4" BLOCKS NAIL BETWEEN STUD FOR NAILING UP VERTICAL BOARDS

BOARD AND BATTEN SIDING

with them. These are rules to set up standards that will assure maximum protection and durability. There may be definite specifications on the size of lumber, spacing of studs, distance between the bottom wooden sections of the house and the ground, or size of foundations and amount of reinforcement required. Many times, a town or a small city will issue simplified versions of the codes that you can keep on hand. As an example of how such infor-

mation can be useful to you, consider the following:

Suppose you want to add a window to brighten up a room. The code will tell you what size lumber to use as a header, so that the overhead weight will be adequately supported across the span you propose. Not only does this keep you on the right track but it also supplies vital information. Some accessory sheets supplied by local building inspectors will provide a nailing schedule

Floor plates are attached to the subfloor, outlining the house's perimeter and its inside rooms. At door openings, floor plate gets cut off, flush to the stud.

Shown here is doubled fire blocking. This can be used with building paper under exterior siding when code omits sheathing. Note wiring and diagonal bracing.

so you will know what size nail to use where—and even how many!

Generally speaking, all house frames are attached to the foundation through a sill which is anchored directly to the masonry Beams span across the foundation walls and are supported between with posts resting on piers. In some construction, the subfloor attaches directly to these beams. Other times the beams are supports for flooring joists. In either case, knowing the location of the structural supports will enable you to nail solidly should you ever want to attach something permanently to the floor.

Once the subfloor is down (over beams or joists), the floor plates are laid. These plates outline the perimeter of the house and the interior partitions. If the house is on a concrete slab, the plates are secured directly to the masonry, being installed with anchor bolts while the concrete is wet

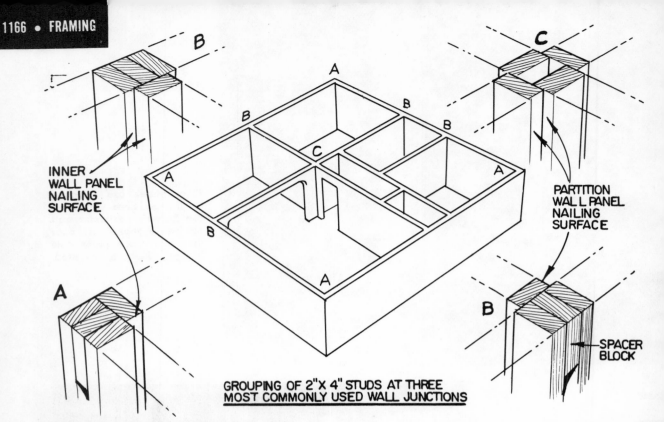

INNER WALL PANEL NAILING SURFACE

PARTITION WALL PANEL NAILING SURFACE

SPACER BLOCK

GROUPING OF 2"X 4" STUDS AT THREE MOST COMMONLY USED WALL JUNCTIONS

or later with special hardened fasteners.

So far, all the building has been horizontal. After the plates are set, vertical construction begins with studs, (usually 2x4 lumber spaced 16 inches apart on centers.) "On center" means that the measurement is taken from the center of one stud to the center of the next. Variations will occur, especially around windows and doors, but the stud spacing is kept as uniform as possible. On top of the studs, running in the same line as the floor plate, is a doubled 2x4 top plate. At corners, three studs are preassembled into roughly an L-shape. At partitions, three studs are assembled like a "T." Where the partitions cross, four studs are assembled into a double "T."

At openings for doors and windows, filler studs are nailed directly to full-length studs. The length of the filler stud is approximately the distance from the top of the proposed window or door to the finished floor. Spanning the opening, across the top of the filler studs, rests the header. This can be a 4x6, a 4x8, a 4x12—it all depends on the length of the unsupported span, which, of course, is actually the width of the window or door. Short block studs are used between the top of the header and the underside of the top plate.

A single 2x4 or double 2x4's will span the opening between the filler studs to mark the lower line of the opening. Short vertical studs are used between this and the floor plate. Halfway between the floor plate and top plate a line of short 2x4's

(fire blocks) is run horizontally between studs. For some types of siding (board and batten, for example) this blocking is doubled. That is, *two* horizontal lines are formed, equally spaced between floor and top plates. This is to provide necessary nailing surface for the vertical siding.

Spanning across the outside walls (resting on the top plates of the wall frames) are the ceiling joists, and rising at an angle to meet at the topmost point of the roof are the roof rafters. The ceiling joists are what the inside, finished ceiling is attached to, and, in a two story house, what the upstairs floor is nailed to. The roof goes on the roof rafters.

One thing to be careful about—remember that inside the walls are electrical and plumbing equipment. When a job comes up that requires cutting into or through a wall, pay some attention to electrical outlets and fixtures and plumbing equipment that may be nearby.

Generally speaking, the bulk of the plumbing is under the house, with pipes running vertically where needed. Electric wires can run horizontally over the ceiling and under the floor, coming down (or going up) where needed. When a wall has more than one outlet, chances are that wire is strung horizontally between the two. Cut carefully—always be aware that there may be something in the walls that shouldn't be cut and not before turning off the water main or throwing the switch at the electrical entrance. •

Below is complete framing, ready for wall and roof coverings to be applied. Because ceiling beams will be left exposed on inside of room, heavy beams (4x12) have been chosen for the 20-foot span.

Picture Framing

Simplicity and neatness amount to protection and decoration if the project happens to be framing either paintings or decorative wall maps

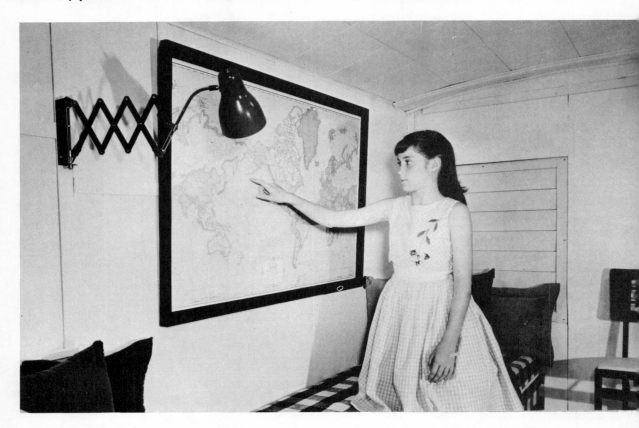

Here framing was used to contain a large map which serves to cover an unused expanse as well as colorfully decorate with a useful news spotter.

HOW often do you find a piece of inexpensive art work, a map, a photograph or a drawing that you would like to frame but don't wish to spend a great deal of money on? It is not difficult to frame it yourself from pieces of wood you have in your cellar. It takes no more than a saw, a bit of glue and a few brads to do a professional job on your own picture frames.

Since the decorating job in this spread involved a den, a large map was used to cover an expanse of wall space. It might just as well have been a large photo of the mother-in-law, since the job of framing would have been exactly the same. Variations to the steps listed here can be found in the different types of wood available for such work. ●——*by Emil E. Brodbeck*

Contact cement is used to join map to Masonite backing. Use a piece of newspaper to separate pieces before joining and ease out for binding.

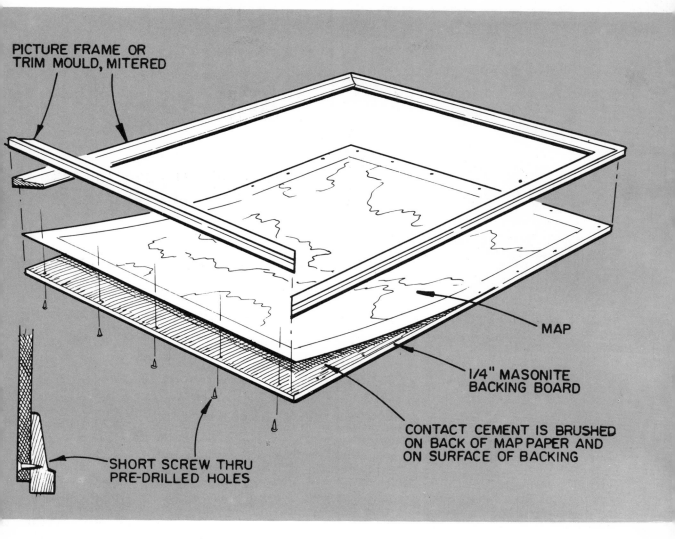

PICTURE FRAME OR
TRIM MOULD, MITERED

MAP

1/4" MASONITE
BACKING BOARD

CONTACT CEMENT IS BRUSHED
ON BACK OF MAP PAPER AND
ON SURFACE OF BACKING

SHORT SCREW THRU
PRE-DRILLED HOLES

Use any of a number of standard moldings for your frame and miter the joints as shown. If a box saw is not available, use care in marking.

Frame can be joined using either metal fasteners or glue. Finish with stain or paint before attaching to map, picture or painting being framed.

fuels and fuel storage

Whatever fuel you use, in whatever system, knowing the "why" and the "how" is equally as important as providing the "where" of your supply.

ACCORDING to 1950 census figures, coal was used in 46% of the homes having central heating equipment, and in about 25% of the homes with non-central heating. In the northeast and the north-central sections of the United States, coal was used as the heating fuel in about half the dwelling units. Thus, coal is by far the most used fuel for home heating.

There are two types of coal, bituminous, or soft coal, and anthracite, or hard coal. The difference between the two is that the soft coal contains a high percentage of volatile gases (hydrocarbons) in relation to the percentage of fixed carbons un-combined with hydrogen or oxygen; while the hard coal consists almost exclusively of fixed carbons. Both have certain percent-ages of rock, slate, ash and water. The content of these impurities varies, and has a direct effect upon the quality of the coal.

Most anthracite coal comes from a sec-tion of Pennsylvania, and due to freight charges, its use is confined to that area. "Egg" is the largest size coal of this type, and burns with a smokeless and sootless flame. The other sizes range downward, for different kinds of heating units.

Bituminous coal is mined in widely scattered areas almost all over the United States. Its size varies from huge blocks downward. The block coal is generally used in hand-fired units.

Some urban areas have ordinances pro-hibiting the use of certain types of coal that produce much smoke.

Coal Storage

If you plan to use coal as your fuel, especially in your new home, you'll have to make allowances early in the planning for a coal storage space, or coal bin, as they are called.

Your building and heating contractors will assist you in determining just where this coal bin should be built, if your plans do not specify. It should be as near the furnace as possible, regardless of whether your furnace will be hand or stoker-fired. Before the coal bin is built, it should be definitely decided just where the furnace will set. Room for easy shoveling of the coal to the furnace door, or to the stoker hopper, should be allowed for. And it should be noted if the person who will fire the furnace is right or left-handed. A little extra planning at the right time can save you much inconvenience later on.

A coal bin can be of masonry, or any kind of lumber, rough or dressed. About forty cubic feet is ample space to allow for each ton of coal. In other words, a space 4'x10' and a foot high would hold one ton of coal, and a bin the same size 8' high would hold eight tons. Incidentally, while you are getting your coal bin built, you might as well make it plenty big. Try to have it hold at least 10 tons.

A metal outside door should be placed near the top of the coal bin, and it should open onto your driveway, for easier and more practical coal deliveries.

If the coal bin is built in a basement corner, then only two walls are necessary. It is a good idea to give the inner side of the masonry wall a coating of the same type of waterproofing substance that is used on the outside foundation walls. This assures, doubly, dry fuel and a non-leaky basement, at least in that corner.

Oil

Oil has become very popular as a fuel for home heating. A few of the advantages of oil for home heating are:

Can be stored outside the home or basement, and requires no handling whatever.

Leaves no ashes.

Requires no kindling for fire building.

Is fired instantly and thereby delivers instant heat.

The annual fuel bill for an oil-burning heating unit, plus the slight additional charge for electricity, is apt to be higher than other fuels. But the fuel selling the cheapest is liable to cost you more in the long run, if you consider your time and labor in terms of money. In short, with oil as your fuel, you usually get more efficient heat, with less time and bother, but it costs you more.

There are three types of oil for home heating. Nos. 1, 2, and 3. No. 1 is the lightest grade, and more expensive than the other two. It is used in the pot-type burners. Nos. 2 and 3 cost about the same per gallon, and are used in both the gun-type and rotary-type burners.

Fuel Storage for Oil-Burning Furnaces

While the installation of an oil furnace eliminates the necessity of a coal bin or storage place, as in the coal furnace, it is still necessary that you have an oil storage tank. The big advantage here is that you can bury the tank outside your basement. This is the usual method of fuel storage where the two-pipe suction feed system it used. With the one-pipe gravity system, the tanks are sometimes stored inside the basement.

Let's consider the single-pipe gravity system first. The drawing shows the general layout of the tank, burner, fuel supply line, valves, etc. The tank should always be placed in the lowest story of the house, if it is to be an inside tank. In deciding just where the tank of this type should be placed, here are a few things to be considered:

The tank, preferably a 275-gallon affair, should be not less than seven feet from the burner, and the bottom of the tank should be at level with or higher than the burner. Put the tank near an outside wall, where the fill and vent pipes will be as short as possible and still be accessible from the outside. These fill and vent pipes must always conform with any and all local ordinances.

As for the piping sizes, 1¼ inch for the fill pipe and 2 inches for the vent pipe are most used, fittings being black malleable and the pipe galvanized. The fuel supply line should be of ⅜ inch pipe, copper tubing if possible, in lines less than 40 feet. Longer lines should be ½ inch. Any of the oil proof compounds are okay for doping the threaded joints. When trenches are chiseled from the concrete basement floor, these should be grouted over smooth with fresh concrete after tubing or piping is

---

The diagram below shows an outside oil tank, in cross-section, using two pipes and suction feed.

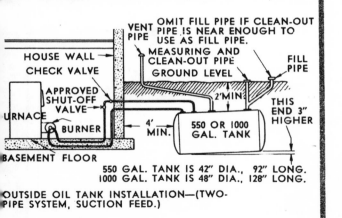

OUTSIDE OIL TANK INSTALLATION—(TWO-PIPE SYSTEM, SUCTION FEED.)

An inside installation of an oil tank may be made as below, using a single-pipe gravity feed system.

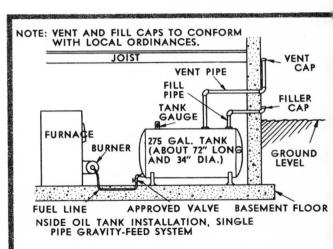

INSIDE OIL TANK INSTALLATION, SINGLE PIPE GRAVITY-FEED SYSTEM

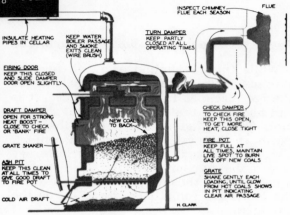

Section through a conventional coal-burning furnace shows most efficient method of using fuel.

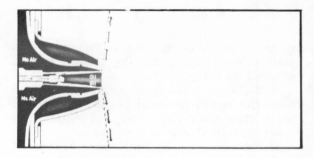

In firing of oil, the fuel is first thrown off in a thin film by a rapidly rotating atomizing "cup."

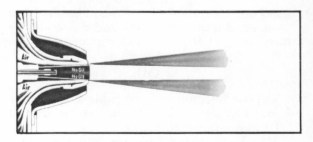

Firing efficiency is then achieved by introducing air into oil film, making it a combustible mixture.

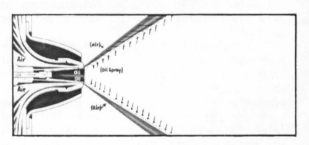

Small arrows show the direction of the oil and air movement that results in well distributed mixture.

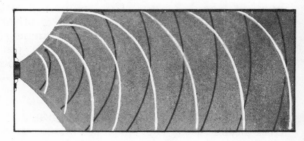

Above, more air is injected into the atomization of fuel by damper action to create fire modulation.

Below, the resulting fire may be varied from long to short flame, depending on special requirements.

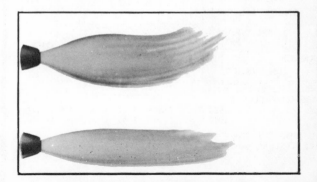

installed. It is quite permissible to run the pipe on the floor surface, the concrete over it, without the trench. This can be done neatest by running the tubing along the base of the wall for as many feet as possible, before running it directly to the burner.

The tank should be at least ten inches off the floor.

The vent pipe should be terminated with a screened hood.

The vent and the fill pipes should always be connected to separate fittings in the tank.

Any holes made in the foundation walls (masonry) should be closed with okum and finished with cement.

Where the authorities demand it, fill and vent pipes should end in double swing joints at the tank.

If a tank larger than 275 gallons is used, it must be protected by a reinforced brick or concrete enclosure. If two tanks of the 275-gallon variety are used, a three-way valve must interconnect the two.

Several years ago, it was advisable to install a larger tank due to the fact that oil companies offered discounts to customers who bought their fuel in larger volumes. In most cases, this practice has been discontinued.

With the two-pipe system, the tank is usually 500, 550, or a 1000-gallon capacity container, and like the smaller tank, must be approved by the National Board of Fire Underwriters. The drawing shows general outline of how tank can be buried and connected to the burner.

In choosing where to excavate for the tank, here are a few things to keep in mind: The end of the tank should be no closer to the building foundation than 4 feet, yet it should be placed so the lines will be as short as possible. The tank should not be more than 10 feet above, or more than 8 feet below the level of the oil burner, and at least two feet below the ground level. It should not be in an area where there is sewage, drainage, water or underground cables.

When the tank is below the burner level, pitch the pipe toward the tank.

All pipe fittings and connections should conform with local ordinances, and be approved by the National Board of Fire Underwriters.

Gas

Gaseous fuels are either natural or manufactured, and must be supplied to the home via pipes, or containers. Gas was used in 28% of the dwelling units with central heating, and about 25% of those with non-central heating, according to the 1950 census.

The use of gas as a heating fuel is more or less confined to certain areas, due to the expense of building main pipe lines to supply outlying districts. Since most of the new housing projects and individual homes being constructed today are in suburban areas of the larger towns and cities, the percentage of gas-heated homes is likely to remain about the same for some time.

Liquid petroleum, or L.P., or "bottled" gas is sometimes used for home heating.

Natural gas contains around 1,100 B.T.U. per cubic foot; manufactured gas about 600, and bottled gas 3,000.

Bottled gas is heavier than air, and a safety control valve is necessary to shut off the gas to the pilot when it goes out, as well as to the burner. Unless any gas that has possibly leaked out can escape through a vent at the floor level, an explosion is likely.

Natural gas is usually found underground near deposits of crude oil. It is collected at the source, and piped to homes.

Manufactured gas is made by one of the many processes of incomplete combustion or chemical breakdown of coals.

Wood

The 1950 census showed that about 20% of the homes heated by non-central systems used wood as their fuel. Most of these homes were in rural areas, or farmhouses.

While wood is bulky, and requires a large storage space, it is easy to start a fire with, burns with little smoke and leaves very little, if any, ash. While it takes labor to cut and stow wood, a lot of rural homeowners have ample supplies close at hand, and continue to use this fuel.

Well-seasoned hardwood has about one half the heat value of good coal, pound for pound. A cord of oak, beech, hickory, sugar maple, or rock elm weighs about 2 tons and will have the same heat value as one ton (2,000 pounds) of good coal. Cordwood lengths are 4 feet long, and a cord of wood stacks 4 feet high and 8 feet long.

Wood is used in cooking stoves that serve both cooking and heating purposes, in regular heating stoves and heaters, in grates, fireplaces and in some boilers. •

Pounds of Coal Necessary to Heat an Average Brick Building Per Season Per Cubic Foot of Building

Heat demand in degree-days	Coal "As Received"									
	10,000 Btu.		11,000 Btu.		12,000 Btu.		13,000 Btu.		14,000 Btu.	
	Hand fired	Stoker fired	Hand fired	Stoker fired	Hand fired	Stoker fired	Hand fired	Stoker fired	Hand fired	Stoker fired
3,000	.83	.65	.75	.58	.69	.53	.64	.49	.59	.46
3,500	.98	.75	.89	.69	.82	.63	.75	.58	.70	.54
4,000	1.12	.86	1.02	.78	.93	.72	.86	.66	.80	.62
4,500	1.27	.96	1.15	.89	1.06	.81	.96	.75	.91	.70
5,000	1.43	1.10	1.30	1.00	1.18	.92	1.10	.85	1.02	.79
5,500	1.59	1.22	1.45	1.11	1.33	1.02	1.22	.94	1.11	.87
6,000	1.75	1.35	1.59	1.22	1.46	1.12	1.35	1.04	1.25	.96
6,500	1.94	1.49	1.76	1.35	1.62	1.24	1.49	1.15	1.39	1.06
7,000	2.15	1.65	1.95	1.50	1.79	1.38	1.65	1.27	1.54	1.18
7,500	2.40	1.85	2.18	1.68	2.00	1.54	1.85	1.42	1.71	1.32
8,000	2.65	2.04	2.41	1.85	2.21	1.70	2.04	1.57	1.89	1.46
8,500	2.95	2.27	2.68	2.06	2.46	1.89	2.27	1.75	2.11	1.62
9,000	3.30	2.54	3.00	2.31	2.75	2.12	2.54	1.95	2.36	1.81
9,500	3.67	2.82	3.34	2.57	3.06	2.35	2.82	2.17	2.62	2.03
10,000	4.10	3.16	3.73	2.87	3.42	2.63	3.16	2.43	2.93	2.25

Hand-fired efficiency figured at 50 per cent; stoker-fired, at 65 per cent efficiency.

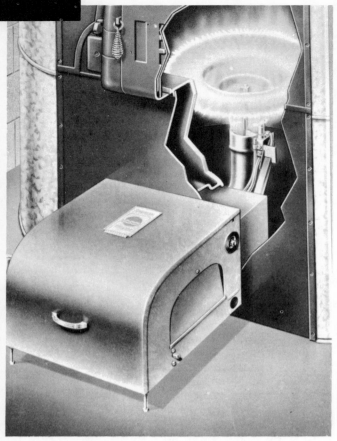

This unit is used for changing from coal to gas. A telescopic burner tube adjustment makes it centered conveniently in almost any coal furnace. It is made by American Standard, has a special retention lip.

converting from one fuel to another

Any number of factors may make a switch advisable. Changeovers are usually simple, can be readily made.

FOR many reasons, it sometimes becomes necessary and advisable for the homeowner to convert his heating plant from one fuel to another. During World War II, many owners of oil-burning furnaces found it much to their advantage (and the country's) to convert from oil to gas, or coal. After the war was over, and more oil was available, they changed back. And even in normal times, the homeowners change their fuels simply for more efficiency and less labor in firing and upkeep.

Here are a few possible changes that can be made, listing the kinds of heating units necessary for the changes. Costs will vary, primarily due to labor costs in your locality. This factor serves as a barometer for most of your heating costs, incidentally.

From Coal to Oil

A typical conversion oil burner is the gun-type. It can be installed in any hand-fired coal-burning heating unit. (It can also be installed in place of a stoker, although it is seldom done.) To do this it is necessary to remove the grates and bricks or lining, and to build a new combustion chamber of special bricks inside the heating unit. From then on the unit is installed in much the same manner as the stoker, right through the ash pit doorway. Once installed, the space around it is bricked and cemented up air-tight. Instead of sand, a special compound called zonolite backfill is used to fill in the dead space in the ash pit. Fuel supply is discussed in another chapter, as well as the piping system. This is identical to that of a regular oil burner.

From Gas to Coal

This cannot be done, unless the heating unit was originally designed as a coal-burning unit in the first place. If such is the case, the furnace may need re-lining and new smoke pipe added, as well as the controls changed. This is another of the changes in fuel that is seldom made by homeowners.

From Oil to Coal

Can't be done, as with the gas, unless the unit was a coal-burner to start with. The furnace lining for an oil-burning furnace is different, as are the controls. Once the homeowner has a satisfactory oil-burning heating system installed in his home, it is doubtful that he would ever desire a change under normal conditions. The possible exception here is, of course, in the event of a fuel oil shortage. But even in this case he would be more likely to convert to gas rather than coal, if he lived in an area where gas was available.

The most versatile of the forced warm air heating units is the regular square-based coal-burning forced air furnace. They are primarily designed for coal, of course, but they are adaptable to all fuels, and once they have been changed to, say, oil-burning, they can just as easily be changed back to coal again. For this reason, when converting from one fuel to another, do not sell or throw away the discarded unit, or any of the parts used in its installation. You might want to change back to your original fuel, due to some unforeseen cause.

From Coal to Gas

Any coal-fired furnace or boiler can be equipped with a gas conversion unit, and thereby changed from a coal-burning heating system to one that is gas-burning. This works out very well for the homeowner who has a good coal-burning system in his home, but wishes the convenience of gas heat and cannot afford a complete change. Of course, such a system will give satisfactory service only if the old system was properly installed in the first place, and the furnace itself must be in good shape. Photo shows a typical conversion burner. This is the single port type with the special flame retention lip. The burner tube has telescopic adjustment for centering in any unit.

From Oil to Gas

Most manufacturers of oil-burning furnaces also design a special conversion

Oil conversion burners may be installed in most all coal and gas-fired heating units. Burner is actually a pump that shoots a stream of oil into the furnace which is mixed with air and ignited by electricity.

burner to convert the furnace from oil to gas. A conversion job of this sort requires little time, but must be done by an expert in this type work. The oil-burner itself must be in good condition. The existing pipes and ducts may be retained, as they are.

From Gas to Oil

The oil conversion burner pictured for coal furnaces is the type used for this, although this change is seldom made.

A final word: Don't expect a conversion job to solve all your problems, if your furnace is already worn out, improperly installed, or just too small for your house. Get the advice of your heating dealer before making any definite plans for changing. •

To convert from oil to gas, a unit may be obtained which fits right into the opening used by the oil-burner—in fact, can be anchored with the selfsame bolts. Existing pipe and ducts may be preserved.

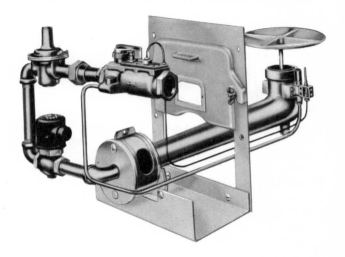

Motor Fuel

Carburetors regulate fuel intake　　　　　by FRED RUSSELL

Leaky fuel lines can cost you money; make sure that all their connections are both tight and dry.

WHILE THE CARBURETOR is the heart of the fuel system its efficiency is closely tied in with several other important units, any one of which can render it helpless. A perfect example is the way you can bring the engine to a halt, and also buckle the gas tank, by substituting a tightly fitting nonvented gas tank cap for the vented cap that was original equipment on your car. Another illustration is water in the gas tank. This is drawn into the fuel filter trap to freeze in cold weather and stop fuel flow as effectively as pinching the fuel line. Main cause of water in gas tanks, incidentally, is failure to keep them as full as possible in cold or changeable weather. The emptier the tank the more condensation there will be.

The fuel pump is one of the most neglected units of the engine, yet its care is reasonably simple. Due to vibration its connections can easily loosen. The same goes for the cap screws for its cover. In addition, the pump may come loose from the engine. Any gasoline around the pump is evidence of such looseness, but an added problem is the air that may be sucked into the system. Air can also be sucked in through loose connections at the ends of the flexible fuel line which joins the main line to the pump, not to mention leakage in this short line itself. Since this line is not under pressure, fuel does not leak out, and we have no easy clue to the situation. It costs little to replace one of these flexible lines and the change often will check what seems to be vapor lock.

The trend has been away from dual type pumps which use vacuum to assist the windshield wipers, partly because of the use of better functioning electric wipers and also because intake manifold vacuum is being used so widely for power braking. If the car has a dual type pump, and you want to know if the vacuum side of the pump is working efficiently you have merely to note if the wipers slow down too much when you are climbing a hill or step on the gas. If there is such evidence the trouble is usually due to a punctured diaphragm on the vacuum pump. An advantage of vacuum operation of wipers is that you can slow the blades down to a crawl if the rain is light. That helps prevent friction damage to the windshield.

Some cars have a vent for the gas tank filler and then use a nonvented cap. The idea is to provide sizable venting while at the same time preventing the chance of rain water leaking into the tank via the cap. Vent pipes have been known to come loose from the filler pipe. In such a condition, powdery road dirt tossed up by the rear tire may pass through the fuel filter's element. If trapped under the seat of the carburetor's needle valve, it would cause flooding and a type of stalling that would turn anyone's hair gray.

So if there is a vent tube make sure it is firmly inserted into the filler pipe and that it is not broken at any point where it travels to the tank. While you are checking this, with the car on a grease lift, take a look at the outlet line of the tank as well as the connection for the tank fuel gauge unit. Make sure things are tight here, otherwise there may be leakage as well as inaccurate reading of the gauge. If you replace the gas tank be sure to have it undercoated.

An important change in fuel filtration has brought into popularity the in-line type of filter. This inserts in the line between the pump and the carburetor. It does not trap out water, unless it is the type with a

U-design. The in-line filter is merely replaced, while the trap type has a bowl which is cleaned out and an element which is either washed in solvent or replaced. Just a little bit of lint on the cleaning cloth which you use to wipe out the bowl may be enough to cause carburetor flooding if it passes out of the filter with the outgoing fuel. Filter care may seem like a simple operation, but you can't be too careful.

Now we have arrived at the carburetor which, while more complicated than ever, need not baffle us. One of the newest developments is use of a rubber-tipped needle valve. This is a real aid in checking flooding because if there is a speck of dirt on the seat it will become embedded in the rubber tip of the needle valve. Thus instead of hanging up the valve the dirt will quickly get out of the picture. There will be no flooding, hence no stalling.

Carburetion has become so critical that many an experienced mechanic will be found sitting on the rear bumper to "feel" his way to a correct idling adjustment. Latest in idling is the use of large screws to meter air to control idle speed, the throttle plates closing fully at idle instead of remaining "cracked" as in conventional design. This is said to eliminate the need for a more critical throttle plate adjustment. Idle speed is always important since it must be fast enough to prevent stalling and not high enough to cause annoying creeping with cars equipped with automatic transmissions. Idle speed should be higher when a car is operating an air conditioner. In some cases this is automatically controlled.

Carburetors are complicated in that some are two-barrel, some four. We find

The newer in-line type of fuel filter is popular because it is inexpensive and easily replaced.

Special rules and care are required for efficient servicing of new types of air cleaner elements.

When you are replacing the air cleaner on the carburetor, be sure it is properly seated.

Watch out: a worn gasket between the carburetor and intake manifold will leak gas.

FUEL PUMP ECCENTRIC

OIL GROOVE
CAMSHAFT

DISTRIBUTOR DRIVE GEAR

This front view of Buick camshaft shows gearing for driving distributor and fuel pump eccentric.

two four-barrel jobs as well as triple two-barrel. Simpler carburetor models on the earlier compacts have been a temporary relief, but to a world where performance is king, simplicity must remain a mirage.

Most of the automatic drives have controls hooked up to the same throttle linkage that operates the carburetor. Some carburetors have a dashpot control—a sort of brake on the throttle to prevent too sudden closing—to prevent stalling when you take your foot off the accelerator pedal suddenly for a quick slowdown or stop. Recent in carburetor design is the use of a water-heated throttle to prevent stalls from "icing" in cold, damp weather. Some of the arrangements have a secondary throttle to bring extra barrels into action during the high speed range, thus providing economy under conditions where top performance and power are not needed.

Before tackling the action of some of the latest carburetors let's note a few hard and fast rules that should help obtain better service from this hard-working unit of the car, regardless of its design. First is the importance of cleanliness, outside and in. A treatment of carburetor cleaner such as Gumout will keep this vital unit operating better and will also put new life into one that has been neglected. Preferably feed solvent to the carburetor while the engine is running, with the car out in the open. There's a new Gumout automatic choke cleaner, in convenient aerosol can form, which can also be used for removing dirt and gummy deposits from the fast idle mechanism. An automatic transmission will often shift better if its throttle control is kept free of dirt and gums.

Mark the best choke setting on the choke cover to guide yourself in future adjustments of unit.

Keep the carburetor cover screws tightened to prevent the development of any gas or air leaks.

A second point to consider is carburetor wear. The needle valve and its seat may need replacing. There is wear, too, on metering rods, the idle adjusting screws and the float mechanism. Carburetor manufacturers make kits which can be used to give new life to the oldest of units.

I have already covered point three in mentioning care of the various other units of the fuel system on which the carburetor depends so we can pass along to point four which is concerned with the business of adjusting the carburetor. Float level that is too high enriches the mixture excessively; too low a level leans it too much. The engine should be well warmed up when adjusting the idle mixture, and it is important to repeat the job several times just to be sure you're right. For setting the idle speed use an electric type of tachometer.

All the standard carburetors have systems, or "circuits," which provide metered fuel and air to take care of idling, power, acceleration, etc. They all have a choke control, a fast idle device, an acceleration pump and usually an unloader. In addition some have anti-stall controls, including an idle compensator which prevents the engine from conking out during prolonged hot idling, a starting switch where cranking is actuated by pressing the accelerator pedal, replaceable leaner or richer metering rods, and other features such as a vacuum switch or a secondary throttle lever.

If the carburetor is one of the simpler ones, it may have an acceleration pump with an adjustable stroke for summer or winter driving. This used to be common practice but is no longer needed on the more complicated carburetor models. To understand the four-barrel carburetor it is necessary to meet the two-barrel job because the former virtually is a double version of the latter. A dual-barrel carburetor has one air intake, a choke and a float chamber, but has a separate fuel jet, venturi tube and throttle for each barrel. It may also have two floats. The idea originally was that each barrel would feed one bank of cylinders in a V8 engine, but this type carburetor also is used for six-cylinder engines. It can be used to provide more uniform distribution of fuel to the cylinders, but also can function in such a way that the second barrel serves as a reserve to amplify the first when power and performance are needed. Use of this type carburetor for such a wide range is partly accomplished by employing two of the throttle plates as secondary and two as primary control.

Since the four-barrels are in one housing, these carburetors are not as complicated in appearance as they might be. Also there is only one acceleration pump, one set of idle needle valves and one power system. Twin four-barrel carburetors have been used but were difficult to adjust. Each make and model, of course, has its own oddities. The triple two-barrel carburetor is especially interesting in that while the center unit only has a choke and power system all three carburetors are involved in the part-throttle system. The engine derives its extra mixture for heavy loads and high speed from the center carburetor's power system.

There are different ways of metering, such as by air bleed jet or metering pins.

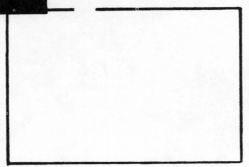

First need is for a place for the supply of gas. The name of this place, officially, is "the bowl."

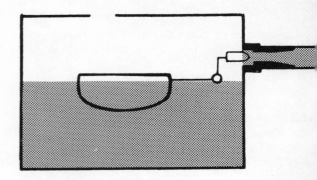

A float (heavy black line) actuates a needle valve to control the level of gas in the bowl.

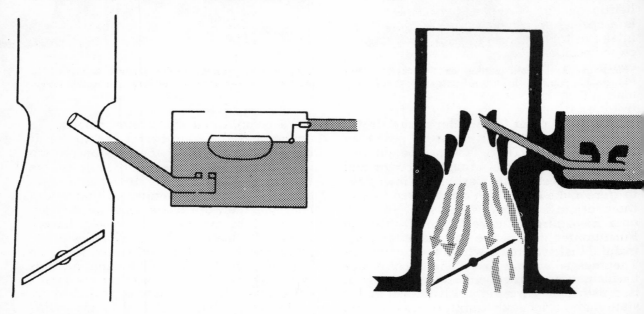

Air and gas are brought together and a restriction is added—the pipe—to passage of the gas.

Here is an elementary carburetor in which the flow of gas is proportional to the flow of air.

The venturi (which is the throat into which fuel is sprayed or injected as air passes through at high velocity) may be plain, double or even triple. That's not all, but enough to explain why the carburetor continues to be a mystery to many and such an important part of car performance.

No matter how advanced or how simple the carburetor, certain rules apply if you want best results. Float level is one of these. It must be exactly as the manufacturer recommends for your make and model car. In adjusting the idle mixture turn the screw, or screws, "in" or clockwise to lean. Here, too, you must have exact specifications, for some screws turn to open (left) in ¼ to ½ revolution while others require from 1 to 2 revolutions.

If the engine is hard starting, idles rough and shows fouled spark plugs (assuming other conditions such as ignition, compression, etc. are normal) the chances are that the carburetor has plugged idle jets or passages. Needle valve stickage or float trouble is indicated by surging when the engine is running, stalling, fuel leakage around the carburetor and low gas mileage. If the carburetor has a vacuum piston in its power circuit, a tendency to run rough, foul plugs and develop flat spots may be evidence of a weak piston spring or sticking of the vacuum piston itself.

Hesitation and pinging when trying to pick up speed, following a sharp turn, may indicate that the floats do not have enough clearance and are binding against the float wall. Overtightening the air cleaner may cramp the choke valve and cause low gas mileage and lack of pep. Be careful that the cleaner is correctly positioned because it may interfere with the automatic choke control.

Strenuous efforts have been made to simplify servicing of modern carburetors. One make can be purged of dirt and sludge by removing the lower bowl screw. It is now also possible to remove and replace a worn needle valve and seat while the carburetor is still on the engine. Use of chromium plated linkage is another forward step. But regardless of the complexity of carburetors the seemingly unimportant attentions are the ones that play such an important role in helping to prevent major servicing.

Because the choke is a fairly simple addition to the carburetor it is skipped over lightly and little understood. Basically it is a special throttle-like valve in the air intake of the carburetor which, when in a closed position, cuts off air supply. Thus the engine can draw in a highly rich mixture for cold starting. This control can be manual or automatic. In either case trouble can develop if the valve is cramped by overtightening the air cleaner, or if there is any binding in the choke shaft or linkage.

In automatic choking there is a thermostatic coil spring which has tension enough to close the choke valve when cold. Since the choke valve is offset, air velocity will open it a little as soon as the engine starts. Further opening is obtained by intake manifold vacuum applied to a choke piston. Then heated air from a "stove" on the exhaust manifold, or from a heat tube in it, is drawn into the housing of the thermostatic coil. The coil then unwinds and gradually opens the choke. Naturally if the tube leaks, the choke will not open soon enough, the engine will operate on a too rich mixture and gas mileage will drop.

Leakage in the heat tube can be even more troublesome because cold damp air entering it may corrode the coil. That prevents normal choking for starting. If the choke coil housing is dirty there may not only be hard starting but tardy opening of the choke valve and thus overchoking. The coil housing usually has provision for adjusting the coil toward a richer or leaner choke. There's also a mechanical unloader to prevent loading conditions during cold starting, and there is linkage to the choke to provide fast idling during the warm-up.

Choke mechanical parts may become gummy and should occasionally be cleaned by spraying with a choke cleanser (solvent). After such treatment a few drops of light engine oil will help insure smooth action of this essential mechanism.

Fuel injection to replace conventional carburetion is designed to improve overall engine performance and to boost gas mileage. In this arrangement pressurized fuel is delivered to the individual cylinders by being injected into the air stream of the intake manifold near the intake valve of each cylinder. To accomplish this there must be a pump to provide controlled pressure, a distributor to meter the fuel, a control for mixing and the individual injection nozzles.

There are a number of different systems each with its special features and provisions for cold starting, warm-up and idling. The pumping and distributing units are complicated but the results seem to justify further development of this newer way of feeding today's—and especially tomorrow's—gasoline engine. •

Driven by the camshaft, the mechanical fuel pump uses a diaphragm to move fuel to the carburetor.

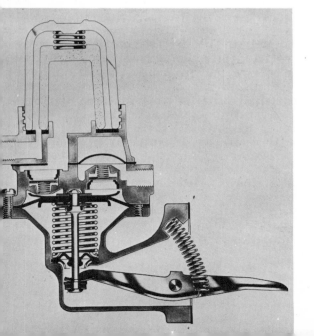

This Rochester fuel injection system has three basic parts—fuel meter, manifold and air meter.

cleaning, servicing and repairing

Why pay maintenance bills, when with a little knowledge you can learn to take care of your heating plant yourself?

IN the installation of new heating systems, there are few chances for the layman to do the complete job, with the exception of the coal-fired gravity furnace. But once the heating plant is properly installed, there are countless ways in which the homeowner can save himself money in cleaning, servicing and repairing bills.

One of the first things the man of the house should do when he buys a new home with an existing heating plant, or invests in a new heating system for his old home, is to learn all about this plant. He should take time to be thoroughly familiar with every part of the heating system, and understand its function. It should contain no "mysteries" whatever. There are several ways of doing this, even with the most complex method of home heating.

Suppose you have moved into a new home, complete with a strange furnace, or suppose you've had a new furnace installed about which you know nothing, except possibly that someone did recommend it. Talk to the original homeowner about the workings of the furnace, if possible. Any mechanical or electrical controls that are not working properly should be checked by a good service man at once. And don't pay a service man so many dollars an hour without asking a lot of questions and watching what he does. In this way you can greatly increase your chances of being about as good a service man as he is . . . with your own furnace.

Heating systems, like people, sometimes are subject to minor ailments and require attention. The home owner should not hesitate to make any necessary repairs at once, if they are needed. But there are countless things that the layman can do himself, when it comes to servicing, cleaning, or repairing a furnace, that will save him money. Some of these he can do almost at once, others can be learned by repeated study of the chronic ailments of a particular furnace, and by asking questions.

Anyone can learn to do all the following things, without help from a service man:

Clean a furnace.

Clean or replace a smoke pipe.

Oil a motor.

Check the gear case oil in a stoker.

Check fan and other belts. Replace worn-out ones.

Check and replace firebricks of lining of furnace.

Check and replace grates.

Blank off an unused heat pipe, or leader.

Adjust the airflow from a stoker fan to retort, inside furnace.

Renew air filters.

Clean heat lines, register boxes and registers.

Replace fuse plugs.

Paint the front of a furnace, and the inside of a stoker hopper.

Eliminate minor rattles in furnace or ductwork.

Splice an automatic damper chain.

Once the new heating plant is completely installed, or it is decided that the old one will have to do, the homeowner should say to himself: "Well, now, here's what I *want* to do: I want to obtain the maximum efficiency from this heating unit, with a minimum cost for fuel, maintenance, and repairs."

1. Fuel. The usual procedure in firing a coal-burning furnace is to shovel coal *into* the furnace, and ashes *from* the ash-pit. So, any man seen shoveling every third shovelful of coal *into the ashes* would be considered foolish. However, figures are available to prove that the average furnace tender wastes that amount of fuel through improper firing or other wasteful ways. The ratio of wasted oil, gas, and other fuels is somewhat lower, of course, but heating experts generally agree that almost any homeowner can show a saving of 10% on his heating bills.

There are three main clasifications of home heating fuels: Solid, liquid and gas.

Solid fuels are coal, coke, charcoal, wood and other carbon-containing materials.

Liquid fuels or oils are what remains from petroleum after gasoline and kerosene is distilled. Different weights run from No. 1 to No. 6, but No. 1 and No. 2 give the best performance in household equipment.

Gaseous fuels are either natural or manufactured, and can be piped to the home, or delivered in containers.

Coal is still used more than any other single fuel, in the American home. Figures from the U. S. Census Bureau show that nearly half (46%) of the dwelling units having central heating used coal as the

the furnace

The humidifier pan should be periodically taken out of the furnace, cleaned and repainted. Scrapings shown on floor are rust and mineral deposits from evaporated water in pan.

Cementing around rings at bottom of a furnace makes inner space airtight and prevents water seepage. When ring of cement chips off, be sure to recement.

principal fuel. Gas was second with 28% while 23% of the units were reportedly heated with liquid fuel.

Among the dwellings not having central heating, such as the home heated with individual stoves, heaters, fireplaces, cookstoves, etc., coal and gas was each used in about one fourth of the units. Wood and liquid fuels were next in line.

The above figures cover the nation as a whole. In the northeast and north central regions, coal is the predominant fuel used for home heating. About three fifths of the dwelling units in the West are heated with gas, while in the South and Southwest, about one third of the units use gas, with coal and wood following closely.

All too often, installations of heating systems are made solely on the basis of first costs of the equipment, and with not enough regard for future fuel costs and maintenance, repair and replacement expenses, and quality of performance. The type of fuel best suited for your heating system, provided of course the latter is the proper system for your home, should be given much consideration. Costs, transportation, nearness of supply, availability; all these are to be considered.

You can save on fuel costs primarily by selecting the right fuel for you in the beginning. From there it is a question of just keeping your heating plant in good condition and working order. Always remember: Less heat needed upstairs means dollars saved downstairs. So keep unused rooms closed off. Don't leave those outside doors open any longer than it takes to get inside or out. A lecture to children

now and then usually helps. When you close a window, *lock it*. Most windows are so designed that when the latch is set, the window becomes more airtight. An investment in insulation will pay for itself in from ten to fifteen years. A good weatherstripping and caulking job on your doors and windows will be well worth your money, too. If you leave a closet door open, a lot of heat can go in there, too, so keep closets closed. Getting back to insulation, if you can't afford to have someone insulate the whole house, the second best thing is to buy at least enough materials to insulate your ceiling. This will make a remarkable saving in your annual fuel bill.

Some people like to sleep with their bedroom window open. Health authorities are on record as saying that this is not necessary, but if you do follow this practice, close your bedroom off from the rest of the house, and cut off the heat as well. Always use the damper at the furnace when cutting off the heat from an individual line. The shutters, or louvres, in the registers are there to close off the register, not the heat. Cutting the heat off at the register wastes all the heat that must be held in the entire length of the line from the furnace to the register, and sometimes causes floors and plastering to crack. Registers are designed to be cut off because it adds to the life of the entire heat line when air is not allowed to circulate through this line, when the furnace is not in use. Circulating air carries moisture, and when this is deposited on the inner sides of the piping, eventually corrosion will result.

Stopping the circulation of air through these lines three months out of the year will add 25% to the normal life of the piping and register system.

Maintenance, Upkeep and Repair: Hand-Fired Coal Furnace

Naturally, the best time to inspect your hand-fired coal furnace for needed repairs, etc., is in the spring, just after the time it has become evident that you will not need further heat.

The first thing to be considered with any heating system, and particularly the coal-burning furnace, is the cleaning. This should be done annually if at all possible, and never less often than two-year periods. You can take the easy way out, in getting your furnace cleaned, by merely letting your dealer do it. It'll cost you about ten dollars, plus any spare parts needed for grates, smoke pipe, or lining. Or you can clean it yourself.

The proper way to clean any furnace is the vacuum way. In fact, a regular furnace cleaning machine is merely an over-sized vacuum cleaner. However, an ordinary vacuum machine can be used.

Take down your smoke pipe when you are ready to tackle the job. Be careful not to damage controls or draft regulators that are or might be attached to the smoke pipe. If the pipe is still in good condition, clean it thoroughly, with any type of brush, mop, broom, or whatever you have handy. Get right down to the metal of the pipe. This increases the draft potential of the pipe. Now lay the pipe aside. Even if you in-

tend to replace the pipe, you'll still need it for the purpose of measuring the new pipe lengths.

The smoke radiator of a furnace is either attached to the rear part of the furnace, or rests atop the combustion chamber. The interior of this radiator can be reached through either the smoke collar at the back, or wherever the collar protrudes; or through cleanout doors. This radiator is designed to catch the smoke and burning fuel gases and retain the heat from them a little longer after they have left the combustion chamber. Radiators invariably need cleaning. In coal-burning equipment, fly ash usually accumulates in the bottom, and soot on the inner walls of both the radiator and the furnace drum. With oil or gas-burning equipment, soot is your big problem. One eighth of an inch of soot clinging to the walls of the furnace radiator or drum has the same insulating effect as about one half inch of real insulation material. So you can see the importance of removing the soot from the walls of the furnace and radiator.

To get the soot and fly ash down to where you can remove it from the heating unit, use a stiff brush. Clean down all the walls and rake out as much as you can before starting the vacuum, if you have one. Don't be afraid of getting a little dirty. You'll look like a chimney sweeper anyhow before the job is done, at best. But the results in fuel savings and heating efficiency will be worth your trouble.

Shake down all the ashes and cinders from the firebox, and clean the grates and furnace lining. By using a light and shak-

The smoke pipe should be cemented airtight where connection is made to the chimney thimble. This is a joint that should be periodically checked up on during firing season.

ing the grates while looking at them, you can easily determine if any of the parts are in need of replacement or repair. You can inspect the lining by cleaning the bricks off and looking. If either is in need of being replaced, do not hesitate to do so. There probably is a dealer in your community who deals with the type furnace you have. Contact him and see if he has the part in stock. Or get the name and address from the furnace itself and order direct from the manufacturer. Replacing a grate part or a furnace brick is a simple task. The methods vary, depending upon the type of furnace, of course. But anyone who can use a wrench and screw driver can take out a set of grates, put in a new piece, and replace the set. The operation for most types consists of a few cotter pins and bolts and nuts. For the aged furnace, it may become necessary to cut off bolt heads with a hammer and cold chisel, and put new bolts back in when the grates are replaced. The important thing to remember about grates is that if they are not in good condition, you lose fuel dollars by the unburned coal going right on through to the ashes.

The bottom row of fire bricks in a furnace is usually a complete ring. They are shaped so they fit snugly, and the heat from the first fires expand them tightly in place. The top row is made up of shorter bricks, and only a partial circle is used, this partial ring of bricks running from the inside of the coal chute door around the drum to the opposite side. These bricks are fitted in and clamped into place with a clamp that is bolted through to the coal chute itself. These clamps have slots, rather than regular bolt holes, and can be adjusted for a tight fitting of the bricks. When replacing bricks, it is usually necessary to remove at least one of these clamps. Remember, you don't have to replace the whole set of bricks just because one or two are melted down or cracked. Most people keep spare

bricks around, for quick replacement when needed. If you have your dealer to replace a set of bricks, the cost will be about $25, but if you buy the bricks and do the work yourself, you'll save about half this amount. A new set of grates will cost about $25, and the installation charge will be about $10, which you can save.

Now let's presume you have the entire furnace cleaned, and the bricks, grates, and shaker mechanism are all in good condition. The next thing to do is inspect the chimney and flue, while you have the smoke pipe down. Most chimneys have a cleanout at the bottom, at the floor level. If so, open this and clean out all the soot and fly ash. Then brush the inside of the thimble and flues with whatever you have (brush, old mop with short handle, etc.). While you're at it, place a light at the bottom of the chimney in the cleanout, or through the thimble, and get up on the roof and have a look. Your chimney may be almost clogged up. If so, here's how to clean it:

Drop a rope or wire down through the chimney, and then tie on a bundle of rags or burlap bags. Make this bundle just large enough to slide through easily, yet snugly. Then simply pull it through, just like you were cleaning your rifle barrel. Another way to clean a chimney from the roof is to use a rope, and a weighted burlap bag. Just lower and pull back out several times. And while you're up there on the roof, don't forget to inspect for leaks, cracks and other damages that might need immediate attention. A lot of homes are burned down each year due to a faulty chimney and leaky flues.

Now the chimney is in good shape, and you're ready to replace the smoke pipe. The average life of furnace smoke pipe, which should be 24 gauge thickness, is from two to three years. If the pipe passes your inspection and is good enough for another year, that's just that much money you'll

Both warm and cold air pipe connections should be sealed by taping the joints with 3-inch wide asbestos tape. Put paste on one side of the tape and lap it about 2".

save. But don't take a chance on losing
your home in order to save that few dollars.
Let's say you want to put up a new smoke
pipe, and you want to save money by doing
the work yourself.

Renewal of the Smoke Pipes

Regardless of the kind of heat you have,
or the fuel you use, the smoke pipe is
going to have to be renewed about every
two or three years, or maybe oftener. This
is one way that any homeowner can save
himself money on his total heating bills.
Anybody can take down an old smoke pipe
and put up a new one.

The best time to renew a smoke pipe,
of course, is during the summer when the
furnace is not in use. Before you actually
take the pipe from the chimney thimble or
collar, remove any controls or check drafts
that are attached to the pipe. Do this only
after you are sure that you can replace
them in the new pipe, at the right place.
If you can, take the old pipe out all in one
piece and lay it aside until the new pipe is
installed. You can get your proper measurements from this old pipe, and determine
just where and how what went.

You can get smoke pipe at any heating
dealer or hardware store. For a furnace,
get at least 24 gauge thickness. Some
lighter gauges are on the market for heating and cooking stoves. Elbows and angles
should be of the adjustable variety, the
same gauge as the pipe.

The only way you can install a new
smoke pipe without tools is if there are no
controls of draft checks on the pipe, and
if you don't wish to metal screw the joints
together, and provided the amount of pipe
comes out exactly the same as the length
of one or more joints of pipe, plus elbows.

But on most jobs, here are the tools you'll
need to do a first-class job: ¼ inch electric
drill, ⅛ inch bit, metal screws and screw
driver, hammer, circle-cutting tin snips, a
trowel and some freshly mixed mortar or
furnace cement for sealing around the pipe
in the thimble. Here's how you go about it,
now that you have the tools. You have the
pipe and elbows that you need, and are
ready for the installation:

Your guide is the old pipe, provided it
gave satisfaction. Take the exact measurements from it, and cut your other pipe the
same. In close quarters, you may have to
put the pipe up a piece at a time, and
then add the controls or draft regulators.
In others, where you have plenty of room, it
is possible to assemble the whole thing on
the floor and install it in one operation.

Cutting holes in the pipe can be done

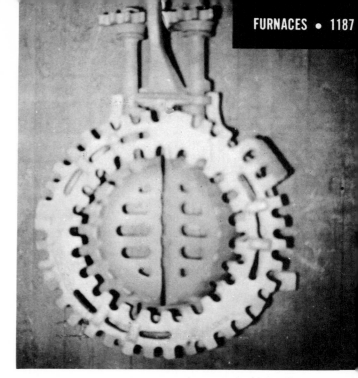

A set of grates for a coal-burning furnace may be
purchased for about $25, can be installed at home.

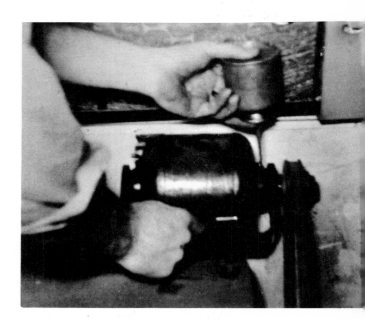

Fan on forced air furnace should have motor oiled
at least two or three times during firing season.

A dangerous oil leak, as shown below, should be
corrected by periodic maintenance of fuel lines.

with the circle-cutting tin snips. A pair of "Aviation" snips is better for cutting the smaller holes. Incidentally, any homeowner will do well to invest in a pair of this type snips. They have many uses, in addition to smoke pipe installation. For instance, running a new heat line from your furnace to a new room, upstairs, or a garage. Getting back to the hole cutting in the pipe, you can first mark the hole, start it by use of a hammer and chisel.

When removing the controls or check drafts from the old pipe, be sure to observe just where they were, at what angle. They are usually metal screwed to the pipe. This is where your electric drill is needed, although it is possible to make the necessary holes with an ice pick, or any sharp punch. You may have to have new screws, but you'll have some on hand anyway, since you'll need them in putting the joints of pipe and elbows together.

If the furnace is equipped with an electric damper control, be sure to connect the chain back just as it was. Try it to make sure by moving the thermostat setting. The draft door at the bottom of the furnace should be closed when the check draft door is open, and vice versa. If this control is operated manually from upstairs, one setting provides for both to be closed at the same time.

Once you have your new or old pipe up, you now are ready to seal it in with mortar or furnace cement, so the seal will be airtight, and have maximum efficiency. Before you actually seal in the pipe, make doubly sure the pipe extends into the chimney only as far as the inner edge of the flue tile, or chimney opening.

Mix about a half-gallon of rich mortar, using about half sand and half Portland cement, and seal in the pipe. Make the mortar "stiff" for better results. The job can be done best with a small trowel. Allow this mortar to dry naturally for at least twenty-four hours before building a fire in the furnace, or it might crack, and fall out.

Next, have a look at your humidifier. If it is the pan type, manually filled or otherwise, take the pan out, scrape out the rust, etc., paint with aluminum heat-resistant paint, and replace. If it is the type that fills automatically and shuts the supply tubing with a float valve, inspect all this and see that it is working properly. Then shut the valve at the source (main water pipe) and leave the pan free of water until the next firing season. This prevents rusting.

Now take your aluminum paint and paint the entire front, and everything else that looks like it might rust. For best and longer

protection, this should be done right after your last fire.

In servicing the forced warm air furnace, if the unit is a coal burner, the procedure is the same as with the gravity coal-burner, so far as the furnace, smoke pipe and chimney are concerned. However, the blower and motor contained in the cold air return should be thoroughly checked and oiled. Filters should be renewed every year, and shaken out during the regular season several times. A good deal of the foreign matter can be removed in this manner.

In the oil-burning furnace, it is, of course, best to have a qualified service man have a look each year, even if everything has been working satisfactorily. But even the homeowner who doesn't know the first thing about an oil burner can detect leaks in the fuel lines, and other such obvious fire hazards. He can also check, clean and replace the smoke pipe and filters, oil the fan and fan motor. The special lining in oil furnaces is designed to last a long time, but should your furnace need a new lining, you'll probably have to get your dealer to do this. One of the main reasons for an oil furnace lining ever needing replacement is: Over-firing has simply melted down the original lining. If the furnace is fired properly, this will not happen in the first place.

1 To clean your heater, open clean-out door and push the accumulated fly ash inside the furnace. Don't be afraid to use your tank vacuum cleaner for this job—it'll save time and effort.

2 The smoke pipe should be taken down at least once a year for a going-over. If rusty or corroded beyond repair, it should be replaced. When fitting in place, be sure joints are tight.

3 Do the doors fit perfectly? This damper door is warped, and must either be made flush by filing or else replaced. Same applies to all regularly-used doors, like the firing and ash pit doors.

4 If your clean-out doors are warped, replacement is not necessary, for they are not opened too often. Gaps can be simply sealed with furnace cement which can be chipped off at cleaning time.

5 Air leaks steal a lot of heat, are easily located by passing a lit candle around door frames, joints and furnace base. When flame is drawn into the heater, you know you've found one.

6 Sealing these leaks can be accomplished easily and quickly with furnace or asbestos cement. Both of these items are inexpensive and can be applied with a putty knife or a spatula.

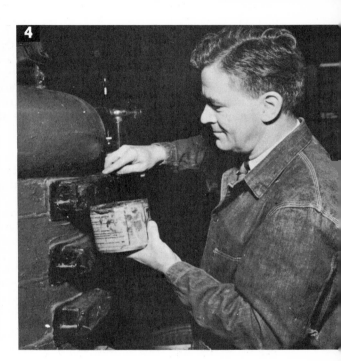

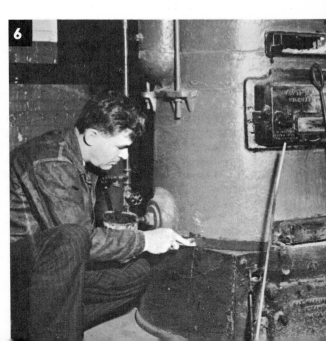

In servicing the gas furnace, it is altogether best to have it done by a regular, qualified service man, especially when it comes to checking the burner and gas supply lines. Of course you can take care of your smoke pipe, filters, etc.

In your annual spring cleaning, it is a good idea to remove all your registers, cold and hot air, and vacuum clean the boxes and pipes as far as you can reach. This removes lint, dirt, and dust particles that have accumulated over the last year.

Repairing the Cast Furnace

The cleaning and repairing of a cast iron furnace is essentially the same as that of a steel furnace, with the exception of the lining. Some cast furnaces are not lined at all. Those that are lined are lined with a type of fire clay or refractory cement, the finished job becoming seamless. For the homeowner who has the cast furnace, it's a good idea to keep some of this refractory material around in case one of the bowls of the firebox crack. A leak in the firebox can put lethal coal gases upstairs in your rooms, and that is bad.

The use of refractory cement is by no means confined to cast furnaces. It can be used to patch the brickwork inside a steel furnace, heating stoves, warm morning heaters and kitchen ranges.

Refractory cement is usually packed and sealed in the proper plastic consistency for immediate use. However, if it has dried out, it can easily be made workable by the addition of water. Just place the cement in a container, barely cover with water, and let it absorb the water for 24 hours. Build a fire immediately after the lining job is completed.

The casing of the furnace should be taken down and the combustion chamber inspected only if you have reason to believe there is a crack or leak in it. Unusually dirty and smoky places on walls around register might be the first tell-tale signs of such a leak. The odor can be detected almost as soon as the leak occurs. Fuel gas in the home *can* be lethal, although most such accidents are caused by the improper firing or banking of heating equipment used in living quarters, other than basement. But any time you think for any reason that you have a leak in your combustion chamber, the time to do something about it is right then. Small leaks can be repaired. If your furnace has about twenty years of service behind it, you just may need a new furnace. To remove the casing from a round-cased furnace, wire the bonnet to the joists and unbolt at the

connections the two wrapper lengths of sheet metal. Place a strong light on the inside of the furnace. In this way you can soon see any leaks. Most likely place is around the radiator connection. Heating experts light a "smoke candle" and place it inside the furnace, closing all doors and drafts. This is an excellent method of finding leaks.

A leak in a steel furnace can be welded, in most cases, although the leak may be a crack so large that it is advisable to replace the cracked part. Should you ever have your cast furnace torn down to this extent, by all means reline it while other work is being done. Also, re-cement all connections.

When checking a servicing and heating system, check all the piping connections for places where the asbestos tape has peeled or cracked. This means of sealing is easy to do, and you should keep a roll of the tape around at all times. Any hardware store or heating dealer will have it, as well as the cold water paste used in applying it. Seal all joints airtight. This adds much to the efficiency of the system.

Don't be too angry with your heating dealer when you get your bills for services rendered. Remember this: A good service man gets paid by the hour, anywhere between $1.50 and $3.50 per hour, depending on what part of the country he works in, wage scales, etc. His company must charge you a certain percentage above this wage for the time he spends on your furnace, plus a charge for the truck he uses to get himself, tools and parts from the shop to your house, plus the cost of the materials used, plus a helper's wages if one is needed, plus sales taxes in some states. So consider these things the next time you think your bill is too high.

But the high cost of repairs is just another reason why you should take it upon yourself to *learn* to do all the repairs in connection with your own heating plant. Get a service manual from your dealer, or write the furnace manufacturer for one. The next time you want heating repairs or service, do it yourself.

Servicing the Floor Oil Furnace

At least twice during each firing season, the floor furnace should be serviced. Of course, this is best done by an experienced service man, but the homeowner with the floor furnace can soon learn to do this checking and cleaning himself, thereby saving the amount of the service call.

This inspection should include:
Cleaning oil strainer in float valve.

Inspection of burner and removal of accumulated carbon through the removable door at the front of the burner.

Removal of all dirt and dust from inside the casing through the cleanout doors.

When replacing the strainer after cleaning with kerosene, be sure that the fibre gasket is cleaned and replaced.

Inspection of oil flow orifice into the burner. Be sure that accumulated carbon is removed from burner end of orifice.

Be sure to always go by the manufacturer's instructions in determining what type oil to use.

Never allow your supply tank to burn completely dry; keep at least partially filled at all times.

Keep all rugs and other combustible material off and away from the grille.

Servicing the Floor Gas Furnace

Gas floor furnaces should be checked, cleaned and inspected at least twice per season. With this type more so than any other, the work should be done by a reliable, experienced service man.

It is not recommended that the home owner attempt any repairs or servicing whatever to this type, unless he is thoroughly familiar with its operation, and knows all the safety rules to be observed.

Don't, under any condition, expose a flame where unburned gas is present.

If the gas pilot has been on but not lighted, purge all gas burning equipment of gas by shutting off the main gas valve to equipment for at least five minutes.

If the gas to the main burner has been flowing with the burner not lighted, the equipment should be purged at least thirty minutes with all valves closed.

L.P. gases such as Propane, Butane, or combinations, are heavier than air, and will not rise out the chimney. They spill out on the floor. Equipment to burn this gas requires special controls, of course, with a 100% shutoff in case the pilot flame goes out. But it takes almost a minute for the safety pilot to shut off the gas supply, and it is therefore possible to get quite a bit of L.P. gas in the base of the heater. Be sure to see that all L.P. gas in the base of the equipment can escape into the surrounding space to dilute it to a safe mixture. •

Filters are an important part of any forced warm air heating system and should be renewed at least once a year, or as often as needed. Shake them out every two weeks during the period of most utility.

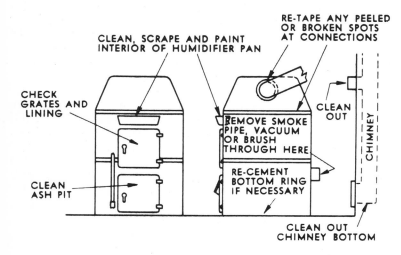

At left is a check chart for guidance in the proper care and servicing of the ordinary gravity coal-burning furnace.

Sheet-metal plenums, as on top of this oil-burning unit, may give greater efficiency to the furnace.

High temperature firebrick in a furnace lining, as below, keeps gas hot and assures full combustion.

alterations to your present system

Sometimes all a furnace needs is some homemade trouble-shooting.

A good humidifier is an excellent investment in comfort and health. Cutaways show proper set-up.

IF your present heating system isn't functioning just as it should, don't rush right out and buy a new plant. Maybe all it needs is a few alterations. In any event, get a heating expert to look the whole works over before doing anything drastic. Here are a few things that might be wrong, and how to fix them.

Not enough cold air return capacity. Hot or warm air weighs about .062 lbs. per cubic foot, while cold air weighs .076 lbs. The cold air being heavier, slips and is pushed downward by the warm air from the ceiling, and goes through your cold air grille back to the furnace. If you have a forced air system, it is drawn back by the suction of the fan. Either way, the capacity of the total of all the heat lines should be about the same as that of the cold air lines. So add up the capacity of each. You may need more cold air return space, and you can have this by enlarging the line or lines you have or adding new ones.

Furnace large enough for house, but doesn't heat adequately. Your home may need weatherstripping, caulking, or even insulating. A good insulation job saves at least 30% fuel in most cases, in addition to providing additional summer comfort.

Some rooms too hot and some too cold. If your furnace is large enough for your house, then the heat is just not distributed in the right proportions. An adjustment of the dampers in all the lines can usually correct this. If no dampers are in the lines, then some should be installed.

Heat from the furnace cracking the floor overhead. About all you can do about a cracked floor is refill the cracks with plastic wood and refinish, but you can insulate the top of the furnace and nail a metal liner to the joists.

Using too much fuel. Either the furnace is just too small, or, if the unit is oil or gas-fired, it's out of adjustment, or needs a smaller nozzle. The service man should have a look at this trouble as soon as you detect it.

Too noisy. Usually just a loose connection that can be fixed, in the case of most automatic furnaces. Electric motors that interfere with radio reception should be checked by electrician.

Heat blows from registers right onto where persons usually sit in living room, dining room, etc. Most wall or ceiling registers have deflectors that can change the directions of warm air streams. If yours doesn't have these, then have your heating dealer change the ones that have become bothersome. Direct, forced warm air should not be aimed directly at anyone.

House cool, although thermostat shows right temperature. This is just a case of the thermostat being in the wrong place, or the house is old, and in need of weather-stripping, etc.

Heat and "smoke" from registers dirty walls and add to decorating bills. While it is entirely possible to have a smoke leak in the combustion chamber of your furnace, thereby causing "smoky" walls, the chances are the dark, sooty-like stuff on your walls is simply baked dust, dirt and lint, especially if you live in an industrial area, or on a dusty road.

Suppose you've just built a new room to your house, or want to add a heat line to the garage, or attic. This is easily done, but before you do anything like this, always be sure that your furnace is large enough to carry another line, especially if you intend to heat this added space all the time. A word of advice here on heating your garage: Automobiles need only a 40 degree temperature to start promptly on cold mornings. The chances are that your garage keeps the car motor that warm most of the winter, just by being enclosed. In short, for the most part, heating your garage just isn't worth it. However, if you use your garage for other purposes, then that's a different story. . . A new line can be run from the bonnet or plenum of your furnace as described in the installation part on gravity furnaces. If you use round pipe and a floor register, you can do the work yourself. A line can be run upstairs right through a closet. Use flat duct, 3x12, insulate with asbestos paper, and paint to match your closet wall. The kind of box and register you'll use will depend upon how your upstairs is finished, but usually it's best to use a floor box and register.

You may want to add an automatic humidifier to your furnace, if your present unit has the plain water pan built in; the type that must be filled by hand. A float type can be added for a few dollars. A saddle clamp fitting is mounted on your cold water pipe and copper tubing run from this fitting to the pan. The pan may have a hole near the top of the fitting for the tubing connection, if not, then one may be drilled, $\frac{5}{16}$ inch. The shut-off valve and float are inside the pan. When the pan fills, the valve shuts off. When a certain amount of water evaporates, the valve lets more in.

Any line changes in your hot or cold air ducts can be accomplished without much time or trouble. There are several reasons why you might wish to alter in some way the existing ducts to your furnace. If the ducts are rectangular, and you find that you need more, you'll have to get this made at a sheet metal shop, but if the ducts are round, you can easily do all the work yourself. With the right tools, such as a drill, tin snips, screw driver and metal screws, hammer, etc., you can get what extra pipe and adjustable elbows you need and get right into the job. The ducts are lightweight and easily handled. If possible, don't use any more elbows and angles than already were in use on each line. Use less, if you can. The more turns the pipe has, the less the gravity pull. Hang all pipes securely by wire hangers, and put at least three metal screws in each joint for greater holding strength.

The thing to remember again is that the more of the work you can do yourself, the more money you can save. Pay for advice on your alterations, yes, but do the work yourself, if you can. Chances are you can save yourself more per hour than you make at your full-time job. •

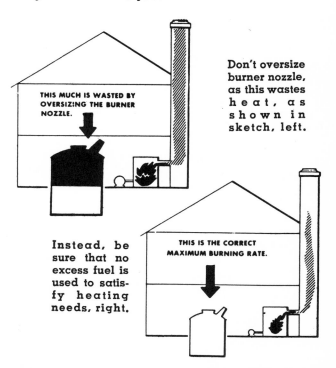

THIS MUCH IS WASTED BY OVERSIZING THE BURNER NOZZLE.

Don't oversize burner nozzle, as this wastes heat, as shown in sketch, left.

THIS IS THE CORRECT MAXIMUM BURNING RATE.

Instead, be sure that no excess fuel is used to satisfy heating needs, right.

chaise

Both comfort and convenience are featured in this folding lounge.

THE chaise illustrated is designed for a maximum degree of reclining comfort with a minimum amount of bulk and weight. The backrest is adjustable to three positions and, when down, the chaise becomes a 68 in. bed with an adjustable canopy to insure a restful, mid-afternoon snooze. If you prefer a face tan, tilt the canopy back or remove it. The footrest is also adjustable to three positions which, in combination with the angles of the seat and backrest, will conform to your particular angles of anatomy. The footrest is removable, transforming the chaise into a luxurious lounge chair.

If you live in a hot-and-cold climate the chaise can be easily disassembled and stored in a space 13 in. deep, 41 in. wide and 58 in. high—an impossible achievement with the conventional-type chaise.

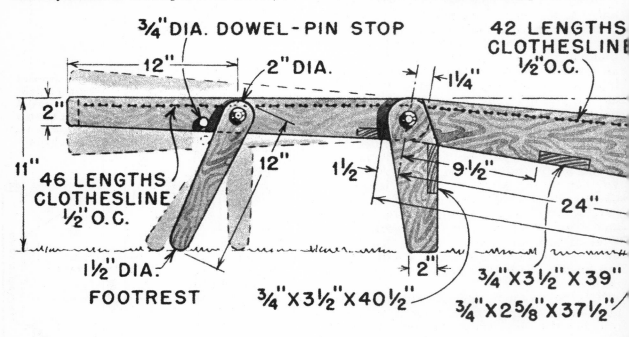

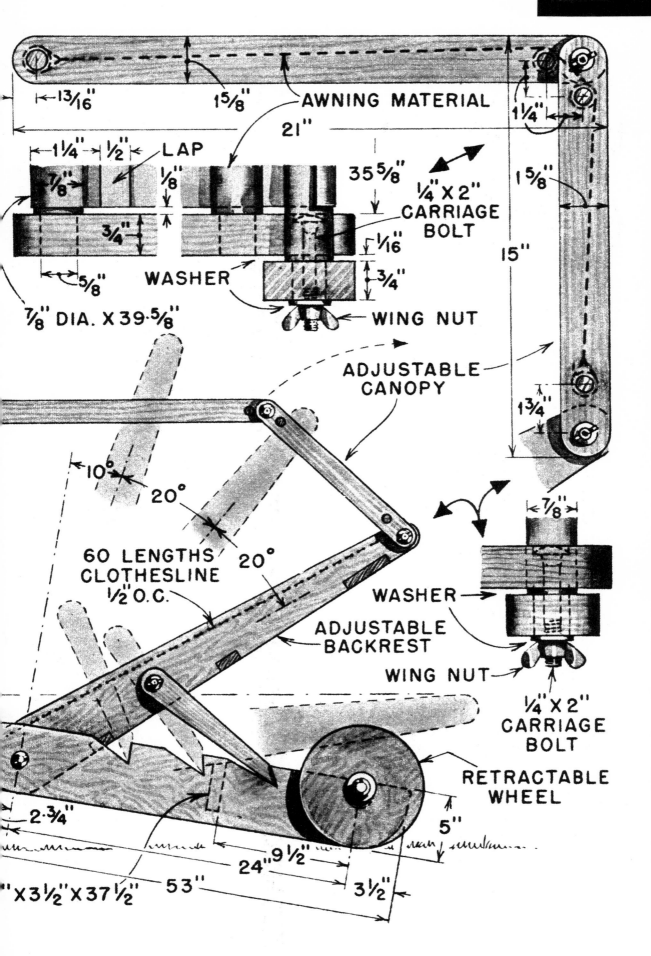

13/16"

1 5/8"

AWNING MATERIAL

1 1/4"

21"

1 1/4" — 1/2" — LAP

1/8"

7/8"

35 5/8"

1 5/8"

3/4"

1/4" X 2" CARRIAGE BOLT

1/16"

3/4"

5/8"

WASHER

15"

7/8" DIA. X 39.5/8"

WING NUT

ADJUSTABLE CANOPY

1 3/4"

10°

20°

7/8"

20°

60 LENGTHS CLOTHESLINE 1/2" O.C.

WASHER

ADJUSTABLE BACKREST

WING NUT

1/4" X 2" CARRIAGE BOLT

RETRACTABLE WHEEL

2. 3/4"

5"

24" 9 1/2"

"X 3 1/2" X 37 1/2"

53"

3 1/2"

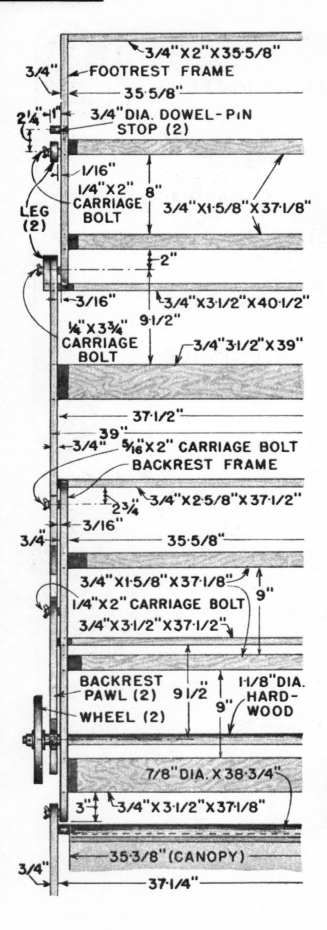

3/4"X2"X35·5/8"
FOOTREST FRAME
3/4"
35·5/8"
2¼" 1"
3/4"DIA. DOWEL-PIN STOP (2)
1/16"
1/4"X2" CARRIAGE BOLT
8"
3/4"X1·5/8"X37·1/8"
LEG (2)
2"
3/16"
3/4"X3·1/2"X40·1/2"
¼ X 3¾" CARRIAGE BOLT
9·1/2"
3/4"3·1/2"X39"

37·1/2"
39"
3/4"
5/16"X2" CARRIAGE BOLT
BACKREST FRAME
2¾"
3/4"X2·5/8"X37·1/2"
3/16"
3/4"
35·5/8"
3/4"X1·5/8"X37·1/8"
9"
1/4"X2" CARRIAGE BOLT
3/4"X3·1/2"X37·1/2"
BACKREST PAWL (2)
9½"
1·1/8"DIA. HARD-WOOD
WHEEL (2)
9"
7/8"DIA. X 38·3/4"
3"
3/4"X3·1/2"X37·1/8"
35·3/8"(CANOPY)
3/4"
37·1/4"

To reduce bulk to a minimum and yet attain maximum structural strength and rigidity, use exterior-grade, ¾ in. fir plywood for the side frame members and wheels. This material is bonded with waterproof resins and will not warp or split. Bracing members can be well seasoned solid wood such as pine, cedar, cypress or redwood. Personally, working with power tools, I prefer plywood and no end-grain weakness. Canopy frames can be made of either solid or plywood. Use fh wood screws and resorcinol resin glue (Cascophen) which is waterproof and heatproof and makes a stronger-than-wood joint for all framing members. Another reason for using plywood for the footrest, seat and backrest is that solid wood will split between the ½ in. o.c. holes required for the clothesline.

Cut the seat side frames from ¾ in. fir plywood to dimensions, and dado bottom edge ¾x3½ in. for one brace. Bore $\frac{3}{16}$ in. holes on a line ½ in. from the top edge,

PARKING SPACE:
13" DEEP
41" WIDE
58" HIGH

½ in. o.c. Countersink holes to an outside diameter of ½ in. and chip out a groove between the pairs of holes retaining the clothesline turns. At the start and finish side, bore a $\frac{3}{16}$ in. hole ½ in. below the first and last hole; countersink and chip a groove between the holes. Bore a $\frac{5}{16}$ in. hole in each piece as dimensioned for $\frac{5}{16}$x2 in. carriage bolts (backrest pivots). Counterbore all bolts for a flush drive of bolt heads. Cut notches for the backrest pawls and wheel axle. Cut braces to size, butt-joining center and back braces with resorcinol resin glue and No. 14 x2 in., fh wood screws. Countersink slightly deeper than flush all fh wood screws and fill with a water-mix, wood putty. Dado-joined members are secured in the same manner.

Cut to shape two pieces for the seat-frame legs, dadoing ¾x3½ in. for a brace. Attach to the frame with glue and three No. 14 x1¼ in. fh wood screws each, from the inner side. Bore ¼ in. holes for two ¼x3¾ in. carriage bolts (footrest pivots). Frame brace to legs with glue and No. 14x2 in. fh wood screws.

Construct the footrest frame, butt-joining the front brace and dado-joining the two bottom braces with glue and No. 14 x 2 in. fh wood screws, first boring $\frac{3}{16}$ in.

MATERIALS REQUIRED

Exterior-grade fir plywood
2 pieces (seat side frames), ¾″ x 5″ x 53″
2 pieces (footrest side frames), ¾″ x 3″ x 25½″
2 pieces (backrest side frames), ¾″ x 5″ x 35″
2 pieces (seat-frame legs), ¾″ x 3″ x 11″
2 pieces (footrest legs), ¾″ x 2″ x 12″
2 pieces (wheels), ¾″ x 9″ dia.
Solid wood or plywood
1 piece (footrest front brace), ¾″ x 2″ x 35⅝″
2 pieces (footrest braces), ¾″ x 1⅝″ x 37⅓″
1 piece (seat-frame leg brace), ¾″ x 3½″ x 40½″
1 piece (seat-frame brace), ¾″ x 3½″ x 39″
1 piece (seat-frame brace), ¾″ x 2⅝″ x 37½″
1 piece (seat-frame brace), ¾″ x 3½″ x 37½″
2 pieces (backrest-frame braces), ¾″ x 1⅝″ x 37⅛″
1 piece (backrest-frame brace), ¾″ x 3½″ x 37⅛″
2 pieces (canopy frame), ¾″ x 1⅝″ x 15″
2 pieces (canopy frame), ¾″ x 1⅝″ x 21″
Oak, maple or plywood
2 pieces (backrest pawls), ¾″ x 2″ x 12″
Hardwood
2 pieces (canopy braces), ⅞″ dia. x 37⅛″
2 pieces (canopy braces), ⅞″ dia. x 38¾″
1 piece (axle), 1⅛″ dia. x 41⅝″ oak round
2 pieces (footrest-leg stops), ¾″ dia. x 1¾″
Hardware
8 carriage bolts, ¼″ x 2″
2 carriage bolts, ¼″ x 3¾″
2 carriage bolts, ¼″ x 5½″
2 carriage bolts, 5/16″ x 2″
38 iron washers for ¼″ and 5/16″ bolts
4 iron washers for ¾″ shaft
2 ¾″ shaft collars
No. 14 x 2″ flat head wood screws
No. 14 x 1¼″ flat head wood screws
Resorcinol resin glue (Cascophen)
Miscellaneous
1 piece, 10 oz. canvas awning material, 41″ x 36″
475 ft. approx. No. 5 cotton braided clothesline (3/16″ dia.)

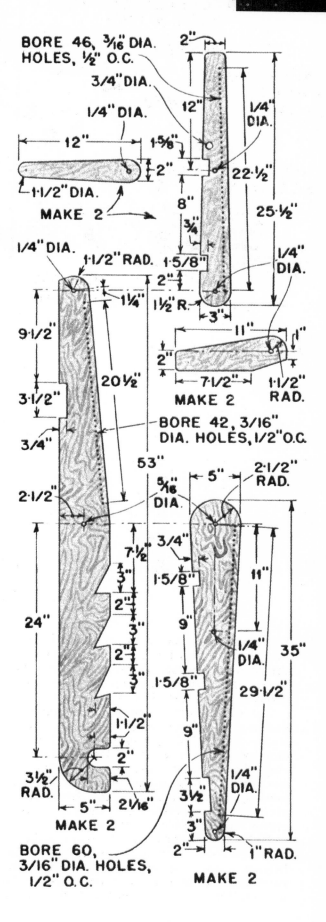

BORE 46, 3/16″ DIA. HOLES, ½″ O.C.
3/4″ DIA.
1/4″ DIA.
2″
12″
1/4″ DIA.
12″
1·5/8″
2″
1·1/2″ DIA.
MAKE 2
22·1/2″
8″
3/4″
25·1/2″
1/4″ DIA.
1·1/2″ RAD.
1·5/8″
1/4″ DIA.
2″
1¼″
1½″ R.
1/4″ DIA.
3″
11″
1″
9·1/2″
2″
7·1/2″
1·1/2″ RAD.
20½″
MAKE 2
BORE 42, 3/16″ DIA. HOLES, ½″ O.C.
3·1/2″
53″
2·1/2″ RAD.
5″
3/4″
5/16″ DIA.
2·1/2″
3/4″
7·1/2″
1·5/8″
11″
3″
2″
3″
9″
2″
1/4″ DIA.
35″
24″
1·5/8″
29·1/2″
3″
1·1/2″
9″
2″
3½″ RAD.
5″
2·1/16″
3½
3″
1/4″ DIA.
MAKE 2
BORE 60, 3/16″ DIA. HOLES, ½″ O.C.
2″
1″ RAD.
MAKE 2

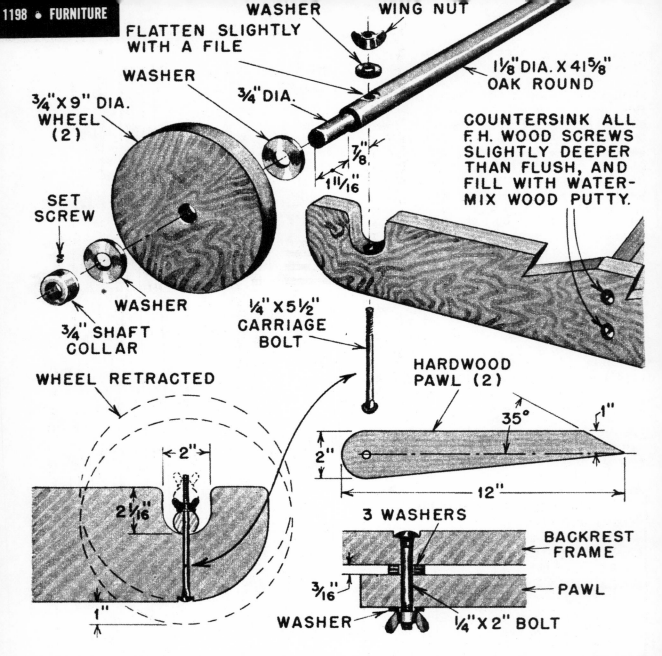

WASHER
WING NUT
FLATTEN SLIGHTLY
WITH A FILE
WASHER
3/4" DIA.
3/4" DIA.

1 1/8" DIA. X 41 5/8"
OAK ROUND

3/4" X 9" DIA.
WHEEL
(2)

7/8"
1 11/16"

COUNTERSINK ALL
F.H. WOOD SCREWS
SLIGHTLY DEEPER
THAN FLUSH, AND
FILL WITH WATER-
MIX WOOD PUTTY.

SET
SCREW

WASHER

3/4" SHAFT
COLLAR

1/4" X 5 1/2"
CARRIAGE
BOLT

HARDWOOD
PAWL (2)

35°
1"

WHEEL RETRACTED

2"

2"

12"

2 1/16"

3 WASHERS

BACKREST
FRAME

1"

3/16"

PAWL

WASHER

1/4" X 2" BOLT

holes, countersunk for the clothesline. Bore four 1/4 in. holes for the carriage bolts for the legs and pivots. Bore two 3/4 in. holes for the dowel-pin leg stops. File spiral glue grooves in the dowel ends and glue.

Cut the backrest frames to dimensions, dadoing the back edges for the braces. Bore 3/16 in. holes, countersunk for the clothesline. Bore 5/16 in. holes for the carriage-bolt pivots and 1/4 in. holes for 1/4x2 in. carriage bolts for the pawls and canopy pivots. Assemble the frame with glue and wood screws. Cut the pawls from either oak, maple or plywood.

Make the canopy frames from solid or plywood stock, boring 5/8 in. holes for the braces. Bore 1/4 in. holes for 1/4x2 in. carriage-bolt pivots. Turn or shape to 5/8 in. dia. the ends of the 7/8 in. stock rounds

and file spiral glue grooves in the ends.

You will require approximately 147 ft. of No. 5 cotton braided clothesline for the footrest; 140 ft. for the seat and 186 ft. for the backrest. The clothesline is usually sold in 100 ft. lengths at most hardware-house furnishings stores. Soak the clothesline in water, then stretch it as tightly as possible between convenient points and let dry. This will reduce the 3/16 in. dia. enough to easily thread the line through the holes and reduce further stretching to a minimum when in the frames.

Assemble the footrest and seat frames, seat frame and backrest, using three 1/16 in. thick iron washers (for 1/4 in. and 5/16 in. bolts) between frames, and one washer between the wing nuts and frames.

Use 10 oz. canvas awning material in

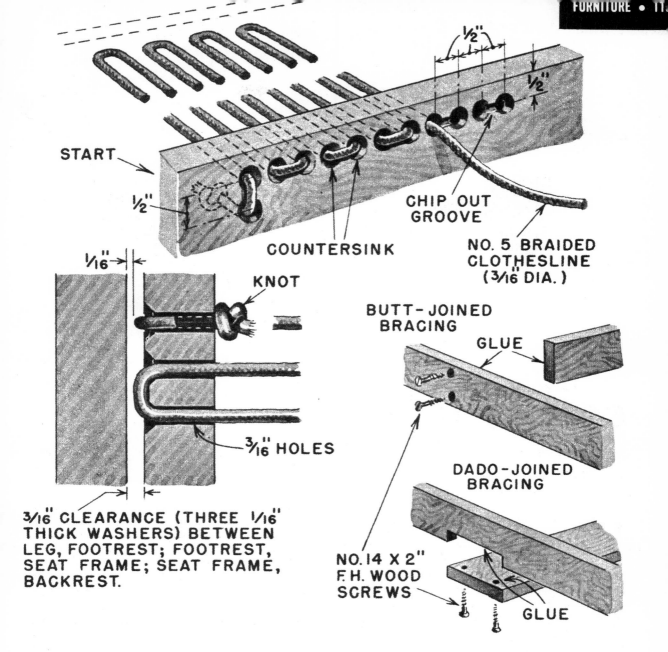

START

½"

COUNTERSINK

CHIP OUT GROOVE

NO. 5 BRAIDED CLOTHESLINE (3⁄16" DIA.)

½"

½"

1⁄16"

KNOT

BUTT-JOINED BRACING

GLUE

3⁄16" HOLES

3⁄16" CLEARANCE (THREE 1⁄16" THICK WASHERS) BETWEEN LEG, FOOTREST; FOOTREST, SEAT FRAME; SEAT FRAME, BACKREST.

DADO-JOINED BRACING

NO.14 X 2" F.H. WOOD SCREWS

GLUE

either solid or striped colors, vat dyed. You will require a piece 41 in. long and 36 in. wide which leaves a $\frac{5}{16}$ in. hem to be sewed on each edge. Turn over the loop ends ½ in. and double stitch for added strength. After the canopy is finished, assemble the braces and frames with glue.

Cut the wheels from ¾ in. plywood stock with either a coping saw or power jig saw.

Then bore a ¾ in. hole through the disks for the axle.

Use a length of 1⅛ in. dia. x 41⅝ in. oak round, which is stock material in most lumber yards, for the axle. Cut and shape to a ¾ in. dia. each end to receive the wheels. Bore ¼ in. holes at each end for the ¼x5½ in. carriage bolts and attach to the frame. Place an iron washer between the axle shoulder and the wheel, and the

wheel and the shaft collar, for turning fit.

Sand the chaise thoroughly, rounding all sharp edges slightly, and finish with two or more coats of spar varnish. Or, if you prefer bright colors, first apply two coats of white Firzite to cover the wild fir grain, and then two or more coats of outdoor paint or enamel.

For the last word in cushioned comfort, foam rubber of from 2 in. to 4½ in. thick, cored and No. 4 compression is the answer. "Airfoam," a product of Goodyear is procurable in most localities, either from distributors or from upholstery firms. Cushions are easily made, using ½ in. solid slab utility stock for open core facing cemented with rubber cement. Tailored slip covers of gaily patterned, waterproof material can be made at home. •

coffee table

Make several of these tables to

unfold for your terrace parties.

OUTDOOR coffee tables are as useful as their indoor counterparts—actually more so—if full enjoyment of outdoor living is to be experienced. On the outdoor coffee table almost everything can be parked clean and dry and near at hand.

This coffee table is generous in size and it, too, can be folded, and stored in a space 3½ in. deep, 24 in. high and 36 in. long. The legs are rigidly braced by a pivoted stretcher which forces them against two end braces. To tuck away, swing the stretcher clear of the hinged legs which, when folded, are again secured by swinging the stretcher to its lock position.

Use exterior-grade fir plywood for the top and the legs and, if you prefer, hard or softwood for the end braces, pivoting block and the stretcher. Use resorcinol resin glue and fh wood screws for strong, lasting joints.

To assemble, first hinge the legs to the top, recessing the hinges ½ their thickness deeper than flush in both the legs and the top, and cut notches to clear the hinge knuckles. Recessing the hinges in this manner insures the edge of the legs fitting tightly and squarely against the underside of the top. With the legs in vertical position, locate the end braces in which you

have bored and counterbored five lead holes each for No. 16 x2 in. fh wood screws. Apply glue, clamp the end braces to the legs and screw in place.

Counterbore the underside of the top to receive and clear the $\frac{5}{16}$ in. carriage-bolt (stretcher pivot) head. Bore a hole for a drive fit of the bolt through the pivot block and, with the bolt in place, attach the block to the top with four No. 10 x1¼ in. fh wood screws countersunk deeper than flush. Cut the stretcher slightly longer than the dimension between the legs and round the corners of the ends slightly. Bore a $\frac{5}{16}$ in. hole for the bolt and attach with a washer between the block and the stretcher. Tighten with a washer and a wing nut. •

MATERIALS REQUIRED

Exterior-grade fir plywood
  1 top, ¾" x 24" x 36"
  2 legs, ¾" x 14" x 19"

Hard or softwood
  2 end braces, ¾" x 1⅝" x 19"
  1 pivot block, ¾" x 3" x 4"
  1 stretcher, ¾" x 1⅝" x 29⅝"

Hardware
  4 tight-pin, 2" butt hinges
  1 carriage bolt, 5/16" x 3"
  2 iron washers
  1 wing nut
    fh wood screws
    resorcinol resin glue (Cascophen)

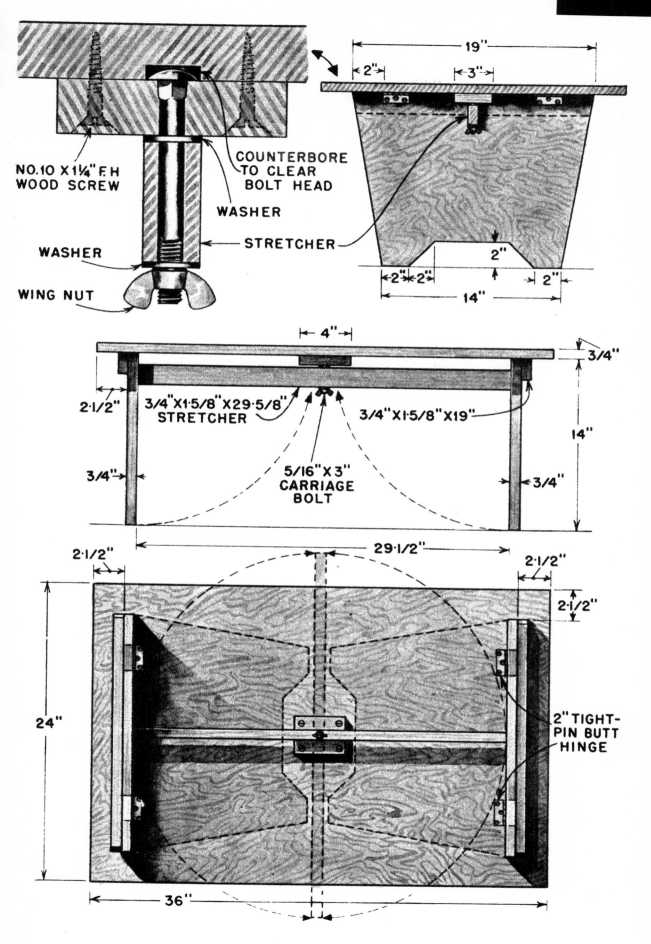

NO.10 X 1¼" F.H
WOOD SCREW

COUNTERBORE
TO CLEAR
BOLT HEAD

WASHER

WASHER

STRETCHER

WING NUT

19"

2"

3"

2"

2" 2"

2"

14"

4"

3/4"

2·1/2"

3/4"X1·5/8"X29·5/8"
STRETCHER

3/4"X1·5/8"X19"

14"

3/4"

5/16"X 3"
CARRIAGE
BOLT

3/4"

2·1/2"

29·1/2"

2·1/2"

2·1/2"

24"

2"TIGHT-
PIN BUTT
HINGE

36"

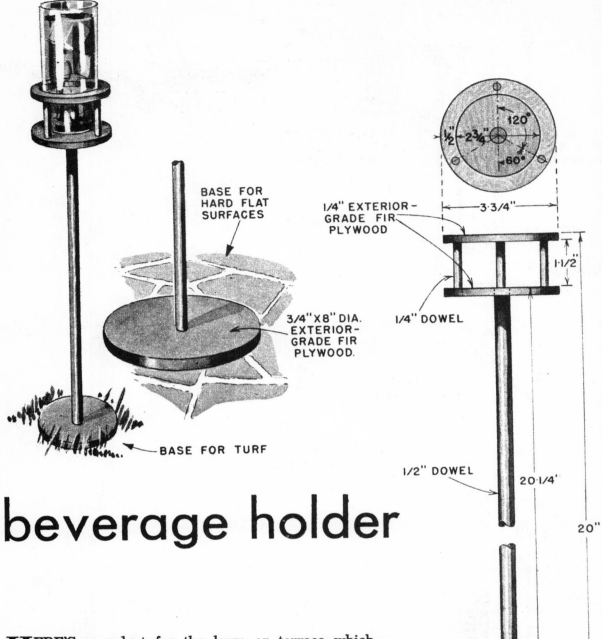

BASE FOR HARD FLAT SURFACES

3/4"X8" DIA. EXTERIOR-GRADE FIR PLYWOOD.

BASE FOR TURF

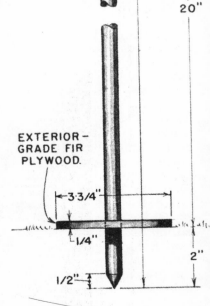

1/4" EXTERIOR-GRADE FIR PLYWOOD

120°

1/2" 2-3/4"

60°

3-3/4"

1-1/2

1/4" DOWEL

1/2" DOWEL

20-1/4"

20"

EXTERIOR-GRADE FIR PLYWOOD.

3-3/4"

1/4"

2"

1/2"

beverage holder

HERE'S a gadget for the lawn or terrace which solves the problem of where to park that short or tall drink wherever you happen to wander. It also cuts down on glassware breakage by those unwary souls who somehow always stumble over a glass trustingly at ease on the lawn or terrace.

You'll want a number of these holders which are easy to make from exterior-grade fir plywood, hardwood dowels and resorcinol resin glue (Cascophen). The inside diameter of the holder is for the average, straight 12 oz. glass. If your glassware is of different dimensions, change the diameter of the holder to fit. File a couple of grooves in the part of the dowels to be glued. Sand the assembly thoroughly and apply two coats of white Firzite. When dry, use gay color enamels. A different color for each holder or group of holders helps identify individual beverages, and colorfully accents outdoor entertaining. ●

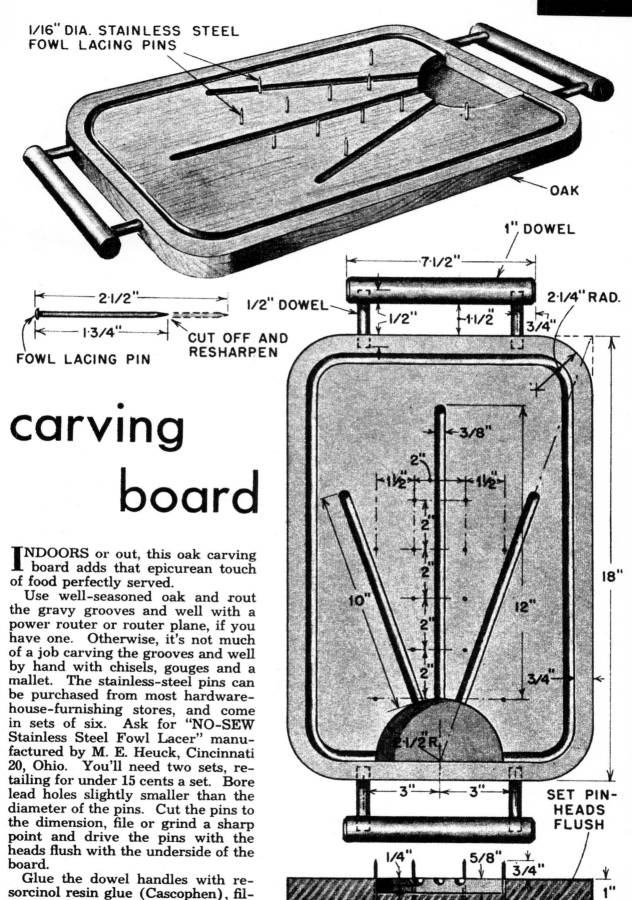

1/16" DIA. STAINLESS STEEL FOWL LACING PINS

OAK

2-1/2"

1-3/4"

CUT OFF AND RESHARPEN

FOWL LACING PIN

1" DOWEL

7-1/2"

1/2" DOWEL

2-1/4" RAD.

1/2"

1-1/2"

3/4"

3/8"

2"

1-1/2"

1-1/2"

2"

2"

18"

10"

12"

2"

3/4"

2"

2-1/2"R.

3"

3"

SET PIN-HEADS FLUSH

1/4"

5/8"

3/4"

1"

12"

carving
board

INDOORS or out, this oak carving board adds that epicurean touch of food perfectly served.

Use well-seasoned oak and rout the gravy grooves and well with a power router or router plane, if you have one. Otherwise, it's not much of a job carving the grooves and well by hand with chisels, gouges and a mallet. The stainless-steel pins can be purchased from most hardware-house-furnishing stores, and come in sets of six. Ask for "NO-SEW Stainless Steel Fowl Lacer" manufactured by M. E. Heuck, Cincinnati 20, Ohio. You'll need two sets, retailing for under 15 cents a set. Bore lead holes slightly smaller than the diameter of the pins. Cut the pins to the dimension, file or grind a sharp point and drive the pins with the heads flush with the underside of the board.

Glue the dowel handles with resorcinol resin glue (Cascophen), filing glue grooves in the dowel ends. •

tray

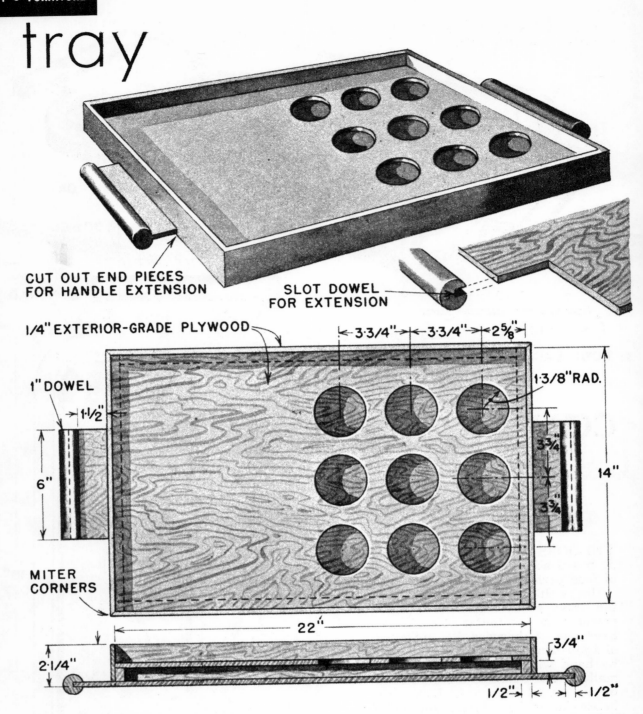

CUT OUT END PIECES
FOR HANDLE EXTENSION

SLOT DOWEL
FOR EXTENSION

1/4" EXTERIOR-GRADE PLYWOOD

3-3/4" 3-3/4" 2⅝"

1-3/8"RAD.

1"DOWEL

1-1/2"

6"

3¾"

3¾"

14"

MITER
CORNERS

22"

2-1/4"

3/4"

1/2" 1/2"

OUTDOOR entertaining has, to a large extent, to do with serving beverages, and here's a tray which will make serving a pleasure. It's easy to make and very little time is required to make it. Openings in one end of the tray prevent filled glasses from sliding and spilling their contents, particularly so on uneven lawns and different-level terraces. If you like, make a number of these trays, some exclusively for glassware and others for canapés and the like. The openings when not used, don't interfere with the service of solid foods.

Use exterior-grade fir plywood which is waterproof, resorcinol resin glue (Cascophen) and brads set slightly deeper than flush, and water-mix wood putty to hide the brad heads. Construct a frame from ½x¾ in. solid stock, butt-joining the pieces with glue and two 2d finishing nails for each corner. Cut the bottom with extensions at each end for the dowel handles, and the end pieces to fit over the extensions. Slot two 1 in. hardwood dowels to receive the extensions and glue. Finish the tray with two coats of spar varnish. ●

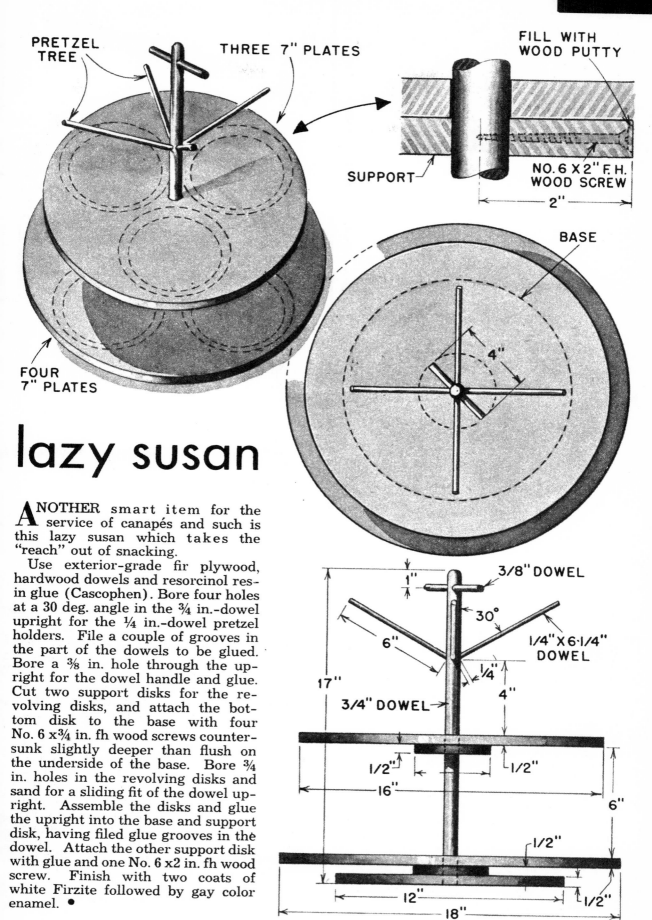

PRETZEL TREE

THREE 7" PLATES

FILL WITH WOOD PUTTY

SUPPORT

NO. 6 X 2" F.H. WOOD SCREW

2"

BASE

4"

FOUR 7" PLATES

lazy susan

ANOTHER smart item for the service of canapés and such is this lazy susan which takes the "reach" out of snacking.

Use exterior-grade fir plywood, hardwood dowels and resorcinol resin glue (Cascophen). Bore four holes at a 30 deg. angle in the ¾ in.-dowel upright for the ¼ in.-dowel pretzel holders. File a couple of grooves in the part of the dowels to be glued. Bore a ⅜ in. hole through the upright for the dowel handle and glue. Cut two support disks for the revolving disks, and attach the bottom disk to the base with four No. 6 x¾ in. fh wood screws countersunk slightly deeper than flush on the underside of the base. Bore ¾ in. holes in the revolving disks and sand for a sliding fit of the dowel upright. Assemble the disks and glue the upright into the base and support disk, having filed glue grooves in the dowel. Attach the other support disk with glue and one No. 6 x2 in. fh wood screw. Finish with two coats of white Firzite followed by gay color enamel. •

3/8" DOWEL

30°

6"

1/4" X 6·1/4" DOWEL

1"

1/4"

4"

17"

3/4" DOWEL

1/2"

1/2"

16"

6"

1/2"

12"

1/2"

18"

table with canopy

HERE'S a table with an adjustable canopy which will seat six comfortably—eight at a pinch—yet can be disassembled quickly and, exclusive of the pole, tucked away in a space approximately 7 in. deep, 48 in. wide and 48 in. high. Its light but rigid construction enables you to move it with ease.

The pivoted table legs lock in place with stove bolts through the table aprons and top leg stretchers, and the bottom stretchers are locked by the hinged cross brace and the canopy pole which is sunk into the ground about 3 in. If the canopy is not desired, one stove bolt (not shown in the illustrations) through the leg cross brace and bottom stretcher will serve.

Canopy braces are uniquely designed to fold into a compact unit when not in use.

Each of the four sections is hinged to its mate, locking into a cross when opened. The tilting crosshead is so designed to support the braces at their juncture, and the canvas canopy when stretched over the braces adds further rigidity to the assembly.

Use exterior-grade ¾ in. fir plywood for the table top, legs and bottom cross brace, and hard, softwood or exterior-grade fir plywood for the table aprons, leg stretchers, crosshead, canopy braces and corner blocks. Use a length of stock 1¾ in. oak round for the canopy pole. Assemble throughout with resorcinol resin glue and fh wood screws countersunk slightly deeper than flush, and fill with water-mix wood putty.

For the canopy braces, use tight-pin

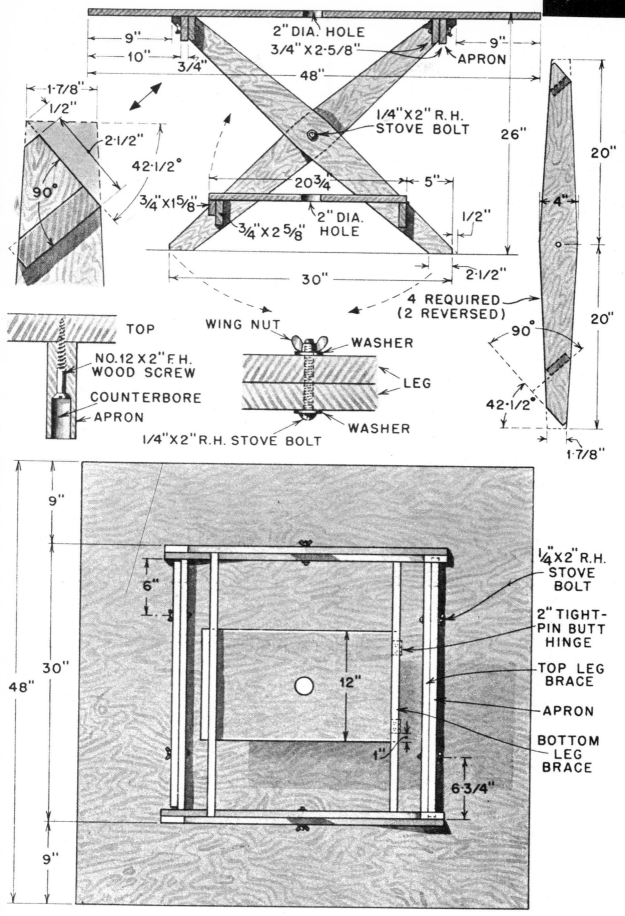

2" DIA. HOLE
3/4" X 2·5/8"
APRON
9"
10"
9"
3/4"
48"
1/4" X 2" R.H. STOVE BOLT
26"
20"
1·7/8"
1/2"
2·1/2"
42·1/2°
90°
4"
20"
3/4" X 1·5/8"
20¾"
5"
2" DIA. HOLE
3/4" X 2·5/8"
1/2"
90°
4 REQUIRED (2 REVERSED)
30"
2·1/2"
42·1/2°
1·7/8"

TOP
NO.12 X 2" F.H. WOOD SCREW
COUNTERBORE
APRON

WING NUT
WASHER
LEG
WASHER
1/4" X 2" R.H. STOVE BOLT

9"
6"
30"
48"
12"
1"
6·3/4"
9"

1/4" X 2" R.H. STOVE BOLT
2" TIGHT-PIN BUTT HINGE
TOP LEG BRACE
APRON
BOTTOM LEG BRACE

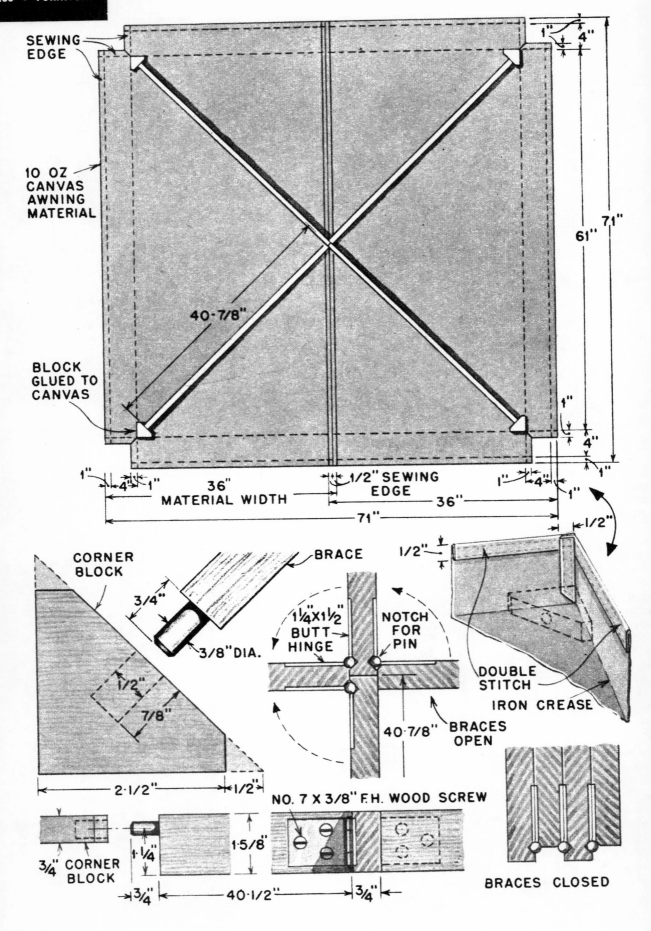

SEWING EDGE

10 OZ CANVAS AWNING MATERIAL

BLOCK GLUED TO CANVAS

40·7/8"

1"
4"

71"
61"

1"
4"

1/2"

1"
4"
1"

36"
MATERIAL WIDTH

1/2" SEWING EDGE

36"

1"
4"
1"

71"

1/2"

CORNER BLOCK

BRACE

3/4"

3/8" DIA.

1/2"

7/8"

2-1/2"

1/2"

1/4 x 1 1/2"
BUTT HINGE

NOTCH FOR PIN

40·7/8"

BRACES OPEN

DOUBLE STITCH

IRON CREASE

1/2"

3/4" CORNER BLOCK

1 1/4"

1·5/8"

3/4"

40·1/2"

3/4"

NO. 7 X 3/8" F.H. WOOD SCREW

BRACES CLOSED

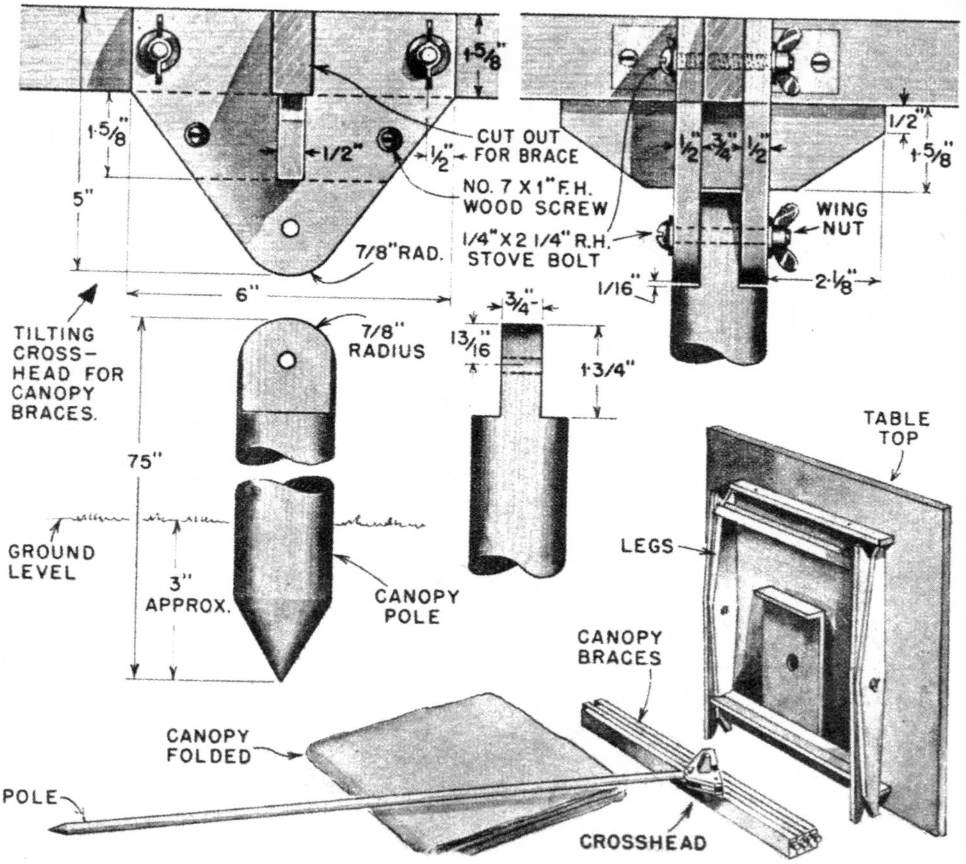
1-5/8"
1-5/8"
1/2"
1/2"
CUT OUT FOR BRACE
NO. 7 X 1" F.H. WOOD SCREW
1/4" X 2 1/4" R.H. STOVE BOLT
7/8" RAD.
5"
6"
1/2" 3/4" 1/2"
1/2"
1-5/8"
WING NUT
1/16"
2-1/8"
TILTING CROSS-HEAD FOR CANOPY BRACES.
7/8" RADIUS
3/4"
13/16"
1-3/4"
75"
GROUND LEVEL
3" APPROX.
CANOPY POLE
TABLE TOP
LEGS
CANOPY BRACES
CANOPY FOLDED
POLE
CROSSHEAD

hinges recessed flush, and notch out the corners of the braces to clear the hinge knuckles as shown in the drawing detail. Apply resorcinol resin glue and use No. 7 x⅜ in. fh wood screws, flattening the screw points slightly with a file so they will clear each other.

Cut the canopy braces longer than dimensioned so they can be fitted to the canopy *after* it has been sewed and the corner blocks have been glued in place with resorcinol resin glue.

To construct the crosshead, cut out two side pieces and a separating piece which constitute a fork for one pair of braces. Cut out each side piece at its top center, ¾x1⅝ in. to receive the other pair of braces, and chamfer the inner edges to clear the hinge knuckles of the braces. Glue and screw from the inner side two bracket supports for one pair of braces. Then assemble the side and separating pieces with glue and fh wood screws. Bore a ¼ in. hole for a ¼x2¼ in. rh stove-bolt pivot, and with the braces and crosshead assembled, bore two ¼ in. holes through the assembly for stove bolts which lock the assembly in place.

Use 10 oz. canvas awning material (matching in color the chaise canopy). Cut to dimensions and sew as shown in the drawings. Ten oz. material can be sewed on most home sewing machines. Press the box-edge crease with a hot iron.

Sand all wood surfaces thoroughly and round all edges slightly. Apply two or more coats of spar varnish or, if you prefer, gay colored outdoor enamel. •

MATERIALS REQUIRED

Exterior-grade fir plywood
- 1 table top, ¾" x 48" x 48"
- 4 legs, ¾" x 4" x 40"
- 1 bottom cross brace, ¾" x 12" x 20¾"

Hard, softwood or exterior-grade fir plywood
- 1 table-top apron, ¾" x 2⅝" x 28¼"
- 1 table-top apron, ¾" x 2⅝" x 26¾"
- 2 leg stretchers, ¾" x 2⅝" x 28½"
- 2 leg stretchers, ¾" x 2⅝" x 27"
- 1 cross-brace piece, ¾" x 1⅝" x 12"
- 2 canopy braces, ¾" x 1⅝" x 41⅝"
- 2 canopy braces, ¾" x 1⅝" x 42"
- 4 canopy corner blocks, ¾" x 3" x 3"
- 2 crosshead side pieces, ½" x 5" x 6"
- 1 crosshead separating piece, ¾" x 1⅝" x 6"
- 2 crosshead brackets, ½" x 1⅝" x 2⅛"
- 1 piece, 1¾" dia. x 75" oak round

Hardware
- 3 tight-pin hinges, 1¼" x 1½"
- 2 tight-pin butt hinges, ⅝" x 2"
- 6 rh stove bolts, ¼" x 2"
- 3 rh stove bolts, ¼" x 2¼"
- 9 wing nuts
- 18 iron washers for ¼" bolts
- fh wood screws
- resorcinol resin glue
- 2 pieces, 10 oz. canvas awning material 36" wide x74" approx.

Two-Tier End Table

A decorative piece used for reading light, storage and convenient table

ALWAYS a favorite with Early American enthusiasts, the two-tier chairside table is a particularly functional piece of furniture.

The entire unit is made of plain, easy-to-work pine boards. The only intricate jointing is with the legs which are doweled to the shelf skirting.

The table is made in two sections: the base including the large shelf, and the top drawer section which fits at the back over projecting dowels.

The legs are made first, of standard 2-by 2-inch pine stock, 15 inches long. They are tapered on only the two inner sides, down to a slim 1- by 1-inch square. This is easy to do on a circular saw with a taper jig made of two hinged boards, as shown in a drawing. The legs will be set in, about ½ inch from each corner edge.

Make the bottom shelf according to the diagram to 17- by 26½-inch size by edge-gluing two pieces of 1- by 9-inch stock, and chamfering or sanding the end-grain edge at the front. Compute from this the lengths of the 3-inch-wide skirting which will join the four legs. Make the curved cuts along an edge, then join the legs and four skirting rails by "blind doweling" and gluing.

The large shelf is attached to the base with ¼-inch dowels in holes drilled through the top into the side skirting rails. Near the front, the dowels are cut off flush, but the dowels near the back are allowed to extend about ¾ inch above the shelf. These will act as anchors for the upper section. The latter will be drilled to match the projecting dowel ends.

The drawer section is made of five parts: the two sides, the back which fits between the sides, a lower shelf which is set into dadoes grooved into the sides, and the top shelf that slightly overhangs the sides. The two shelves form an opening for one or two drawers, according to taste. Drawings show measurements for two drawers.

The top shelf of this section is secured with glued dowels which protrude about ¾ inch above the shelf to secure the shaped 3-side topmost edging.

The drawer has a fully recessed front, made of the same ¾-inch stock, but the drawer sides, back and bottom should be of thinner material if available. Use round wood knobs. •

The two-step table done in soft pine is a worthy chairside companion with accommodations for needed articles.

The legs are tapered on two sides only to a slim one inch square at the bottom. Use a tapering jig on a table saw.

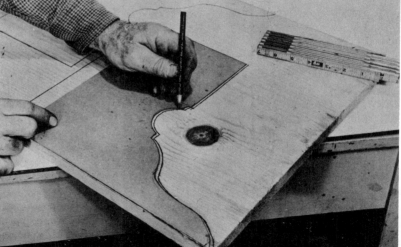

Top section has an interesting profile design. Draw the curved side on heavy paper and trace directly on wood.

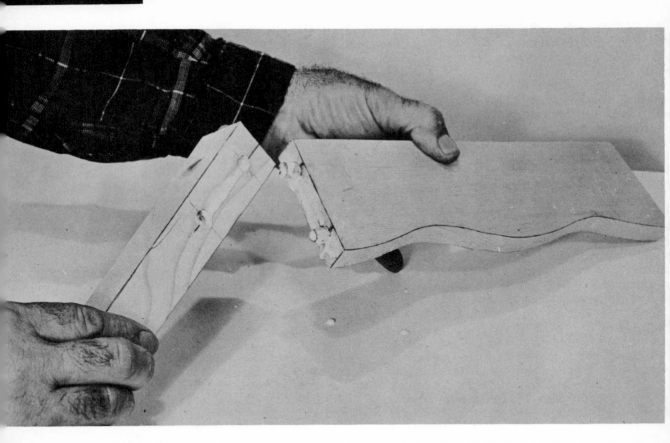

Legs are joined to shelf skirting by blind doweling glued together. Drill dowel holes at center lines.

The center shelf is held in dado grooves that are
cut into the sides to form the drawer compartment.

RIPPING A LEG TAPER

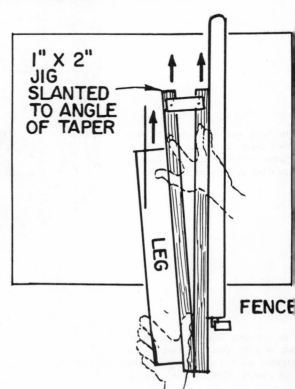

1" X 2"
JIG
SLANTED
TO ANGLE
OF TAPER

LEG

FENCE

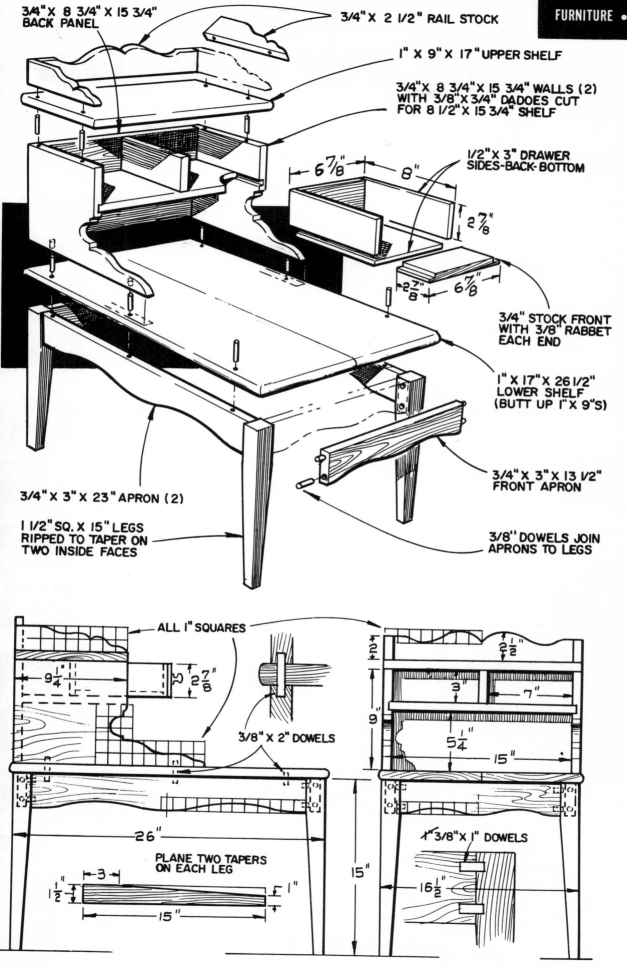

3/4" X 8 3/4" X 15 3/4" BACK PANEL

3/4" X 2 1/2" RAIL STOCK

1" X 9" X 17" UPPER SHELF

3/4" X 8 3/4" X 15 3/4" WALLS (2) WITH 3/8" X 3/4" DADOES CUT FOR 8 1/2" X 15 3/4" SHELF

1/2" X 3" DRAWER SIDES-BACK-BOTTOM

6 7/8"

8"

2 7/8"

2 7/8"

6 7/8"

3/4" STOCK FRONT WITH 3/8" RABBET EACH END

1" X 17" X 26 1/2" LOWER SHELF (BUTT UP 1" X 9"S)

3/4" X 3" X 13 1/2" FRONT APRON

3/4" X 3" X 23" APRON (2)

1 1/2" SQ. X 15" LEGS RIPPED TO TAPER ON TWO INSIDE FACES

3/8" DOWELS JOIN APRONS TO LEGS

ALL 1" SQUARES

9 1/4"

2 7/8"

3/8" X 2" DOWELS

2 1/2"

3"

7"

5 1/4"

15"

9"

26"

PLANE TWO TAPERS ON EACH LEG

3

1/2"

1"

15"

15"

3/8" X 1" DOWELS

16 1/2"

Furniture With Metal Legs

Using easy-to-attach metal legs, you can quickly turn out a variety of tables, stools and chairs

SAW OUT A PERFECT CIRCLE for round-topped table and stools by mounting a pivot-point on which stock rotates, as shown below. Material shown is plasticized paper surface on exterior grade plywood.

MOUNTING wooden legs on tables, chairs, and benches is a difficult job —often wobblingly unsuccessful—which accounts for the tendency to make outdoor furniture of timbers heavy enough for building railroad bridges.

The slimmer, more attractive look that modern outdoor furniture has won't take such massiveness. And it doesn't have to if you use metal legs. Sturdy, weather resistant, good looking, they come with various installation methods built ruggedly into them. Normally, it is possible to fasten these legs securely to a piece of ¾-inch plywood, with a light look that can match the finest of recent Swedish, Danish, and Italian designs.

Steel or brass legs come in a selection of lengths suitable for use on tables of dining, coffee, or cocktail height, as well as for benches of standard seating height or the somewhat lower "lounging" type. They cost very little.

Other Styles

Perhaps a little more rugged even than prefabricated metal legs, are those you can put together yourself, using steel water pipe and a plumber's item called a "floor flange." In the ungalvanized version, such pipe is inexpensive as are the flanges. They have the advantage of being demountable for storage of the furniture during winter. Merely unscrew the pipe from the flange, and you have a handful of legs and a top which require little storage space. Other types of tubing and flanges can be purchased.

Water pipe is designated by its inside dimension, and is a little larger as to outside dimension. For legs half an inch in diameter use ⅜-inch pipe. You get ¾-inch legs from ½-inch pipe. A pipe called ¾-inch has an outside dimension of a good full inch. Normally, that is the largest you'll need—and that only for a fairly big table of dining height.

Since pipe threads are tapered, not every piece of pipe screws the same distance into a fitting such as a flange. Therefore, when you cut pipe legs to be identical in length, first screw the pipes into their flanges and then measure them in combination with the unit. It is a good idea if you disassemble, to mark each pipe for its flange by a code marked on the pipe and flange with a center punch. This difference may be slight, but often enough to make a table rock annoyingly.

For light construction, the flanges can be screwed directly to plywood, using screws just short of coming through. For heavier pieces, it is better to glue a circular piece of plywood underneath the actual top to form a stronger anchor for longer screws. If you want the legs splayed, as so many metal legs are, make these blocks slightly wedge-shaped.

Steel used for outdoor furniture sooner or later will rust, regardless of the finish. To refinish such steel or to put an initial finish on legs you make yourself, first remove all rust, down to bare, gleaming metal. Then apply a coat of primer, such as zinc chromate or red lead. Then apply two coats of the final paint, sanding lightly between all coats.

These days almost any good quality enamel is based on the same alkyd resin formula used for automobile paints and will work well outdoors. Keep in mind, however, that a high-gloss enamel has better outdoor life than semi-gloss or flat.

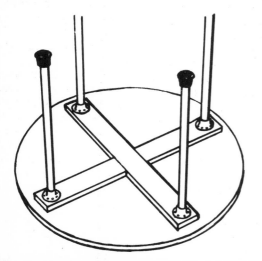

CROSS OF 1x6 BOARDS gives 4-foot round table extra stiffness, provides deep anchor for longer screws in standard floor flanges. Use ¾-inch pipe for high tables, ½-inch for cocktail height.

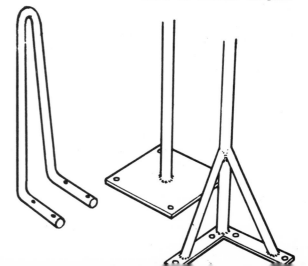

THREE COMMON TYPES of fabricated metal legs: (1) simple flange with welded leg (2) hairpin leg bent of steel rod (3) braced leg with bracket. Hardware stores sell them in several lengths.

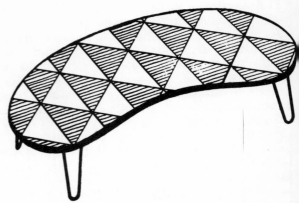

BIG AND USEFUL, yet slim and graceful is picnic table made of slab top and pipe-fitting legs. Use exterior-grade slab door or glue up 2x6s or 2x4s with cleats beneath of oak or rugged angle iron.

FREE-FORM TABLES are particularly adaptable to use with hairpin legs, although straight legs or those made of steel pipe can be used. Be careful leg position doesn't allow enough overhang to tip.

Outdoor finishes, like those indoors, are protected and given better life through the application of wax.

What sort of outdoor furniture is best and easiest to make with metal legs? Almost anything with a top that you sit on or put things on and which needs to be supported at some convenient distance above the floor. Let's take a few basic designs— and you can create your own from there.

The Round Dining Table:

This is as simple to make as a milking stool. Half a sheet of plywood will make a table big enough to seat more people than most rectangular outdoor tables.

Cut the 4x4 sheet of plywood into a circle. Owing to the flat arc, this can be done with a handsaw if necessary, better still with a keyhole saw. Clean up the rough spots with a plane. Even better, if you have access to a band saw, is this trick:

Mount a pivot point the same *height* as the bandsaw table, which is exactly 23⅞ inches from the band saw, and which is exactly at *right angles* to the flat side of the blade. The pivot point can be a nail with the head cut off—anything that will slip into a shallow predrilled hole in the center of the bottom of the plywood sheet. Support it any way you can devise. (The support shown in photograph on page 1214 is a stand normally used to catch the end of a long piece of lumber as it goes through the ripsaw. A vertical piece of wood is clamped to it, a nail in the end.)

With such a jig, you cut a perfect circle that hardly needs touching up with a plane before it is sanded.

On the bottom of the circle mount a cross made of 1x6 lumber, the arms of the cross at right angles to each other. One piece is solid, the other in two parts butting the solid one. Let the ends of these crosspieces hang in about two inches from the edge of the circle to minimize them in appearance. Use plastic resin glue and screws.

The four legs mount on the ends of the cross pieces about 5 inches in from the edge of the table. Use ¾-inch pipe and flanges. Put caps on the ends of the pipes to make them smooth on the bottom, or use crutch tips.

When you paint this table, give the bottom the same number of coats of the same kind of enamel you use on the top. This will equalize the moisture intake on both sides of the plywood and prevent it from warping. *Always paint both sides of all pieces of wood* used out of doors if the stock is of a width that invites warping.

Use Exterior Grade Plywood

It hardly seems necessary to mention that the plywood used for this round table and for all outdoor purposes should be exterior grade. There is a type of plywood particularly well suited to outdoor tables which has a layer of heavy, plastic-impregnated paper bonded to both sides. It is smoother than regular exterior grade fir plywood, for painting.

It is even simpler to construct round stools to match the round table. Cut circles of ¾-inch plywood about 14 inches in diameter (you'd get nine of them out of the other half of the sheet of plywood) and mount ½-inch pipe-flange legs in about 1½ inches from the edges of the circles. For a normal dining table 30 inches high, make stools 16 inches high.

FREEFORM

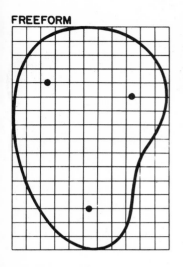

KIDNEY

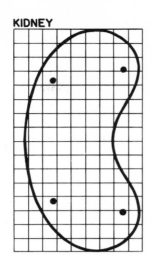

FREEFORM TRIANGLE

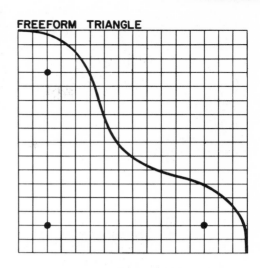

THREE STANDARD FREE-FORM TABLES are shown above: (1) true free-form (2) kidney (3) free-form triangle. Dots show leg positions. Grid represents 3-inch squares. To copy, lay out squares on plywood sheets.

You can have fun with color on these stools. Why not paint them white, orange, red, gray, with a bright blue for accent. They'd be interesting and gay around the terrace, strikingly modern around a dark red or rich brown table.

Nesting Stools:

A variation of the stool to be used equally well with the round table is that with a square top. These can be stacked in a nest. Cut the tops about 16 inches square (again, there are 9 in a half sheet of plywood and you can use that many) and mount the legs as close to the corners as the flanges will allow.

These sturdy and useful stools stack up by putting each one at a slight twist over the preceding one, so that the legs go down over the sides. That is one reason for keeping the legs as far apart as possible, the other reason being to guard against tipping.

Triangular Tables:

There is variety in a set of triangular tables. They can be used singly or in groups. The same technique of plywood with metal legs is used, although in the case of low, cocktail-style tables, the hairpin or simple welded flange leg is strong enough. If the legs are splayed, set them in far enough so they strike the ground beneath the top and do not interfere with other tables when two or more are used together.

These triangular tables can be made as big as 4 feet on the two right-angled sides (four of them out of a sheet of plywood) although in this size the diagonal side gets pretty long and would spring somewhat if anyone sat on it as someone is sure to do.

Holding them to three feet on the short sides would obviate this, or you could nail 1x2 around the edges of the plywood to give it a little less flexibility.

Free Form Cocktail Table:

Since nature seldom makes things exactly rectangular, the free-form shape for outdoor furniture is particularly appropriate. The shapes of leaves, lily pads, flower petals, seeds, etc. are well imitated in putting variety and interest into the things you make of exterior grade plywood.

A band saw, jigsaw or portable saber saw take a lot of the work out of making free forms, but for the patient and willing, the job can be done with a keyhole saw or even a handpowered coping saw fitted with the widest blade it will take.

Three types of free forms are illustrated here. They are the classic, accepted shapes which appear often in furniture design and other art forms. Adapt them exactly from the drawings or let yourself go! It is easy to sketch a good free-form. Doodle on a piece of paper, then on a piece of plywood, and cut out a shape you like.

In the drawings, circled Xs indicate proper positioning of the legs. On any design of your own, follow the general leg spacing indicated, making sure that spans are not too great, and that too much overhang will not make tables insecure.

L-Shaped Table:

A lot of size and importance can be produced for very little in an L-shaped table or bench. If you rip a sheet of plywood down the middle, you end up with a pair of 2x8-foot sheets. With one butting the other, your table or bench measures 8 feet

Set of triangular tables, three hairpin legs to each, can be used in a variety of ways on terrace, as shown above. At cocktail height, slim, good-looking legs like these give plenty of solid support, see page 2140.

on one arm, 10 feet on the other—both 2 feet wide.

That's big, so big it calls for five pairs of legs. Use the kind you buy or pipe-and-flange legs of half-inch pipe. Set them in about two inches; space them evenly on each arm.

For a piece of this size, you may want to face the edges with 1x2 pine to give the top the look of slightly greater thickness, as well as to give it increased stiffness at the edges. Normally no reinforcement for the legs will be necessary unless you happen to make the L-shaped table 24 inches high or more.

When you butt the two pieces together, you'll get the best joint if you put the uncut end of one half against the uncut edge of the other. Few of us can make a cut as true and straight as that put on the sheet by the manufacturer when he made it. Secure this joint with a scrap of ¾-inch plywood about 8 inches wide and 20 inches long. Center it over the joint on the bottom. Use plastic resin glue and screws. Drive these screws at a slight angle, the heads leaning toward the joint on either side, and they will tend to draw it up tight. The remaining crack is easy to fill with plastic wood.

Pipe-Leg Picnic Table:

About as slim and delicate a table as you can make for your terrace is one using a plank top and legs and stretchers of pipe and pipe fittings.

The top of this table can be a flush door if you can find one that is made entirely with waterproof adhesives. Otherwise,

glue up a top using two-inch lumber, with the edges carefully jointed for a good glue job. If you do not have a jointer, perhaps the lumberyard will true up the edges for you, or you can have it done at a local cabinet shop.

You can use fir for the top with excellent results *if* the edge of the grain runs up and down; that is, if the narrow, parallel grain pattern is on the surfaces. It is sometimes hard to find edge-grain fir, but in the interest of economy look for it, even if you have to talk the lumber dealer into letting you riffle through his entire stack of framing stuff.

Minimize Warping

To minimize warping, do not use planks wider than 2x6 which will dress down for edge-joining to a little over 5 inches. Six of these give you a table a little over 30 inches in width. Make it about seven feet long. Sometimes the boards run better in the 2x4 pile, and if they do, use 8 lengths for a table a little under 30 inches.

Plastic resin glue like Weldwood is adequately waterproof. Use at least four bar-clamps on a table 7 feet long. Make the faces as nearly flush as possible. On the under side, screw and glue three cleats of oak which you can get at any lumberyard by asking for stair tread. Or use cleats of steel angle about 1½x1½x¼ which you can usually buy at welding shops. Miter the ends of steel or oak cleats back to make them less noticeable.

Make the table top smooth by planing first across the grain, then lengthwise with

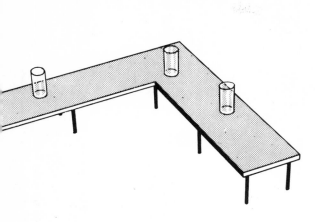

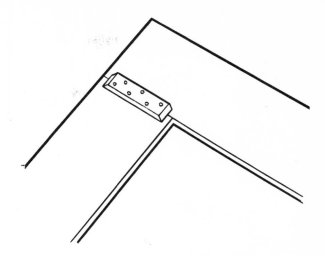

L-shaped bench or table is big, impressive, quick to make from one sheet of plywood. Use five sets of legs, spaced as this drawing shows. Nail 1x2 to edges with glue for thicker look, more strength.

This is how one end is joined, butted, to one edge of L-shaped table. Bevel ends of cleat to make it inconspicuous. This style can be varied to make T table or offset T if that would suit terrace better.

a plane at least as big as the Stanley No. 5 Jack plane to make it flat. Finish with a belt sander—again working first across the grain then with it.

Give the top its finish, equal amounts of the same enamel or varnish on both top and bottom, before you put the legs and stretchers on.

The pipe legs are assembled entirely from nipples and fittings except for the long stretcher down the center. For that piece, buy a length of regular pipe threaded on both ends. Compute its length this way: Length of table less 18 inches (legs hang in 9 inches from each end) less 3 inches (approximate length added by the Ts at each end). Figure on ¾-inch pipe for the job.

Assemble in this order:

(1)—Screw Ts on the ends of the long stretcher, making them tight and ending up with the Ts parallel.

(2)—Screw a 10-inch nipple into each side of the Ts with Ts on the end of those nipples. By shoving a wooden dowel through the Ts you'll be able to screw them tight enough without marring them as a pipe wrench would. These Ts end up at right angles to the ones in the middle.

(3)—Screw four 12-inch nipples into the four Ts. Screw caps on the ends of those nipples.

(4)—Screw four 10-inch nipples into the tops of the four Ts with floor flanges on their upper ends.

(5)—Turn the table-top upside down, position the pipe frame in relation to ends and sides, and screw the flanges on. •

Small tables or stools 16 inches square with steel legs at corners can be used individually or grouped. By turning each stool slightly in relation to the one below, several can be stacked easily.

Room divider that separates living and dining areas cost $72.70 to build. Note cabinet, right; p.1223

Budget Furniture

These four beautiful units were built at a cost of little more than $200

BEAUTIFUL furniture need not be expensive. And built-in furniture—or furniture that looks built-in—adds interest to a conventional house or apartment, costs little if you wield the hammer with modest skill. The room-divider storage cabinet that separates the living room from the dining area of this typical small apartment is a good example.

Room-Divider Construction

Because of its size, begin assembly of room divider on floor, front side down.

Following bill of materials and diagram, glue and nail sides to bottom and first shelf, using 2½" finishing nails. Attach base dividers through bottom and shelf. Attach shelves for three-drawer section through side and divider. Drill and countersink cleats for 1¼" No. 8 screws and attach to each side of base cabinets. Glue and nail remaining shelves to cleats. Attach drawer stops to sides and dividers, flush with back edges. Nail hardboard to base section.

Using first shelf dividers as spacers on either side, glue and nail 2nd shelf in position. Nail dividers in place through shelf at top, toenail bottom at back and sides. Repeat this process for 3rd and 4th shelves. Notch top shelf as shown and attach to sides. Glue and nail 4th shelf dividers in place flush with notches. Attach hardboard to shelves as shown in back view, cutting corners that meet to fit and leaving side over 4th shelf divider unattached.

Stand room divider upright. Toenail all shelf dividers at bottom front edges. Following diagram, attach ¾" strips to top shelf dividers; apply glue and slide dividers into place through notches; nail strips to 4th shelf dividers.

Frame doors with 1½" strips; drill for knobs; notch for hinges and attach to cabinets. Install door catches.

To build drawers, cut false fronts and check fit in drawer openings for free movement in and out. Sand or plane if necessary; remeasure; cut fronts and backs 1" shorter.

Following diagram, glue and nail sides to front with 1½" brads. Attach back between sides, ½" from ends and flush with top edges. Attach false front, nailing from the inside with ¾" brads. Glue and nail ½" strips to front and sides, flush with bottom edges. Slide hardboard bottom in over strips and under back. Using ½" brads, nail bottom to strips; turn drawer over and nail bottom up into back. Drill for knobs.

Finish and paint. Glue screening to hardboard shelf backs. Cut lattice for trim and paint; let dry. Nail to backs, omitting glue. Touch up nailheads. Attach knobs.

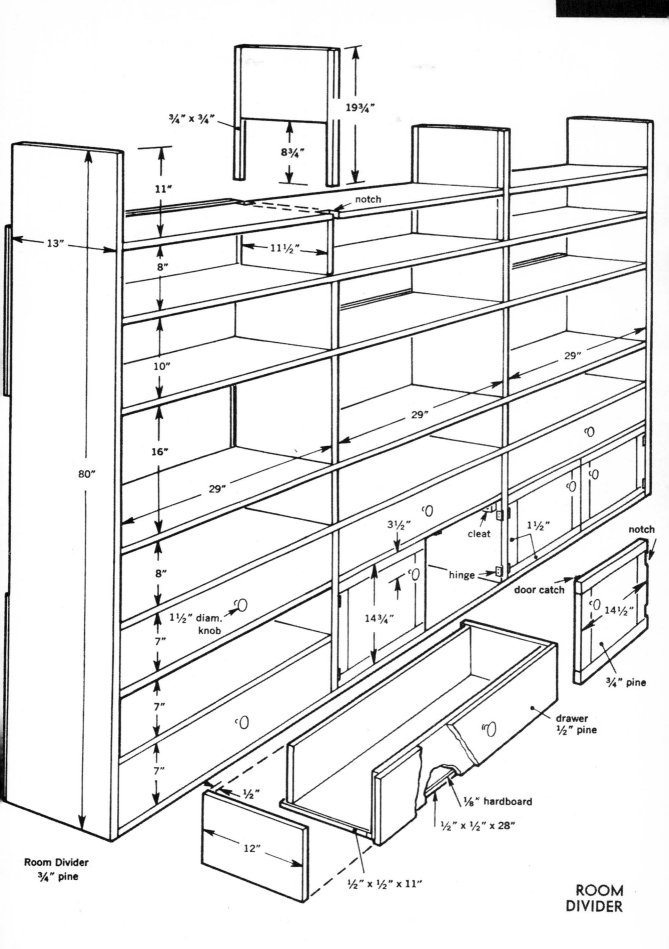

3/4" x 3/4"

19 3/4"

8 3/4"

notch

11"

13"

11 1/2"

8"

10"

29"

29"

29"

16"

3 1/2"

cleat

1 1/2"

notch

hinge

door catch

14 1/2"

80"

29"

8"

1 1/2" diam. knob

14 3/4"

3/4" pine

7"

7"

drawer 1/2" pine

7"

1/2"

1/8" hardboard

1/2" x 1/2" x 28"

12"

1/2" x 1/2" x 11"

Room Divider
3/4" pine

ROOM DIVIDER

Rear view of the room divider; note construction details below. The handsome unit provides drawer and shelf storage for books, china, table linens.

Bill of Materials

ROOM DIVIDER:

92 feet of ¾" x 11½" pine and 104 feet of ¾" x 1½" pine:

(Note: Piece boards before cutting 13" widths.) Two 13" x 80" pieces for sides; six 13" x 88½" pieces for bottom and five shelves; two 13" x 22½" pieces for base dividers; four 13" x 29" pieces for base shelves; two 8" x 13", two 13" x 16", and two 10" x 13" pieces for shelf dividers; two 8" x 11½" and two 11" x 11½" pieces for 4th and 5th shelf dividers; four 11½" x 11¾" pieces for doors; eight 1½" x 11¾" and eight 1½" x 14½" strips to frame doors; four 1½" x 12" pieces for cleats.

8 feet of ¾" x ¾" pine:

Four 19¾" lengths to face 4th and 5th shelf dividers.

One 4' x 4' and one 4' x 8' sheet of ⅛" hardboard:

One 24" x 90" piece for back of base; one 17½" x 60¼" and one 20¼" x 30½" piece for backs of shelves; five 11" x 28" pieces for drawer bottoms.

48 feet of ½" x 7½" pine for drawers:

Five 7" x 29" pieces for false fronts; five 7" x 28" pieces for fronts; five 6⅜" x 28" pieces for backs; ten 7" x 12" pieces for sides.

28 feet of ½" x ½" pine:

Ten 5" pieces for drawer stops; five 28" and ten 11" strips for drawer bottoms.

26 feet of ¼" x ¾" lattice:

One 90", one 60¼", three 16", one 30½", one 29" and two 18¾" strips to trim hardboard shelf backs.

Miscellaneous: ½", ¾", 1" and 1½" brads; 2½" finishing nails; eight 2½" hinges; nine 1½" brass knobs; four door catches; 1¼" No. 8 screws; screening to cover shelf backs (to match lattice blinds used in study alcove).

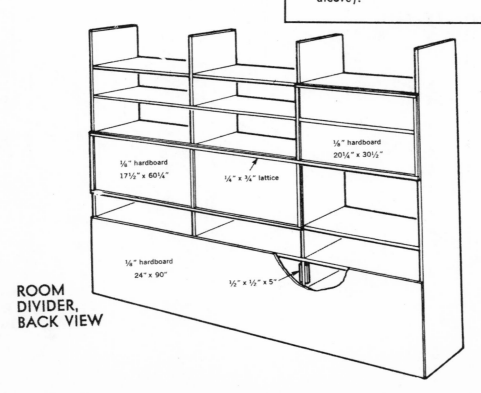

⅛" hardboard 17½" x 60¼"

¼" x ¾" lattice

⅛" hardboard 20¼" x 30½"

⅛" hardboard 24" x 90"

½" x ½" x 5"

ROOM DIVIDER, BACK VIEW

Cabinet Construction

Following bill of materials and diagram, cut top, bottom and sides. Notch sides for toe base. Glue and nail top to sides and sides to bottom with 2½" finishing nails.

Attach cabinet divider through top and bottom. Nail shelves for drawer section through side and divider and attach drawer stops flush with back edges. Drill and countersink cleats for two 1¼" No. 8 screws and attach to divider and side, flush with back. Glue and nail cabinet shelf to cleats.

Attach hardboard to back, flush with edges, then nail to divider and shelves. Glue and nail toe base to sides and bottom. Attach a glide at each corner.

Build drawers, following assembly instructions and detail of Room Divider. Drill for knobs 3½" in from sides on center. Check fit and sand or plane if necessary.

Piece cabinet doors with 1½" strips at top and bottom; drill for knobs 1¾" in from sides on center. Notch for hinges and attach to cabinet. Install door catches.

Finish, paint, and attach knobs to the drawers and doors.

Bill of Materials

CABINET:

24 feet of ¾" x 11½" pine and 26 feet of ¾" x 1½" pine: (piece boards before cutting 13" widths.)

One 13" x 44¼" piece for top; one 13" x 42¾" piece for bottom; two 13" x 22½" pieces for sides; one 13" x 19½" piece for divider; two 13" x 24" pieces for drawer shelves; one 12" x 18" piece for cabinet shelf; two 9" x 16½" pieces for doors; one 2¼" x 44¼" piece for toe base; two 1½" x 11" pieces for cleats; four 1½" x 9" strips for doors.

24 feet of ½" x 7½" pine for drawers:

Three 6" x 24" pieces for false fronts; three 6" x 23" pieces for fronts; three 5⅜" x 23" pieces for backs; six 6" x 12" pieces for sides.

15 feet of ½" x ½" pine:

Six 11" and three 23" strips for drawer bottoms; six 4" pieces for drawer stops.

One 4' x 4' sheet of ⅛" hardboard:

One 21" x 44¼" piece for back; three 11" x 23" pieces for drawer bottoms.

Miscellaneous: ½", ¾", 1½" brads; 2½" finishing nails; 1¼" No. 8 screws; four 2" hinges; four ½" glides; eight 1½" brass knobs; two door catches.

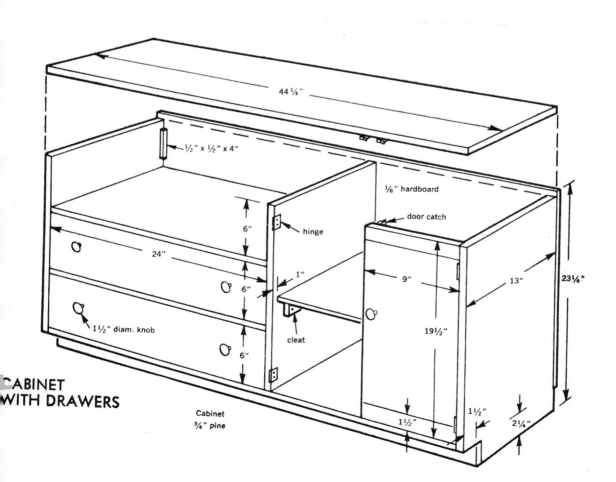

CABINET WITH DRAWERS

Cabinet ¾" pine

Storage units that flank desk cost $89.82 to build including blinds; desk (with file baskets) $17.25.

Study Alcove

Concealed storage shelves are built into units on each side of a wall to form a study alcove 17″ deep. Other dimensions depend on the height and length of the wall.

To work out an individual plan, first make a layout of the available wall space. When determining the size of the storage shelves, keep in mind that the desk top should be at least 40″ long to allow for an adequate kneehole. From your measurements, you will be able to figure out the amount of lumber required.

Desk Construction

Following bill of materials and diagram, cut and notch sides of desk. Using 1″ brads, glue and nail ¾″ quarter round to sides for hardboard shelf supports. Attach sides to bottom shelf with 2″ finishing nails. Nail base to sides and shelf. Using ½″ brads glue and nail hardboard shelves to supports, working from bottom to top.

Cut 2″ strips for framing. Drill and countersink end piece of frame and side of left-hand storage unit from inside for two 1¼″ No. 8 screws. Attach front and back framing to end piece and to sides of desk with 2″ finishing nails. Set desk in place and attach to side B at each end, omitting glue. Cut top to fit and nail to framing and sides of desk. Finish and paint the desk.

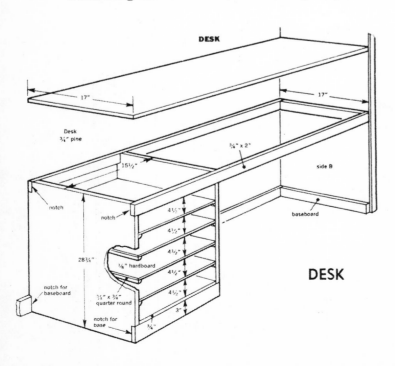

DESK

Bill of Materials

DESK:
¾″ x 11½″ and ¾″ x 5½″ pine: (Note: boards before cutting 17″ widths.)
  One length to fit between storage un desk top; two 17″ x 28¾″ pieces for one 14″ x 17″ piece for bottom she 3″ x 15½″ piece for base.
¾″ x 2½″ pine:
  Two pieces 2″ x length of desk top fo and back framing; one 2″ x 15½″ pi end framing.
One 4′ x 4′ sheet of ⅛″ hardboard:
  Four 14″ x 17″ pieces for shelves.
12 feet of ¾″ x ¾″ quarter round:
  Eight 17″ lengths for shelf suppor
Miscellaneous: Corrugated fasteners; 1″ brads; 2″ finishing nails; 1¼″ screws; five baskets to fit shelves.

Storage-Unit Construction

Measure from top of baseboard to molding, if any, or to ceiling for sides A and from floor to ceiling for sides B. Piece 5½" and 11½" boards and cut sides. Cut side A extensions and notch for baseboard.

Temporarily hold side A in place against the corner wall and check with a level. Shift its position if necessary until front edge is plumb. Draw a line on the wall where side A is to be installed. Rest extension on floor or baseboard molding, if any, and mark side along top edge.

Next drill and countersink for 1½" No. 8 screws, making two holes at top and two centered on baseboard. Glue and screw extension to side A, along the line and flush with front edge. Set side in position, drill through side and wall near upper back corner and attach with a Molly bolt. Screw extension to baseboard.

Notch side B for baseboard and cut top corner with coping saw to fit around ceiling molding, if any. Glue and nail strip to match baseboard to bottom, flush with front edge. Round front end slightly. Place side B in position and attach to floor and baseboard with 3" angle irons.

Repeat same steps to build second unit.

Cut side facings 5½" shorter than floor-to-ceiling measurement. Notch two to fit around baseboard and temporarily nail in place on sides A and B.

Measure overall length and cut valance from 5½" pine, using more than one board length if necessary. Cut corners for molding, if any; attach to sides A and B, flush with ceiling. Remove side facings.

To make shelf support from 5½" pine, cut two 11½" side pieces and one back piece 1½" shorter than shelf. Drill and countersink side pieces for two 1¼" No. 8 screws. Attach sides to back with 2½" finishing nails. Screw support to sides A and B, 18" from ceiling. Drill through back piece and wall and attach with two Molly bolts. Nail shelf to support along sides and back. Repeat steps if additional shelves are desired, omitting Molly bolts from lower supports.

Attach facings permanently to sides A and B. Face valance with 2½" strip extending 1¾" below bottom edge. Nail molding or ¾" x ¾" quarter round to valance, flush with ceiling.

Finish and paint storage units. Attach lattice blinds to back of valance so that bottom touches floor when blinds are fully unrolled. •

Bill of Materials

STORAGE UNITS:

¾" x 11½" pine:
   Two lengths for sides A; two lengths for sides B; two (or more) lengths for shelves; two 9½" x 17" pieces for side A extensions; one length to match baseboard for side B of right-hand unit.

¾" x 5½" pine:
   Two lengths for sides A; two lengths for sides B; two (or more) lengths for backs of shelf supports; four (or more) lengths for sides of shelf supports; one length for valance.

¾" x 2½" pine:
   Four lengths to face sides A and B; one length to face valance.

Ceiling molding to match room or ¾" x ¾" quarter round:
   One length to fit.

Miscellaneous: Corrugated fasteners; 2½" finishing nails; 1¼" and 1½" No. 8 screws; four 3" angle irons; six Molly bolts; two roll-up lattice blinds to fit.

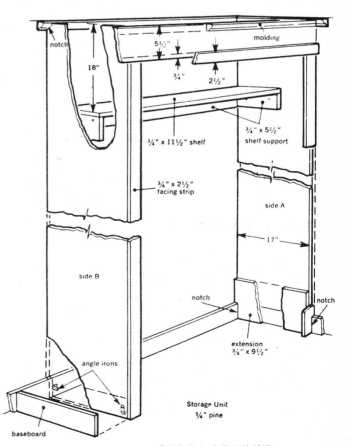

STORAGE UNIT

Tea Wagon

Its three spacious shelves are protected against heat by a tough oil finish

IT only takes a weekend or two to build this attractive tea wagon. And you'll love it for its many practical uses: to serve coffee, tea, party snacks, small buffet meals; to stack dishes from the table; to roll meals to a bedridden patient; and to serve lunch outdoors.

Check diagram to determine amounts of materials to be purchased. Check diagram for dimensions; saw out pieces. Cement all edges before joining them with brads or screws. When using contact cement, follow manufacturer's directions. The cement forms an immediate and permanent bond. Therefore, carefully position pieces before pressing them together. When cementing long strips, such as tray edging, press the end of edging flush with edge of tray and gradually press remainder of strip against tray. Countersink screws; set brads.

POSTS: From ⅞" walnut saw out and

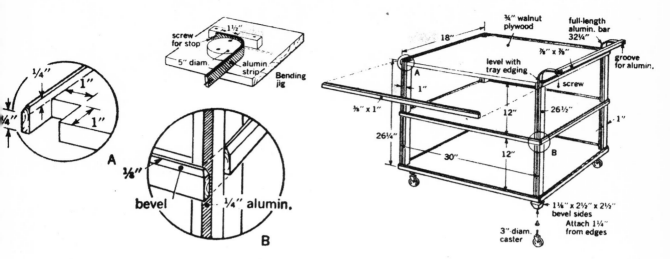

plane six ⅜" x 1" x 26¼" strips, and two ⅜" x 1" x 26½" strips. Saw off two 26¼" strips and two 32¼" strips of aluminum bar. Cement 26¼" strips of walnut for back posts. Curved handle bar supports are a continuation of long strips of aluminum in front posts. To bend aluminum, make a bending jig (see detail). Clamp jig to workbench, bend ends of aluminum around disk. To assemble front posts cement 26¼" walnut strips to back of bent aluminum strips and 26½" strips to front.

TRAYS: From walnut plywood, saw out three trays, each 18" x 30". Saw out 1" x 1" notch from four corners of each tray (see detail "A"). Fit one back post into notched corners of three trays. Mark post where each tray will be attached to it. Drill screw holes through post at marks. Cement, then screw post to trays. Repeat for other three posts.

From ⅞" walnut saw out and plane six ⅜" x 1" x 30¾" strips and six ⅜" x 1" x 18" strips. Bevel outside top edge of each strip (see details "A" and "B"). Edging strips should butt joint at tray corners. Cement edging around each tray flush with tray bottoms.

HANDLE BAR: From ⅞" walnut, saw off 18" strip for handle bar. Groove ends of strip, ¼" x 1". Round edges with sandpaper. Through underside of handle bar only, drill hole ½" in from each end. Slip end of aluminum into handle bar and make a pencil mark through hole onto aluminum. Remove handle bar and make a slight dent with a nail at pencil mark. Drill through aluminum at marked spot. Repeat for opposite side. Replace handle bar; screw through underside with number 5 screws.

CASTERS: From 1¼" pine saw out four caster blocks, 1⅛" x 2½" x 2½". Bevel sides of each block and drill hole at center of underside. Cement and nail blocks to underside of bottom tray at each corner, 1¼" in from edges. Apply walnut stain to caster blocks. Insert caster sockets in blocks, then attach casters.

FINISHING: Fill where necessary with wood filler. Sand plywood surfaces with fine sandpaper. Use medium, then fine sandpaper on all other wood surfaces. Polish aluminum with very fine steel wool. For oil finish: mix two parts boiled linseed oil to one part turpentine. With soft cloth, apply oil mixture generously to all wood surfaces. Let oil soak into wood for four hours. Wipe off excess. (Oil finish protects wood from spilled liquids and hot dishes. However, a very hot pot direct from heat should not be set down on wood.) Rub wood with clean cloth. After 24 hours, apply second coat of oil, allow to soak in, then remove excess. Rub wood with clean cloth. Surface stains can be removed by rubbing a little oil finish over them. •

Bill of Materials

⅞" walnut; ¾" walnut plywood; 1¼" pine; ¼" x 1" do-it-yourself aluminum bar; Contact cement; brads; Two number 5 screws, ⅝"; Twelve number 6 screws, 1½"; Walnut plastic wood filler; Medium and fine sandpaper; Very fine steel wool (No. 0000); Walnut stain; Four 3" diameter clear plastic casters and sockets; Boiled linseed oil; turpentine; ¾" scrap lumber and five No. 8 screws, 1½", to make bending jig.

Boys' Room

Center floor space remains free in this room designed for play and study

Noteworthy are divider between beds that have drawers below, L-shaped table and sliding window-door.

TO leave center floor space free in this room for growing boys, the beds are built along one wall. Each has two storage drawers beneath. The divider between the beds and the sliding window door are designed to simulate barn doors. Wall behind the bed is covered with cork-tile squares and serves as a bulletin board. Closet walls, which jut out into the room, are capitalized on with an L-shaped work and study table, and shelves for books and miscellany. The study table has five drawers and is topped with washable plastic-coated hardboard.

Beds with Storage Drawers

Diagram gives dimensions for beds to fit 30"-wide mattresses; adjust dimensions for wider mattresses.

Cut bed pieces, following diagram. Glue, then nail ends to back; nail front rail to ends. Attach center divider to front and back, then framing strips at each end and at center front. Cut strips for V braces;

attach at either side of center divider. Add stripping for drawer guides above V braces and along ends, back and center divider. Between center divider and each end, attach support from front to back. Cut hardboard to fit flush with bed edges; attach. Make drawers to fit; drill fronts for pulls. Attach casters to each drawer, two at front and one at back.

Bed Divider

Cut pieces to fit width of bed and floor to ceiling height. Glue, then nail framing strips and attach to both sides of plywood. Cut to fit baseboard and molding. Attach divider to ceiling, wall, baseboard and floor with angle irons.

Sliding Window-Door

Cut pieces to fit size of your window and height of room. Glue, then nail framing strips to one side of plywood only. Cut 2 half circles and attach to top strip. Attach

Bill of Materials

BEDS WITH STORAGE DRAWERS (TWO):

¾" x 11½" pine; ¾" x ¾" and ⅝" x ⅝" stripping; ¼" hardboard; 1" quarter round; glue; finishing nails; screws; eight 2½"-diameter metal drawer pulls; twelve 1" square-plate swivel casters.

BED DIVIDER:

¾" x 5⅝" pine; ¼" plywood; glue; finishing nails; four 2" angle irons.

SLIDING WINDOW-DOOR:

¾" x 5⅝" pine; ¼" plywood; glue; finishing nails; door handle; overhead single door track.

WORK AND STUDY TABLE:

¾" x 11½" pine; ¾" x ¾" stripping; ¾" quarter round; ⅛" hardboard; ⅛" coated hardboard; glue; corrugated fasteners; contact cement; nails; five 1¼" drawer pulls and five 1" screw eyes; six 3" angle irons.

WOOD BENCHES:

¾" x 11½" pine; glue; corrugated fasteners; finishing nails; 1½" No. 6 screws.

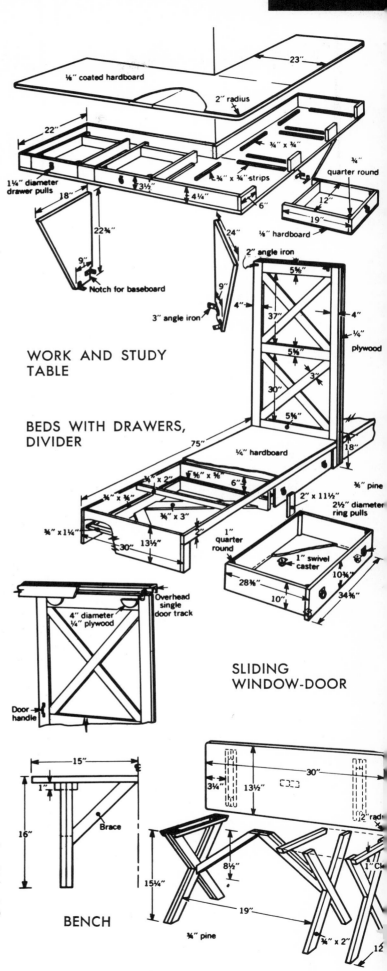

WORK AND STUDY TABLE

BEDS WITH DRAWERS, DIVIDER

SLIDING WINDOW-DOOR

BENCH

...oor handle. Hang door with ceiling track, ...ollowing manufacturer's directions. Con-...eal track with valance strip.

Work and Study Table

Cut pieces for L-shaped worktable, fol-...owing dimensions in diagram and adjust-...ng length to fit your room. Piece top, ...ottom and legs, using glue and corrugated ...asteners. Glue, then nail back pieces and ...nds to bottom; add front drawer dividers ...nd strips for drawer guides. Make drawers ...o fit; reinforce front corners with quarter ...ound; drill fronts for pulls. Notch legs at ...ack to fit baseboard; attach legs to bottom ...t corner and either end. Attach pine top, ...hen cement coated hardboard to it. An-...hor legs to wall and floor with angle irons.

Build L-shaped shelves as in photo-...raph, if desired; attach with standards and ...etal brackets; finish to match table.

Wood Benches

Cut benches, following dimensions in ...iagram; piece tops, using glue and cor-...ugated fasteners. Join leg pieces, forming ...X's. Attach 1" cleats to top of legs. Screw ...hrough cleats into underside of bench top. ...ttach braces to each leg unit and to top ...t center. ●

Teen-Age Girls' Room

The two ingenious space savers that "make" this one are easily constructed

Quarter-circle table, foreground, tops file drawers. Bed slides under corner table, night table for both.

THIS room for two teen-age girls doubles as a sitting room and study and is a place to entertain friends. The furniture includes two ingenious space savers you can build yourself: a quarter-circle corner study table with two-drawer filing cabinet beneath it, and a square corner table with opening at one side that enables a bed to slide under it during the day.

Square Corner Table

From 2 x 2 pine cut three posts to fit from floor to ceiling and one leg to fit from floor to table top. Notch leg and two posts for baseboard and wall molding. Piece table top and bottom, using glue and corrugated fasteners. Cement coated board to top; notch corners of top and bottom. Cut three sides to fit between posts and leg. Glue, then nail sides, top and bottom to posts and leg. Cut door framing; attach. Cut door; drill for knob; hinge to framing at bottom. Attach door catch. Cut and attach two top strips between posts and two to walls, just below ceiling. Screw bottom of posts and leg to baseboard.

QUARTER-CIRCLE STUDY TABLE

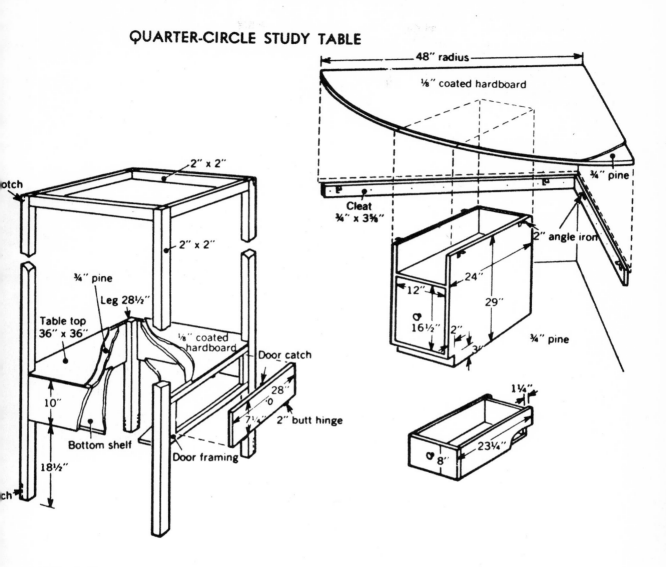

- 2" x 2"
- 48" radius
- ⅛" coated hardboard
- ¾" pine
- Cleat ¾" x 3⅝"
- 2" angle iron
- 24"
- 12"
- 29"
- 16½"
- 2"
- ¾" pine
- otch
- 2" x 2"
- ¾" pine
- Leg 28½"
- Table top 36" x 36"
- ⅛" coated hardboard
- Door catch
- 28"
- 10"
- 7¼"
- 2" butt hinge
- Bottom shelf
- Door framing
- 18½"
- ch
- 1¼"
- 23¼"
- 8"

SQUARE CORNER TABLE

Quarter-Circle Study Table

Piece pine for top, using glue and corrugated fasteners. Cement coated hardboard to top, then saw out to shape, following diagram. Cut and assemble pieces for drawer unit. Make drawers to fit; drill drawer fronts for knobs. Position table top on drawer unit. Draw pencil line along underside of top on each wall. Screw cleats to walls along pencil lines. Join underside of top to cleats with angle irons, then underside of top to drawer unit. •

Bill of Materials

SQUARE CORNER TABLE:

2" x 2" pine; ¾" x 11½" pine; ⅛" coated hardboard; glue; corrugated fasteners; contact cement; finishing nails; 2" No. 8 screws; two 2" butt hinges; 1½"-diameter wooden knob; door catch.

QUARTER-CIRCLE STUDY TABLE:

¾" x 11½" pine; ⅛" coated hardboard; glue; corrugated fasteners; contact cement; finishing nails; 2" No. 8 screws; eight 2" angle irons; two 1"-diameter wooden knobs.

Fuses and Circuit Breakers

These are the vigilant watchmen that protect your home from electrical fires. Learn how they work and keep them in repair

THE PASSAGE of electric current through a conductor generates heat. The heat results from resistance to the free flow of electrons. All wires and other conductors offer some resistance except when at the temperature of 459.69 degrees Fahrenheit *below zero.*

Because of their resistance, wires have a limited capacity to conduct current without becoming overheated. Their current carrying capacity depends upon their size and the material of which they are made. Large wires can carry more current without heating than small wires. When more current than it should carry is forced

through hidden wiring in the walls, or when connections are improperly made or soldered, dangerous heating occurs. The leading causes of fire of electrical origin are overloading of circuits, sockets and outlets, abuse of extension cords, obsolescent wiring and worn-out appliance motors. Low line voltage, which causes appliance motors to continue running on their starting coils, is a frequent cause of overheating and fires in refrigerators, washing machines, air conditoners, etc.

To prevent the rise of *too much* heat, use is made of fuses and circuit breakers, which limit the current-carrying capacity of circuits. Fuses and circuit breakers of proper size open an overloaded circuit and shut off the current before any damage can be done.

Main And Branch Fuses

In most modern domestic electrical systems there is a main fuse or main breaker through which *all* the current used on the premises must pass. In a system supplied by a three-wire service, there are two main fuses or two main circuit breakers housed in a metal box at the main control center. There is one exception to this arrangement. According to the National Electrical Code, residential wiring protected solely by breakers and having six or less branch circuits does not need an entrance switch, a main breaker or main fuses.

Each branch circuit must be protected by its own fuse or breaker. It is advisable that the wiring supplying the motor in an air conditioner, oil burner, washing machine, etc., be provided with its own fuse, preferably of the "slow" type.

Fuse Construction

A fuse consists of a thin strip of lead alloy which has more resistance than an equivalent length of the copper wire it protects. It becomes heated sooner than this wire and it melts at a much lower temperature. It melts under a 25 per cent current overload and opens the circuit so that no current can flow.

The screw-in plug type fuse fits in a socket in the same manner as an incandescent lamp. The cylindrical cartridge type is held in clips mounted on porcelain or plastic blocks. Main fuses are always of the cartridge type. Branch fuses may be either plug or cartridge type. Cartridge fuses are used in branch circuits only when the wires are large enough to carry more than 30 amperes safely. Plug fuses range from 5 to 30 amperes. The numerals stamped on the contact terminal on the bottom of a plug fuse indicate its current carrying capacity. Fuses carry their rated current if all connections are clean, bright and tight. If overloaded they blow out in a fraction of a second. Cartridge fuses are available in many sizes up to 600 amperes.

Types Of Circuit Breakers

Circuit breakers have the same purpose as fuses, but after they open on overloads they can be reset to "on" so as to close the circuit again, whereas burned-out fuses are useless and must be thrown away. There are two types, the thermal and the electromagnetic circuit breaker. When a bimetal strip inside a breaker of the thermal type expands due to the heat generated by an overload, it releases a spring-loaded switch which opens the circuit. An electro-

Three types of common fuses. Ampere ratings of plug and slow-blow fuses are on center contact button.

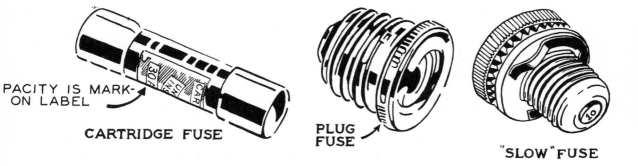

PACITY IS MARK-
ON LABEL

CARTRIDGE FUSE

PLUG FUSE

"SLOW" FUSE

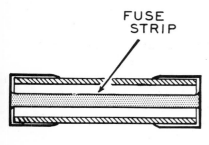

FUSE STRIP

CROSS SECTION OF A CARTRIDGE FUSE

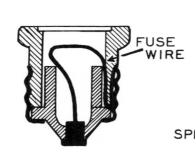

FUSE WIRE

CROSS-SECTION OF A PLUG FUSE

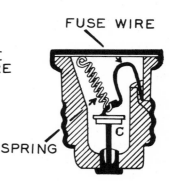

FUSE WIRE

SPRING

C

CROSS-SECTION OF A FUSETRON

1. Normally, current flows through a coil wrapped around a tube containing a hydraulic fluid and a movable iron core rod kept in place by a spring.

2. When too much current starts flowing in the circuit, it creates a magnetic force strong enough to pull the iron core toward the opposite end of the tube. The hydraulic fluid and the spring retard movement of the core, thus providing a time delay. This delay prevents disconnecting the circuit when there is a temporary overload (starting a motor, for example) that can't cause any trouble in the circuit. The greater the overload, the faster the core travels through the tube.

3. When the core touches the end of the tube the increased magnetic forces "trips the breaker" disconnecting the circuit. On very heavy overloads, the magnetic force in the coil itself is sufficient to trip the switch. This eliminates the time delay.

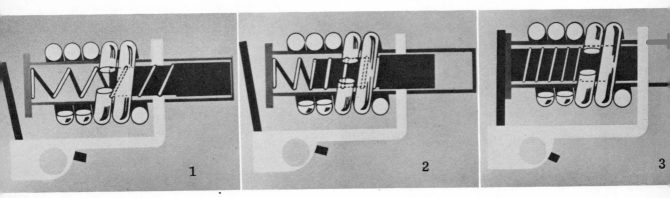

Fully magnetic circuit breaker provides complete protection of electrical circuit under all conditions.

magnetic circuit breaker is also an automatic switch. When the current exceeds the rated capacity of the breaker, the pull of an electromagnet operates the switch and opens the circuit.

When you wish to turn off the current in a fuse-equipped branch circuit to do repair work, the fuse must be removed. If the circuit is protected by a breaker, the handle is merely flipped to the "off" position.

When The Lights Go Out

When a lamp or appliance fails to operate, check other lamps or devices on the same circuit to see if they function. If they also fail to perform but there is power on elsewhere in the house, a branch circuit fuse or breaker has opened.

If no lamps in the house light:
1. The power in the neighborhood is off.
2. One or both main fuses or breakers have opened.
3. There is a loose connection at the service entrance.
4. The service wires leading into your home are cut or broken.
5. A practical joker has removed a main fuse or opened a main switch or circuit breaker.

The most common causes of blown fuses:
1. A short circuit in a lamp cord or appliance cord.
2. Overload caused by too many appliances connected to the same circuit at the same time.
3. Overload caused by jammed motor or two motors starting at the same time.
4. Hairpins, coins, nails, scissors or other metallic objects pushed by children into outlets or sockets.
5. Wet lamp cords and appliance cords.
6. An appliance in which the insulation has broken down coming into contact with a radiator, hot-air register, pipe or other grounded object.
7. A fuse which does not make a good contact and develops excessive heat at that point.

How To Replace Fuses And Reset Breakers

The first step is to locate and remove the cause of the blown fuse or open circuit breaker. Otherwise, a new fuse will blow out immediately, or a reset circuit breaker will pop back instantly to its "off" position.

Fuses and circuit breakers are located in a steel box which is part of the service en-

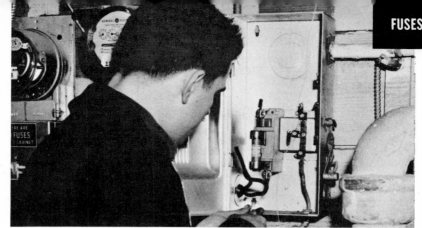

The fuse box which is being installed here is a good size. There is enough room for expansion as needed.

Circuit breakers look like toggle switches. Connections are enclosed, protected, in steel cabinet.

If paper strip goes between end cap and clip, the clip jaws need tightening. Test with power OFF.

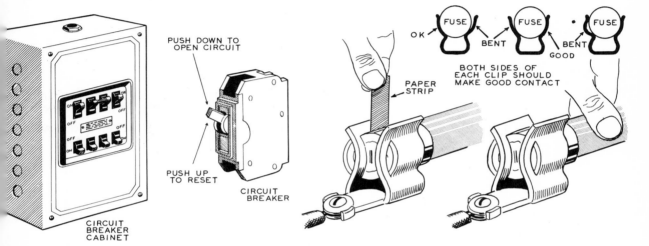

trance equipment. It is possible, however, to have smaller fuse boxes remotely located from the service panel to protect some special circuit for a dryer, air conditioner, refrigerator, etc.

The next step is to open the entrance switch or main breaker. If a main fuse has blown and the entrance switch is of the fuse or combination type, it is a simple matter to grasp the handle and pull out the insulated holder on which the fuses are mounted and then to pull the burned-out fuse from its holder and replace it.

Electricians use insulated pliers made of fiber and called "fuse pullers" to remove and replace both main and branch fuses of the cartridge type. This is only one of the precautions an electrician takes to avoid shock.

It is possible to get a *dangerous* shock when changing fuses. It is advisable to use the following safety precautions:

1. Make certain that all power is shut off at the entrance switch before touching any fuse.

2. Remember that one of the power wires is grounded. If you are in electrical contact with the ground you can get a shock by touching ONE wire. Use only one hand. Keep the other hand always out of

the way behind your back or in pocket.

3. Do not stand on a stone, earth or concrete floor when changing fuses. If the fuse box is located where the floor is damp, wear rubbers over your shoes or stand on a dry board or wooden box.

4. A pair of slip joint pliers wrapped with two layers of plastic insulating tape can be used as a substitute for fuse pullers to remove cartridge type fuses.

Why A Main Fuse Blows

A main fuse may burn out or a main circuit breaker may open because:

1. Something connected to the hot side of a circuit has come into contact with a pipe, radiator, armored cable, outlet box or other grounded object.

2. There are oversize fuses in the branch circuits. When such a branch circuit becomes overloaded or short circuited the main fuse or circuit breaker "goes."

3. The branch circuits, collectively, are carrying too much current for the capacity of the main fuse or breaker.

Why Branch Fuses Blow

When a branch fuse blows out, the cause for it will be found in a branch circuit. Such causes may be:

GOOD FUSE

YOU CAN SEE
FUSE STRIP
THROUGH WIN-
DOW IN TOP

BLOWN FUSE

STRIP HAS
MELTED AND
WINDOW IS
DISCOLORED

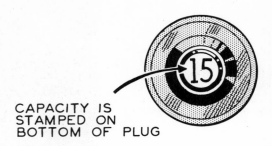

CAPACITY IS
STAMPED ON
BOTTOM OF PLUG

CONSULT THE TABLE FOR CORRECT
FUSE FOR EACH WIRE SIZE

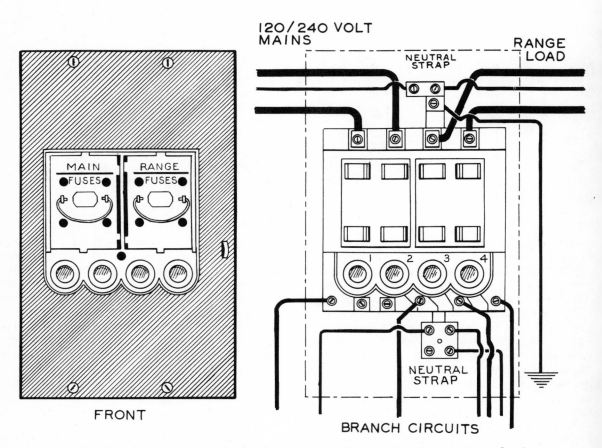

FRONT

120/240 VOLT MAINS

RANGE LOAD

NEUTRAL STRAP

NEUTRAL STRAP

BRANCH CIRCUITS

External appearance and internal wiring of typical entrance box for house having electric range, four branch circuits. Main and range fuses are cartridge type, set in removable box with handle outside. Four branch fuses are of plug type.

1. An undersized fuse.
2. A short circuit.
3. An overload caused by operating too many lamps or appliances on the circuit at the same time.
4. A ground.
5. A defective motor.

List all the electrical equipment which was in operation at the time that the fuse blew or the breaker opened. Ascertain the number of watts each lamp and appliance consumes when in operation. All lamps ar[e] marked with their rating in watts. This in[-] formation is also given on the name plate of electric irons, motors, toasters, etc. I[n] the case of motors, the number of ampere[s] consumed for a couple of seconds whil[e] starting may be several times the figure fo[r] a normal load. Add together the number o[f] watts consumed by the devices and divid[e] this figure by 115. The answer will be th[e] approximate number of amperes con[-]

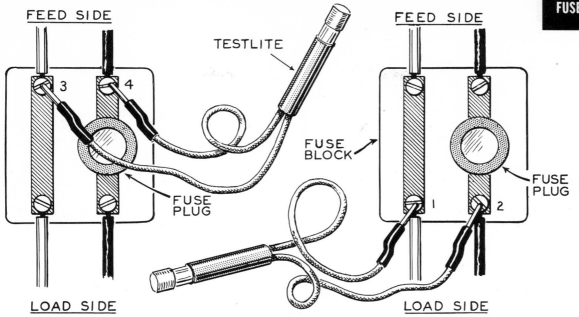

FEED SIDE

FEED SIDE

TESTLITE

FUSE BLOCK

FUSE PLUG

FUSE PLUG

LOAD SIDE

LOAD SIDE

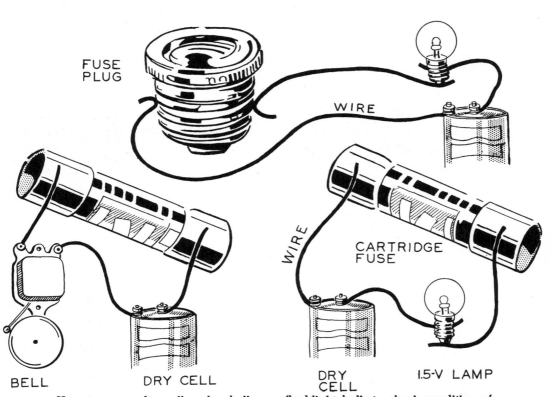

FUSE PLUG

WIRE

BELL

DRY CELL

WIRE

CARTRIDGE FUSE

DRY CELL

1.5-V LAMP

How to use a dry cell and a bell or a flashlight bulb to check condition of fuses. If the fuse is OK, the bell rings or the lamp lights; if blown, no reaction.

sumed. This figure will tell you whether or not the circuit is overloaded and whether or not the fuse is too small.

It is usually not difficult to locate a burned-out fuse of the plug type. The top is transparent and you can see whether the fuse strip has melted or not. If the under surface of the transparent top is blackened or spattered with particles of fuse metal, you can be certain that the fuse is burned out. To remove a burned-out plug fuse,

unscrew it from the fuse block by turning it in a counterclockwise direction. Screw new fuse in place in clockwise direction.

Fuse Directory

A fuse chart or directory pasted on the inside of the door of a fuse box is a time saver in locating burned-out fuses. An open circuit breaker is quickly located because it will be in the "off" position.

A fuse chart will show which lamp

sockets and outlets are in circuit with each branch fuse. You can make a chart if you turn on all the lamps in the house and then remove one branch fuse. Check each room and make notes showing which lamps were extinguished by removal of the fuse. Outlets can be checked by plugging in a table or floor lamp and noting which outlets are dead when a certain fuse is removed. Continue this procedure until you have discovered which lamp sockets and outlets are controlled by each branch fuse. Mark each

branch fuse block with an identifying letter or numeral. Then make a list or chart of lamp sockets and outlets in the house and mark each one with the numeral or letter of the fuse which protects it. When lights go out because of a blown fuse or open circuit breaker, a glance at the chart will show which branch circuit is involved.

You cannot ascertain by looking at a cartridge fuse whether or not it has burned out. Both cartridge and plug fuses can be quickly tested by removing them from the

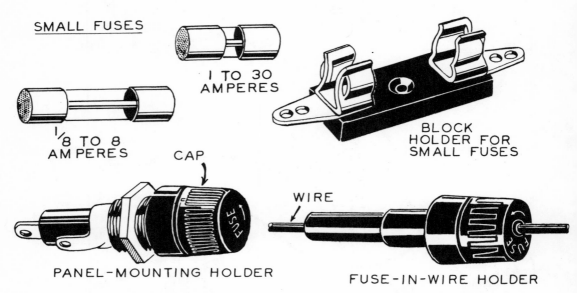

SMALL FUSES

1 TO 30 AMPERES

1/8 TO 8 AMPERES

CAP

BLOCK HOLDER FOR SMALL FUSES

WIRE

PANEL-MOUNTING HOLDER

FUSE-IN-WIRE HOLDER

Small cartridge fuses with clear glass bodies are used in variety of lengths and diameters in radio and television receivers and automobile electrical systems.

In some older systems, both sides of line are fused. Illustration shows methods of testing with neon light

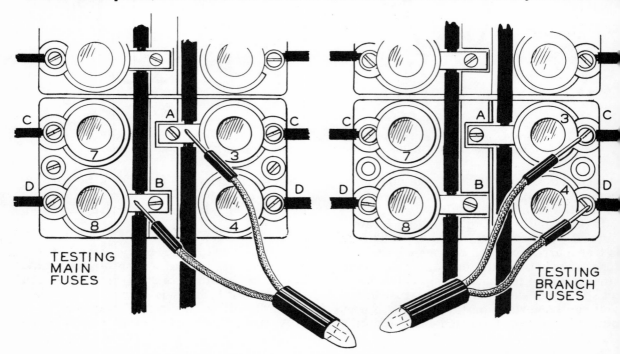

TESTING MAIN FUSES

TESTING BRANCH FUSES

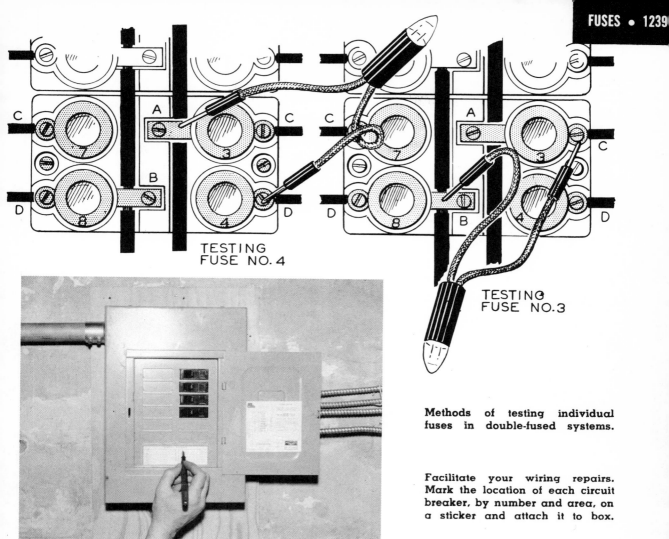

TESTING FUSE NO. 4

TESTING FUSE NO. 3

Methods of testing individual fuses in double-fused systems.

Facilitate your wiring repairs. Mark the location of each circuit breaker, by number and area, on a sticker and attach it to box.

fuse box and placing them in circuit with a flashlight battery and a flashlight lamp or doorbell. The lamp will light or the doorbell will ring if the fuse is a good one.

Fuses For Electric Motors

Small motors such as those used to run sewing machines, fans and mixers do not ordinarily draw enough current to blow fuses. They are usually of the series or universal type and their starting current is not much more than their normal operating current. Larger motors of the induction type, usually ¼ hp or more and made for AC operation only, used for washing machines, oil burners, coal stokers, refrigerators and workshop tools, may draw 35 amperes or more for a couple of seconds while starting. As soon as motor gets up to speed, it may draw only 5 or 7 amps.

The overload in the circuit caused by the heavy starting current is normally harmless because it is of short duration. However, it will usually cause ordinary fuses to blow out. Installing a larger fuse

which will not burn out under the starting overload is the *wrong* solution to the problem. It would reduce protection and be contrary to the rules of the National Electric Code. A circuit on which an induction motor is operated should be protected by a special type of fuse known as the "slow blow" and sold under the trade names Fustat and Fusetron. These have a time lag. They remain inactive and do not burn out on an overload of short duration, but on a short circuit or a permanent overload they act as quickly as an ordinary fuse.

If a Fusetron or Fustat of the correct capacity burns out when a motor is started, the trouble may be due to any one of the following conditions:

1. A new stiff motor belt.
2. A belt that is too tight.
3. A motor load that is too heavy.
4. Starting too frequently or reversing motor too quickly.
5. An armature which does not rotate freely due to misaligned bearings or gummy lubrication. •

Put a Gable
on Your Dormer

Not only will it give you additional space
but it will add prominence and beauty to your home.

By Henry Clark

WE ARE ALL quite familiar with the term "Expansion Attic" and we all realize how attics are made to expand. *You just put rooms up there.* But this procedure is often abused and the owner soon realizes that he has not taken full advantage of his upstairs real estate.

Usually, two shed dormers, one in front and one in back yield two large or three small rooms which seem the ultimate any owner of a bungalow-type house, needing additional space for a growing family, can ask. But we have gone this happy situation one better and gained an additional 33 square feet out front by embellishing, what would otherwise be a plain front shed dormer, with a gable! A gable is a peaked wall, and every bungalow has one on each end, terming its roof a gable roof. A third gable, out front, not only adds highly desirable square feet, but adds such prominence to the frontage that your home will be the envy of the area. And if your home is on a street where all the houses look alike, the change is most welcome.

All these advantages were in mind when we planned to enlarge our home with a gabled dormer. We took into account how little extra effort would be expended as against the resulting space gain. The major components were six lengths of 2x6 rafters about 14 feet long, three on each side of the gable, and joined at the top with a 2x8 ridge that ran 90 degrees to the ridge of the house. Drawings and photographs herewith explain this quite simply. Actually, if you now have a complete shed dormer across the front of the house you can add this gable, as shown on one of these drawings, and not even disturb normal living in it, by building right over the dormer. Tear out the wall later.

Another feature of this type of construction is that you can do it alone, and in spare time; weekends only if you want. All this without letting in a drop of rain. The trick is to build the new structure over the old roof which goes right on protecting the house.

Holes were cut in the roof only where the studs had to penetrate the roof for anchorage to the 2x4 plate laid on the attic floor. After a row of studs were stood, the studs were tarred well at the point where they entered the old roof. Careful plumb bob work gives the points of the cuts.

For the shed dormer portion, each stud must enter next to an old rafter since you must nail it to the rafter, and make the rafter cut later when closed in. A good four feet on the rafter will continue out front permanently. On the gable this does not apply, as will be mentioned later.

We made a model of balsa wood to study the method of erecting a gable most efficiently, and the results are pared down for your convenience in the accompanying drawings. It was decided that the dormer plate, of double 2x4's, should extend clear across the shed portion, unbroken at the gable, to create a small cheek dormer on the left side of the gable. Thus the headroom was not lessened, remaining a constant seven feet. Likewise, a full-length plate gave the structure maximum strength. All studs were erected under this plate for the shed portions, being omitted only at the gable portion, since that is where the extra three feet of space out front is gained. Studs here will come out even with the front of the house, and form the gable wall.

Holes were cut in roof only where studs had to penetrate for anchorage to plate on attic floor.

After a row of studs were set, they were tarred well at points where they entered the old roof.

For the shed dormer portion, each rafter extended from the front top plate to the house ridge.

Gable rafters were laid out on lawn at 90 degrees in accordance with procedure shown in sketches.

After both gable rafters were anchored, the gable ridge was butted and secured to the house ridge.

Dormer plate of double 2x4's extended unbroken through gable to form small cheek dormer on left.

With the shed half done, shingles of the old roof were taken off and the roofer boards pulled out.

Old roof rafters were cut next, sawed off flush inside new studs and pulled off the house ridge.

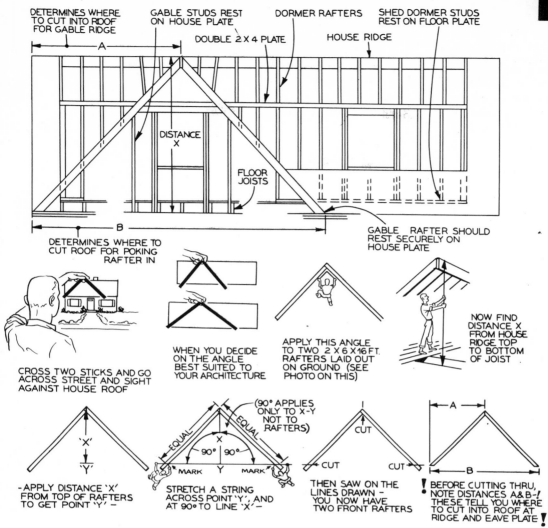

DETERMINES WHERE TO CUT INTO ROOF FOR GABLE RIDGE

GABLE STUDS REST ON HOUSE PLATE

DORMER RAFTERS

SHED DORMER STUDS REST ON FLOOR PLATE

DOUBLE 2 X 4 PLATE

HOUSE RIDGE

DISTANCE X

FLOOR JOISTS

DETERMINES WHERE TO CUT ROOF FOR POKING RAFTER IN

GABLE RAFTER SHOULD REST SECURELY ON HOUSE PLATE

CROSS TWO STICKS AND GO ACROSS STREET AND SIGHT AGAINST HOUSE ROOF

WHEN YOU DECIDE ON THE ANGLE BEST SUITED TO YOUR ARCHITECTURE

APPLY THIS ANGLE TO TWO 2 X 6 X 16 FT. RAFTERS LAID OUT ON GROUND (SEE PHOTO ON THIS)

NOW FIND DISTANCE X FROM HOUSE RIDGE TOP TO BOTTOM OF JOIST

-APPLY DISTANCE 'X' FROM TOP OF RAFTERS TO GET POINT 'Y' —

(90° APPLIES ONLY TO X-Y NOT TO RAFTERS)

EQUAL   EQUAL

X

90° | 90°

MARK   Y   MARK

STRETCH A STRING ACROSS POINT 'Y', AND AT 90° TO LINE 'X' —

CUT

CUT

CUT

THEN SAW ON THE LINES DRAWN — YOU NOW HAVE TWO FRONT RAFTERS

A

B

! BEFORE CUTTING THRU, NOTE DISTANCES A & B-! THESE TELL YOU WHERE TO CUT INTO ROOF AT RIDGE AND EAVE PLATE !

The rafters went on the shed portion next. It was sheathed over with 1x6 roofer boards, waterproofed with asphalt felt paper, and battened down temporarily. With the shed half done, proceed to tear out the old roof under it, taking off all the shingles, pulling out the roofer boards (which can be used for flooring since they are well seasoned), then cutting out the rafters. These were sawed off flush inside the studs of the shed dormer and pulled from the house ridge by using a jimmy bar. If carefully removed, these can be reused for the roof, over to, and past the gable, since they are all short. Before cutting out any rafters, brace up the house ridge with a few 2x4's. In our case we had a center wall, which supported the ridge firmly when the old rafters were removed.

A word about that center wall. It forms another two rooms out back, because we had put up the first dormer there a few years before, and went right out to the house plate with it, gaining us a 12-foot room. The back of the house went straight up, forming two stories. It would have looked too tall, and unbecoming, except that we broke the two floors in half with a false eave line along the middle.

The plan view shows the space gained there. If you are going to build front and back dormers, that plan will quickly show you how much real estate you can own. You might increase your taxes, but the livability and the salability are highly motivating factors.

With half your front dormer now complete, you can use that point as headquarters for working out to the gable, storing tools and lumber. You should put up the gable rafters next because the remaining dormer work will all be built around the gable structure, and up to it.

First thing to know is the angle of the gable, which determines the length of the rafters in front. For maximum head clear-

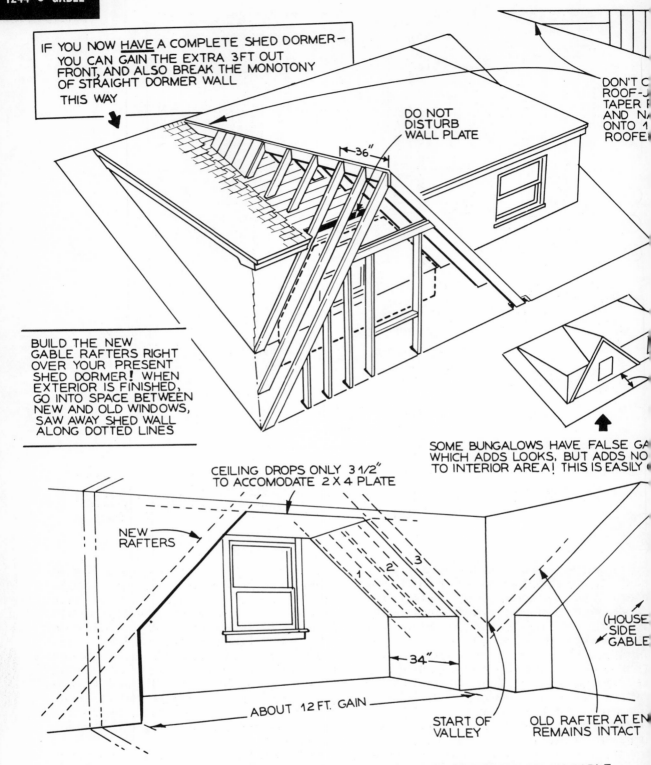

IF YOU NOW <u>HAVE</u> A COMPLETE SHED DORMER—
YOU CAN GAIN THE EXTRA 3FT OUT
FRONT, AND ALSO BREAK THE MONOTONY
OF STRAIGHT DORMER WALL
THIS WAY

DO NOT
DISTURB
WALL PLATE

←36"→

DON'T C
ROOF-J
TAPER F
AND N/
ONTO 1
ROOFE

BUILD THE NEW
GABLE RAFTERS RIGHT
OVER YOUR PRESENT
SHED DORMER! WHEN
EXTERIOR IS FINISHED,
GO INTO SPACE BETWEEN
NEW AND OLD WINDOWS,
SAW AWAY SHED WALL
ALONG DOTTED LINES

SOME BUNGALOWS HAVE FALSE GA
WHICH ADDS LOOKS, BUT ADDS NO
TO INTERIOR AREA! THIS IS EASILY

CEILING DROPS ONLY 3 1/2"
TO ACCOMODATE 2 X 4 PLATE

NEW
RAFTERS

1 2 3

(HOUSE
SIDE
GABLE

←34"→

——ABOUT 12 FT. GAIN——

START OF
VALLEY

OLD RAFTER AT EN
REMAINS INTACT

<u>GENERAL INTERIOR VIEW SHOWS FLOOR AND WALL SPACE GAINED BY GABLE</u>

ance and floor area they should spread just about 90 degrees, or true square. Any less will look too thin and lose room; any more, too squat for a small house. A photograph shows these rafters being laid out on the lawn in accordance with the procedure shown in small sketches.

After this, you will know two vital things: where to butt the new gable ridg to the house ridge, and where to ancho the right hand rafter on the house plat. The one on the left will anchor on the cor ner of the house, of course. Chop or sav away these anchorage points, secure th 2x8 ridge in place on the house ridge, brin it dead level, and brace it on the dorme

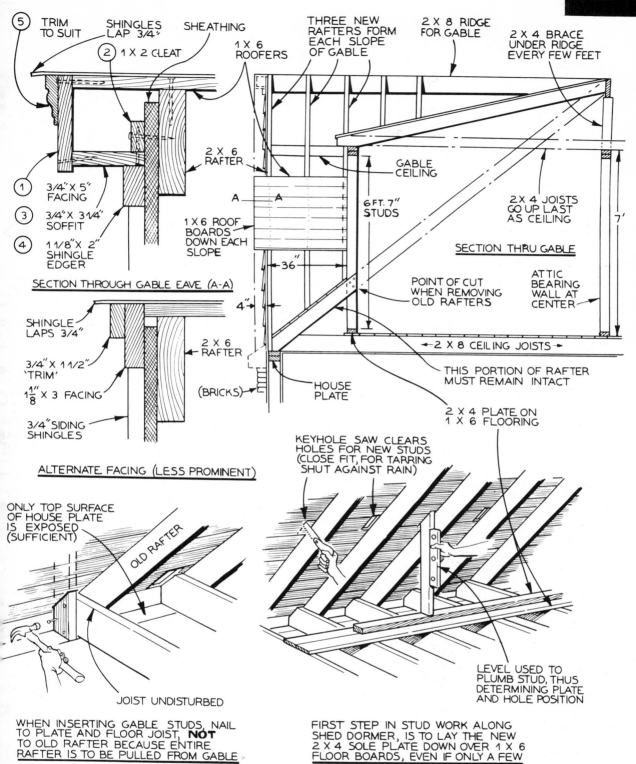

⑤ TRIM TO SUIT

SHINGLES LAP 3/4"

SHEATHING

② 1 X 2 CLEAT

1 X 6 ROOFERS

THREE NEW RAFTERS FORM EACH SLOPE OF GABLE

2 X 8 RIDGE FOR GABLE

2 X 4 BRACE UNDER RIDGE EVERY FEW FEET

2 X 6 RAFTER

① 3/4" X 5" FACING

③ 3/4" X 3 1/4" SOFFIT

④ 1 1/8" X 2" SHINGLE EDGER

SECTION THROUGH GABLE EAVE (A-A)

1 X 6 ROOF BOARDS DOWN EACH SLOPE

A — A

GABLE CEILING

6 FT. 7" STUDS

2 X 4 JOISTS GO UP LAST AS CEILING

7'

SECTION THRU GABLE

36"

4"

POINT OF CUT WHEN REMOVING OLD RAFTERS

ATTIC BEARING WALL AT CENTER

SHINGLE LAPS 3/4"

3/4" X 1 1/2" 'TRIM'

1 1/8" X 3 FACING

3/4" SIDING SHINGLES

2 X 6 RAFTER

(BRICKS)

HOUSE PLATE

THIS PORTION OF RAFTER MUST REMAIN INTACT

2 X 8 CEILING JOISTS

2 X 4 PLATE ON 1 X 6 FLOORING

ALTERNATE FACING (LESS PROMINENT)

ONLY TOP SURFACE OF HOUSE PLATE IS EXPOSED (SUFFICIENT)

OLD RAFTER

KEYHOLE SAW CLEARS HOLES FOR NEW STUDS (CLOSE FIT, FOR TARRING SHUT AGAINST RAIN)

LEVEL USED TO PLUMB STUD, THUS DETERMINING PLATE AND HOLE POSITION

JOIST UNDISTURBED

WHEN INSERTING GABLE STUDS, NAIL TO PLATE AND FLOOR JOIST, **NOT** TO OLD RAFTER BECAUSE ENTIRE RAFTER IS TO BE PULLED FROM GABLE

FIRST STEP IN STUD WORK ALONG SHED DORMER, IS TO LAY THE NEW 2 X 4 SOLE PLATE DOWN OVER 1 X 6 FLOOR BOARDS, EVEN IF ONLY A FEW

plate, 90 degrees to the house ridge. Juggle the left hand rafter into its niche on the house plate and rest its mitered top end against the ridge. Now juggle the right hand rafter into its niche on the house plate, and rest its top against the ridge. The mitered ends of both rafters should meet the ridge flush and true.

Nail lightly for a moment. Go down to the street and stand some distance away from the house so that you can check your gable angle with a wood square held at arm's length. Make your corrections now, with shims or wedges where needed, because that is your last chance to avoid a lopsided gable.

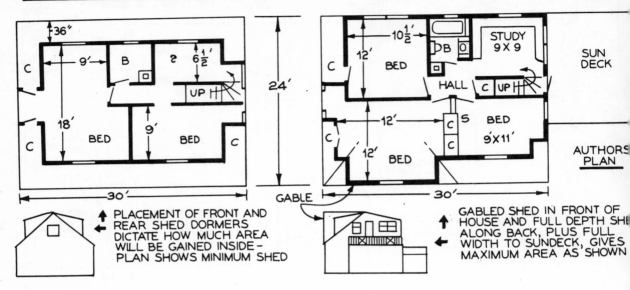

INTERIOR WALLS ARE ARRANGED
TO SUIT NEEDS, BUT THE EXTERIOR
WALLS MAKE OR BREAK YOUR EXPANSION

ATTACHED GARAGE PERMITS BUILDING
DORMER END FLUSH WITH SIDE OF HOUSE
(CAN EVEN BE DONE WITHOUT GARAGE)

↑ PLACEMENT OF FRONT AND
← REAR SHED DORMERS
DICTATE HOW MUCH AREA
WILL BE GAINED INSIDE—
PLAN SHOWS MINIMUM SHED

↑ GABLED SHED IN FRONT OF
← HOUSE AND FULL DEPTH SHE
ALONG BACK, PLUS FULL
WIDTH TO SUNDECK, GIVES
MAXIMUM AREA AS SHOWN

The other four rafters go in now and each is shorter than the next. Place the innermost left hand rafter first, securing the ridge, plate and corner dormer stud group, and making certain it is parallel and in plane with the front rafter pitch. Do the same with the right hand inner rafter. This can end at the roof slant, or go through and anchor inside. (See drawing.)

The intermediate two rafters are simply placed to line up with the other four, now in position. They can be nailed to the old roof, each resting on its slant with a compound mitered base. Its position will not be disturbed when you tear away the inside. None of the rafter base anchor points will be affected by the removal of the old roof.

Your gable frame is now ready for studding and sheathing, and with it you have automatically braced the entire shed dormer frame well beyond the usual building requirements, which demand a diagonal at each corner. Your house looks outstanding already, and you will want to hurry it along now, though not on the weather's account.

Proceed to cut the remaining shed dormer rafters, because regardless of weather, we want to get the roof up. Two of these roof rafters form the valley down each side of the gable top ridge slope. These run from a joint with the ridge, down behind the innermost gable rafter. Now, with roofers all on, cover with asphalt felt, and battens. Leave shingles until later.

The short 1x6 roofers that run down the gable slopes should be cut to extend be yond the front rafter by about 5 to 6 inche to afford you a beefy box eave. Don' shortchange yourself by trimming th gable facing with skinny 1x2 trim. Thi gable is your baby, and it should b trimmed heavy.

The gable wall studs can go in now, an these must likewise pierce the roof. Bu this time they are placed low, down by th house eave, which is where you gain th full 3 feet room bonus. There will be n bearing force on these studs, but they mus still be spaced 16 inches on center to tak the insulation batts and the inside wa board. It is best to rip the entire eav board away, here, even though we were s apprehensive about rain, we had poke the studs into holes, cut small, after whic the points of entry were tarred.

Frame in the opening for the windov doubling the studs on each side. Provid a double 2x4 header, which spans the tw front rafters. The opening you allow de pends upon the size window frames yo will use. Know the size first.

Proceed to sheathe over these studs wit boards or insulation panels, ¾ inch thicl Likewise, finish off the remaining dorme walls. Protect the sheathing with aspha felt, and batten.

You are now ready to go inside and pu away the old roof in the gable section. Her you will be pulling out full length rafter from the house ridge down to the floor lin Previous care made sure you did not na the studs to these rafters, as you did in th

With old rafters removed, interior construction, facing gable and cheek dormer, is clearly seen.

Sheathing, with compound mitered base nailed to dormer roof, is attached to gable ridge, at top.

Framework clearly shows gable rafters and studs, and double 2x4 corner post of the cheek dormer.

Insulation panels cover gable studs, and boards, sheathing dormer, are protected by asphalt felt.

Shingle ends were turned up on dormer sheathing. The siding overlap would make waterproof valley.

Opening for window had double studs on each side and a double 2x4 header spanned two front rafters.

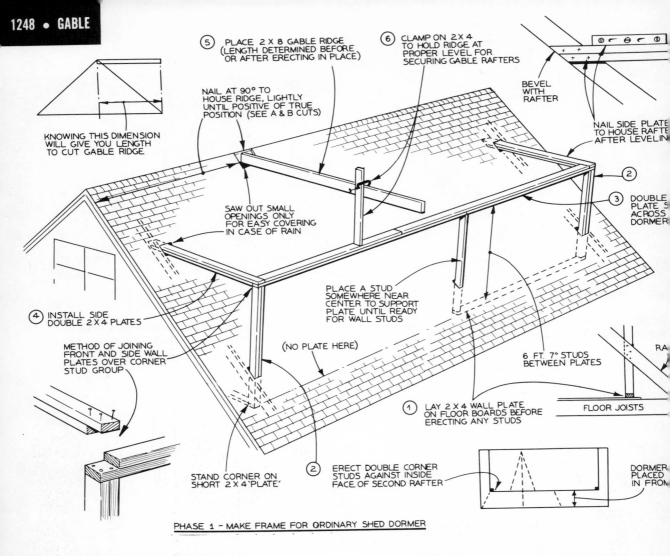

KNOWING THIS DIMENSION WILL GIVE YOU LENGTH TO CUT GABLE RIDGE.

⑤ PLACE 2 X 8 GABLE RIDGE (LENGTH DETERMINED BEFORE OR AFTER ERECTING IN PLACE)

⑥ CLAMP ON 2 X 4 TO HOLD RIDGE AT PROPER LEVEL FOR SECURING GABLE RAFTERS

BEVEL WITH RAFTER

NAIL SIDE PLATE TO HOUSE RAFTER AFTER LEVELING

NAIL AT 90° TO HOUSE RIDGE, LIGHTLY UNTIL POSITIVE OF TRUE POSITION (SEE A & B CUTS)

②

③ DOUBLE PLATE ACROSS DORMER

SAW OUT SMALL OPENINGS ONLY FOR EASY COVERING IN CASE OF RAIN

④ INSTALL SIDE DOUBLE 2 X 4 PLATES

METHOD OF JOINING FRONT AND SIDE WALL PLATES OVER CORNER STUD GROUP

PLACE A STUD SOMEWHERE NEAR CENTER TO SUPPORT PLATE UNTIL READY FOR WALL STUDS

(NO PLATE HERE)

6 FT. 7" STUDS BETWEEN PLATES

① LAY 2 X 4 WALL PLATE ON FLOOR BOARDS BEFORE ERECTING ANY STUDS

FLOOR JOISTS

RA

STAND CORNER ON SHORT 2 X 4 'PLATE'

② ERECT DOUBLE CORNER STUDS AGAINST INSIDE FACE OF SECOND RAFTER

DORMER PLACED IN FRONT

PHASE 1 – MAKE FRAME FOR ORDINARY SHED DORMER

Dormer eave had six-inch overhang under which were openings for air circulation.

shed section, because it is necessary to pull out as much of the rafters as is possible, sawing close to the floor, chiseling out the root, and pulling the top from the house ridge. Again, be sure something is bracing the house ridge before pulling a single rafter. All the new rafters are now bearing on it.

With all sections of the old roof removed, you must now provide ceiling joists. These are 2x4 members running from the center wall, out to the dormer plate where they are nailed to the roof rafter end, and the plate, as well. These, again, are spaced 16 inches on center to assure proper ceiling paneling or tiling, and insulating. If there were no center wall, these joists would have to lap the ceiling joists from the rear dormer to form the needed structural truss, or tie. If you have no center wall up, as yet, keep the ridge braced until one is built, then brace the ridge on this center bearing wall. Aim to keep the house ridge level, and allow no sag. The trick is simply to maintain the level you found in the ridge from the beginning. You can jack an inch, but don't sag an inch.

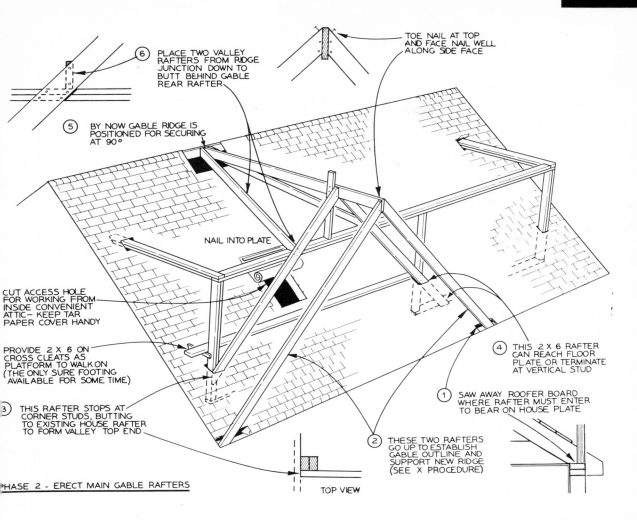

TOE NAIL AT TOP AND FACE NAIL WELL ALONG SIDE FACE

⑥ PLACE TWO VALLEY RAFTERS FROM RIDGE JUNCTION DOWN TO BUTT BEHIND GABLE REAR RAFTER

⑤ BY NOW GABLE RIDGE IS POSITIONED FOR SECURING AT 90°

NAIL INTO PLATE

CUT ACCESS HOLE FOR WORKING FROM INSIDE CONVENIENT ATTIC— KEEP TAR PAPER COVER HANDY

PROVIDE 2 X 6 ON CROSS CLEATS AS PLATFORM TO WALK ON (THE ONLY SURE FOOTING AVAILABLE FOR SOME TIME.)

④ THIS 2 X 6 RAFTER CAN REACH FLOOR PLATE OR TERMINATE AT VERTICAL STUD

① SAW AWAY ROOFER BOARD WHERE RAFTER MUST ENTER TO BEAR ON HOUSE PLATE

③ THIS RAFTER STOPS AT CORNER STUDS, BUTTING TO EXISTING HOUSE RAFTER TO FORM VALLEY TOP END

② THESE TWO RAFTERS GO UP TO ESTABLISH GABLE OUTLINE AND SUPPORT NEW RIDGE (SEE X PROCEDURE)

PHASE 2 - ERECT MAIN GABLE RAFTERS

TOP VIEW

Asbestos siding on dormer overlaps old roof shingles for water-proof valley, but copper valley is needed where gable joins roof.

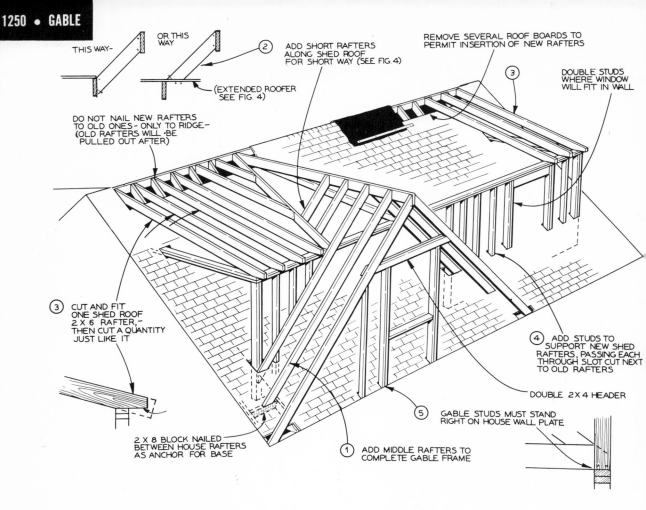

THIS WAY— OR THIS WAY

② ADD SHORT RAFTERS ALONG SHED ROOF FOR SHORT WAY (SEE FIG. 4)

(EXTENDED ROOFER SEE FIG. 4)

REMOVE SEVERAL ROOF BOARDS TO PERMIT INSERTION OF NEW RAFTERS

③

DOUBLE STUDS WHERE WINDOW WILL FIT IN WALL

DO NOT NAIL NEW RAFTERS TO OLD ONES - ONLY TO RIDGE - (OLD RAFTERS WILL BE PULLED OUT AFTER)

③ CUT AND FIT ONE SHED ROOF 2 X 6 RAFTER, - THEN CUT A QUANTITY JUST LIKE IT

④ ADD STUDS TO SUPPORT NEW SHED RAFTERS, PASSING EACH THROUGH SLOT CUT NEXT TO OLD RAFTERS

DOUBLE 2 X 4 HEADER

2 X 8 BLOCK NAILED BETWEEN HOUSE RAFTERS AS ANCHOR FOR BASE

⑤ GABLE STUDS MUST STAND RIGHT ON HOUSE WALL PLATE

① ADD MIDDLE RAFTERS TO COMPLETE GABLE FRAME

Roof shingles are placed
a covering of roofing pa
and from the shed dormer
brought at least eight inc
up each side of the gable
help form a waterproof r

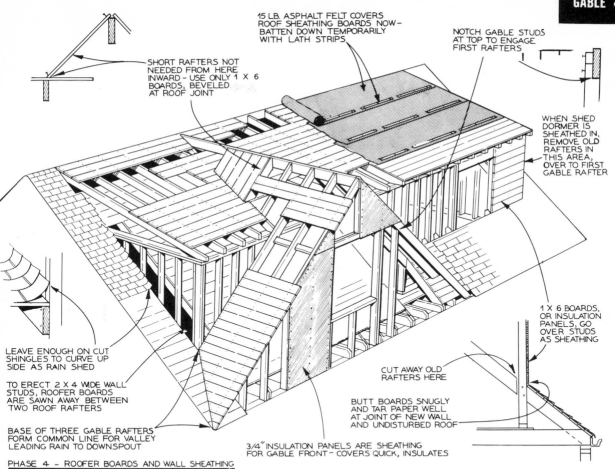

15 LB. ASPHALT FELT COVERS ROOF SHEATHING BOARDS NOW— BATTEN DOWN TEMPORARILY WITH LATH STRIPS

SHORT RAFTERS NOT NEEDED FROM HERE INWARD — USE ONLY 1 X 6 BOARDS, BEVELED AT ROOF JOINT

NOTCH GABLE STUDS AT TOP TO ENGAGE FIRST RAFTERS

WHEN SHED DORMER IS SHEATHED IN, REMOVE OLD RAFTERS IN THIS AREA, OVER TO FIRST GABLE RAFTER

LEAVE ENOUGH ON CUT SHINGLES TO CURVE UP SIDE AS RAIN SHED

TO ERECT 2 X 4 WIDE WALL STUDS, ROOFER BOARDS ARE SAWN AWAY BETWEEN TWO ROOF RAFTERS

BASE OF THREE GABLE RAFTERS FORM COMMON LINE FOR VALLEY LEADING RAIN TO DOWNSPOUT

CUT AWAY OLD RAFTERS HERE

BUTT BOARDS SNUGLY AND TAR PAPER WELL AT JOINT OF NEW WALL AND UNDISTURBED ROOF

1 X 6 BOARDS, OR INSULATION PANELS, GO OVER STUDS AS SHEATHING

3/4" INSULATION PANELS ARE SHEATHING FOR GABLE FRONT — COVERS QUICK, INSULATES

PHASE 4 — ROOFER BOARDS AND WALL SHEATHING

ιble shingles run at right
ιgle to those on dormer and,
ιerlapping the latter, rise
ι ridge. A row of shingles
ιpping ridge lap each other
ιcording to prevailing winds.

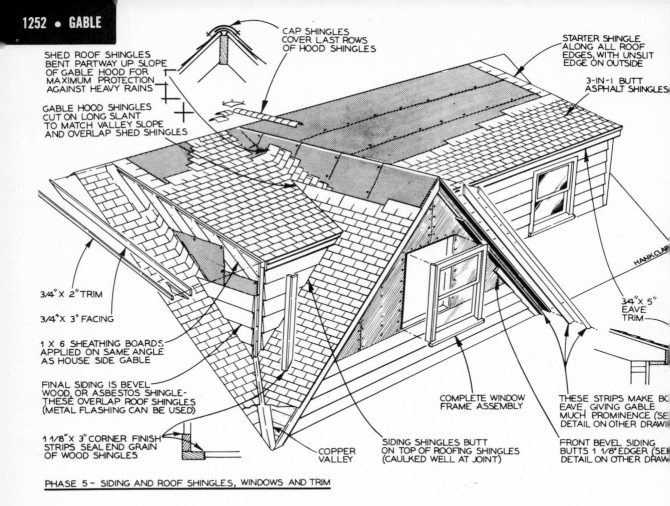

CAP SHINGLES
COVER LAST ROWS
OF HOOD SHINGLES

STARTER SHINGLE
ALONG ALL ROOF
EDGES, WITH UNSLIT
EDGE ON OUTSIDE

3-IN-1 BUTT
ASPHALT SHINGLES

SHED ROOF SHINGLES
BENT PARTWAY UP SLOPE
OF GABLE HOOD FOR
MAXIMUM PROTECTION
AGAINST HEAVY RAINS

GABLE HOOD SHINGLES
CUT ON LONG SLANT
TO MATCH VALLEY SLOPE
AND OVERLAP SHED SHINGLES

HANKCLAP

3/4" X 2" TRIM

3/4" X 3" FACING

3/4" X 5"
EAVE
TRIM

1 X 6 SHEATHING BOARDS
APPLIED ON SAME ANGLE
AS HOUSE SIDE GABLE

FINAL SIDING IS BEVEL
WOOD, OR ASBESTOS SHINGLE-
THESE OVERLAP ROOF SHINGLES
(METAL FLASHING CAN BE USED)

COMPLETE WINDOW
FRAME ASSEMBLY

THESE STRIPS MAKE BO
EAVE, GIVING GABLE
MUCH PROMINENCE (SE
DETAIL ON OTHER DRAWI

1 1/8" X 3" CORNER FINISH
STRIPS SEAL END GRAIN
OF WOOD SHINGLES

COPPER
VALLEY

SIDING SHINGLES BUTT
ON TOP OF ROOFING SHINGLES
(CAULKED WELL AT JOINT)

FRONT BEVEL SIDING
BUTTS 1 1/8" EDGER (SE
DETAIL ON OTHER DRAW

PHASE 5 – SIDING AND ROOF SHINGLES, WINDOWS AND TRIM

View at left illustrates best how gable brings front wall out three feet to give extra room. Compare it with shed dormer on neighbor's house.

Completed structure shows how gabled dormer enhances appearance of property and gives maximum space obtainable from the average bungalow.

Comparison of original bungalow home with photo above shows how full advantage was taken to give growing family added space and a beautiful home.

It is always neighborly to clean up your exterior litter first, and finish the inside later. This means you should apply the roof and the side shingles now, and finish off with trim along the eaves. If you used board sheathing, any siding can be used. If insulation panel sheathing was used, it is best to stick to bevel wood shingling.

Our frontage was all bevel boards, the dormer cheeks being asbestos shingle to match that on the house side gables. On those dormer cheeks you can turn up the old roof shingle ends against the sheathing, and apply the asbestos shingle overlapping them, which makes a watertight valley. Where the gable meets the old roof, however, a copper valley must be provided.

As the photos show, our dormer eave was just as prominent as the gable eave. No rain gutters were needed, since it dripped off and into the lower eaves gutters. However, we took advantage of the good 6-inch overhang of the dormer eave (gained by making the rafters extend that much) by inserting a screened opening every six feet, or so, for ventilation of the hot dead air space over the ceiling. Now, the breeze will keep the heat out of our dormer roof since entry and escape is plentiful.

As plans show, we came up with three full-size bedrooms, a study—where passage is made to the stairs, and a bath. The study opened onto a sundeck. The latter not only formed the roof of our garage, but it enabled us to build the dormers flush with the side of the house, gaining us another two to three feet of space.

You now have the maximum space upstairs that you can obtain from the average bungalow. Only one other course remains open for getting the same space upstairs as downstairs, and that is to build straight up, like a box. This is English and Dutch practice. However, compared to the gabled roof, it has no beauty.

To add color and beauty to your gabled home you should have contrasting siding: brick on the first floor, white shingles on the second floor. It is all up to you—the handy man and builder. Examples are to be seen on any Sunday drive in the suburbs. •

TABLE TENNIS
BASE AND TOP

No nails, no screws are needed in this construction of interlocking parts. And the base of the finished table comes apart for storage.

TABLE tennis, anyone? Here is a good and different table designed by the M & M Plywood Corporation. Its base comes apart completely for storing and it assembles without a single nail or screw.

The parts simply interlock. The center brace has its notches two inches farther apart than those of the ends, thus spreading the side rails to give rigidity to the table. The legs notch into the end pieces on a slant, and thus are braced by the side rails. All parts of the base are cut from ¾-in. plywood on your table saw—and this is a good place to use those long plywood strips left over from other projects.

Your planer or fine-toothed crosscut blade is the best to use for both ripping and crosscutting on the plywood. The various notches in the base are cut with either of the above blades (by making several

passes) or with the dado blade. Here, us your miter gauge with its wood extensio: to hold the work, and utilize the extensio: table on the longer pieces. For the slantin notches in the end braces, set your sav table to 11-degree tilt. Take advantag of the 12-in. disc sander on your powe tool to smooth all outer edges of the vari ous pieces, including the top.

The top is made of ½- or ⅝-in. plywooc You can order a 60 x 108-in. panel fror your dealer—yes, it is available on order i 5-ft. widths. Or you can gain the 108-ir length from two 4 x 5-ft. panels, adding 1 x 5-ft. panel in the middle and connect ing all by hinges on the bottom side. Th hinges shown are satisfactory and the mos inexpensive; piano hinges of 5-ft. lengt} have an advantage in eliminating the pos sibility of warp between them.

The clamps on the ends of your table tennis net will lock the table top to the center brace so that it cannot shift. However, as shown in the drawing, it is better to permanently secure the center brace to the bottom of the top with 1-in. No. 8 f.h. wood screws—in case the table is used for other purposes. You will find that it serves well as a cutting table for dressmaking, as an outdoor table for picnics, as a place for the electric train, and the like. If it is to be left outdoors, make certain the plywood is of the waterproof type, that it is branded "EXT-DFPA" (exterior type plywood for permanent outdoor use) on one end. A fairly dark green paint is generally used to finish a table tennis top. The best job is gained on the plywood by a first coat of a resin sealer, which will reduce any grain rise. ●

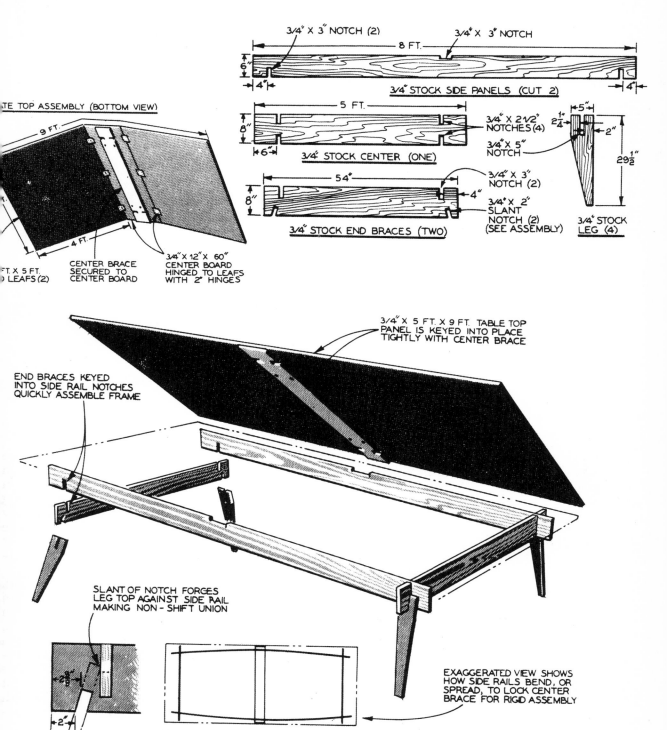

Train-

Game Table
folds into the wall

Cabinet conveniently stores all of children's toys, and opens to give ample room for a boy's train set.

DIVIDENDS in enjoyment for your children and reduced time and effort keeping things in order will be paid for many years by this versatile cabinet. When train equipment is out of sight, its blackboard stimulates children's creativeness; with only slight modification from the plan, you can install a blackboard in the lower half of the table's outer face and a cork "bulletin board" in the upper half, which is beyond the youngsters' reach.

Broken down into its three elements, construction is extremely simple. Glue and nail all joints throughout. The drawing explains assembly of wall cabinet ends, top and shelves. The only rabbeted joints are at top. Relieve the

PARTS SCHEDULE

CODE	NO. REQ'D	SIZE	PART IDENTIFICATION
A	1	46½"x58½"	Table
B	2	23½"x24"	Doors
C	2	10"x22"	Ends—Moving Cabinet
D	1	11"x46½"	Shelf
E	1	11"x47¼"	Top
F	1	10"x46"	Top—Moving Cabinet
G	1	9¾"x44½"	Bottom—Moving Cabinet
H	2	9¾"x44½"	Shelf—Moving Cabinet
I	2	8"x46½"	Shelf
J	1	4"x46½"	Bottom Tie
K	2	11"x84"	Ends
L	1	21⅝"x45¼"	Back
	18 Lin. Ft.	2"x2"	Frame
	2 Pr.	—	Semi-concealed Hinges
	20 Sq. Ft.	—	Cork
	1 Pr.	—	Broad Butt Hinges
	4 Ea.	—	Casters
	2 Ea.	—	Pulls
	2 Ea.	—	Catches
	2 Ea.	—	Hook and Eyes

Miscellaneous—4d and 6d Finish Nails and Glue

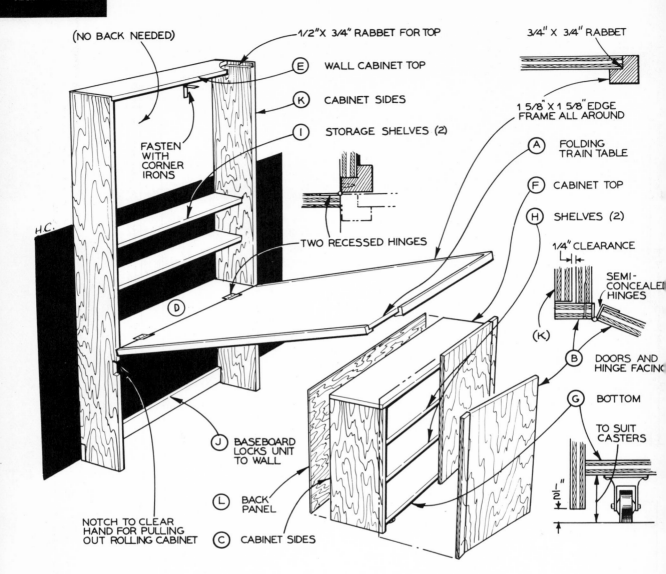

(NO BACK NEEDED)

1/2" X 3/4" RABBET FOR TOP

3/4" X 3/4" RABBET

(E) WALL CABINET TOP

(K) CABINET SIDES

(I) STORAGE SHELVES (2)

1 5/8" X 1 5/8" EDGE FRAME ALL AROUND

(A) FOLDING TRAIN TABLE

(F) CABINET TOP

(H) SHELVES (2)

1/4" CLEARANCE

SEMI-CONCEALED HINGES

FASTEN WITH CORNER IRONS

H.C.

TWO RECESSED HINGES

(D)

(K)

(B) DOORS AND HINGE FACING

(G) BOTTOM

TO SUIT CASTERS

1/2"

(J) BASEBOARD LOCKS UNIT TO WALL

(L) BACK PANEL

(C) CABINET SIDES

NOTCH TO CLEAR HAND FOR PULLING OUT ROLLING CABINET

back edge of ends "K" at the floor and locate stringer "J" to allow for your baseboard. Be sure you keep the entire assembly perfectly square. Fasten to wall at studs, if you wish, with 1½" steel corner braces.

Cut, fit, assemble and hinge table panel "A."

Rabbet ends and top of movable table for ¼" back. Nail through top into ends, install back and bottom panels, then attach shelves. Before locating bottom, check with casters in place to make sure cabinet fits easily under wall cabinet shelf "D." Cut, fit and hang face strips and doors, install casters and finish completely as recommended. Be careful to seal all door edges thoroughly and finish both faces alike. •

Folded against the wall, the table is out of the way and permits mother to clean the floor easily

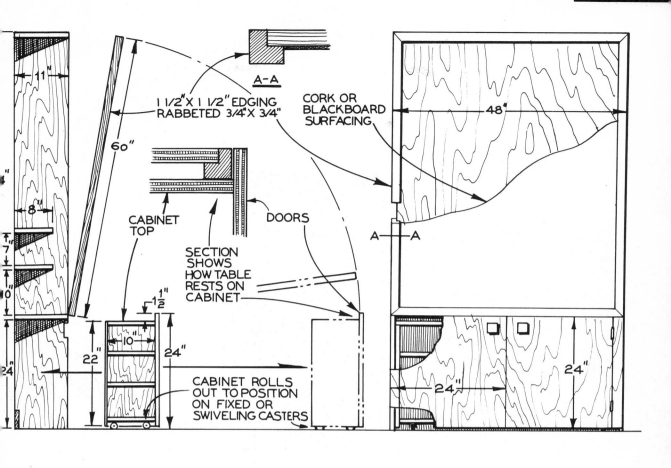

11"

60"

A-A

1 1/2" X 1 1/2" EDGING
RABBETED 3/4" X 3/4"

CORK OR
BLACKBOARD
SURFACING

48"

CABINET
TOP

DOORS

SECTION
SHOWS
HOW TABLE
RESTS ON
CABINET

A — A

8"

7"

1 1/2"

22"

24"

10"

24"

CABINET ROLLS
OUT TO POSITION
ON FIXED OR
SWIVELING CASTERS

24"

24"

24"

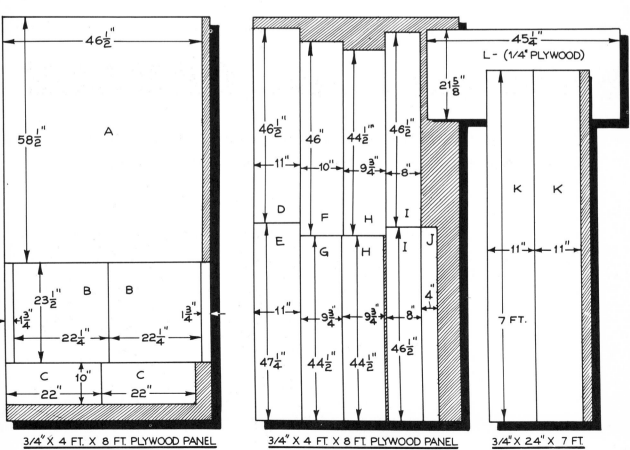

46 1/2"

58 1/2"

A

23 1/2"

B   B

1 3/4"

1 3/4"

22 1/4"   22 1/4"

C   10"   C

22"   22"

3/4" X 4 FT. X 8 FT. PLYWOOD PANEL

46 1/2"   46"   44 1/2"   46 1/2"

11"   10"   9 3/4"   8"

D   F   H   I

E   G   H   I   J

11"   9 3/4"   9 3/4"   8"   4"

47 1/4"   44 1/2"   44 1/2"   46 1/2"

3/4" X 4 FT. X 8 FT. PLYWOOD PANEL

45 1/4"

L — (1/4" PLYWOOD)

21 5/8"

K   K

11"   11"

7 FT.

3/4" X 24" X 7 FT.

build your own GARAGE

This trim, sturdy 12x20-ft. garage saves you hundreds of dollars in construction costs, and requires only three weeks of spare time.

By Henry Clark

Regardless of land slope (see side), this garage stands firmly on level, keeps car snug and dry.

IF you are one of the hundreds of thousands who have just moved into brand-new, garage-less homes, you are probably worrying about shelter for your car. Perhaps you have gazed enviously at neighbors building their own garages, and marveled at their skill and daring in attempting so prodigious a feat. If so, cheer up—building your own garage need take no more than a very few weeks, even if you work only evenings and weekends. Further, the job will cost you about half of what any contractor would charge.

You will have a much clearer picture of your future garage if you think of it as a project in four parts. First, there's the concrete footing and block foundation. Second—framing, roofing and sheathing. Third—nailing of siding and shingling. The fourth part is only a matter of hours—the concrete floor for your garage.

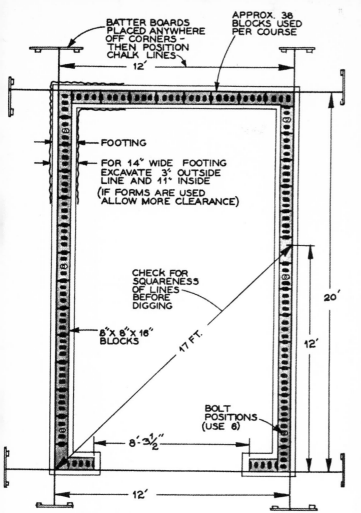

BATTER BOARDS PLACED ANYWHERE OFF CORNERS - THEN POSITION CHALK LINES

APPROX. 38 BLOCKS USED PER COURSE

12'

FOOTING

FOR 14" WIDE FOOTING EXCAVATE 3" OUTSIDE LINE AND 11" INSIDE (IF FORMS ARE USED ALLOW MORE CLEARANCE)

CHECK FOR SQUARENESS OF LINES BEFORE DIGGING

8"X 8"X 16" BLOCKS

17 FT.

20'

12'

BOLT POSITIONS (USE 6)

8'-3½"

12'

TO BUILD 12 X 20 FT. GARAGE, CHALK LINES MUST BE STRETCHED THAT DISTANCE, AND SQUARED PROPERLY

Chalk lines square off dimensions of garage. Bottom of trench is level, insures level sill.

Truck pours concrete into trench. Use spade to help flow to all sides and trowel to level off.

Frequent use of level in all parts of trench gives level footing, insures an easier, trouble-free job.

As soon as you've decided on the location for your garage, square off the site (in this case, 12x20 ft.) with chalk lines stretched between stakes driven in the ground shortly beyond the boundaries. An absolute "must"—critically important—is the checking of the bottom of the trench all the way around. Use your bubble level over the entire length. If this is done, your sill planks will be level—and you will avoid plenty of grief.

Call for one of the Transit-Mix trucks at this point, and have them dump in 2 or 3 cubic yards of concrete. When this is done, level the surface with a shovel and wooden trowel. Let the concrete footing set for a day, and, meanwhile, make certain you have a trowel, level, mixing board or pan (your wheelbarrow), mortar and clean sand—the only tools you need for block work. First, drop plumb lines from intersecting chalk lines to determine the exact corner point for the first blocks. Now—dampen the top of the footing, apply mortar

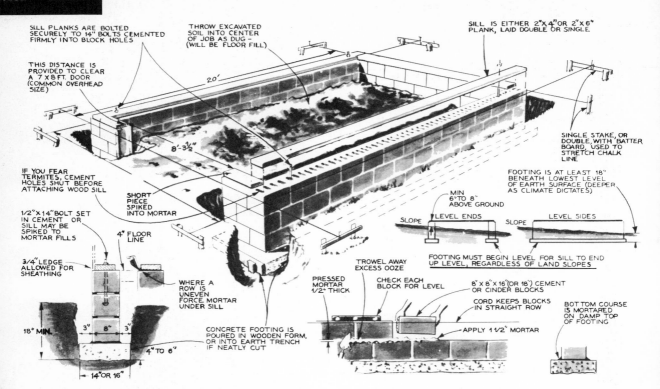

SILL PLANKS ARE BOLTED SECURELY TO 14" BOLTS CEMENTED FIRMLY INTO BLOCK HOLES

THROW EXCAVATED SOIL INTO CENTER OF JOB AS DUG — (WILL BE FLOOR FILL)

SILL IS EITHER 2"x 4"OR 2"x 6" PLANK, LAID DOUBLE OR SINGLE.

THIS DISTANCE IS PROVIDED TO CLEAR A 7 x 8 FT. DOOR (COMMON OVERHEAD SIZE)

20'

8'-3½"

SINGLE STAKE, OR DOUBLE, WITH BATTER BOARD, USED TO STRETCH CHALK LINE

IF YOU FEAR TERMITES, CEMENT HOLES SHUT BEFORE ATTACHING WOOD SILL

SHORT PIECE SPIKED INTO MORTAR

FOOTING IS AT LEAST 18" BENEATH LOWEST LEVEL OF EARTH SURFACE (DEEPER AS CLIMATE DICTATES)

MIN 6"TO 8" ABOVE GROUND

SLOPE   LEVEL ENDS   SLOPE   LEVEL SIDES

1/2"x14"BOLT SET IN CEMENT OR SILL MAY BE SPIKED TO MORTAR FILLS

4" FLOOR LINE

3/4"LEDGE ALLOWED FOR SHEATHING

WHERE A ROW IS UNEVEN FORCE MORTAR UNDER SILL

FOOTING MUST BEGIN LEVEL FOR SILL TO END UP LEVEL, REGARDLESS OF LAND SLOPES

TROWEL AWAY EXCESS OOZE

PRESSED MORTAR 1/2" THICK

CHECK EACH BLOCK FOR LEVEL

8"x 8"x 16"(OR 18") CEMENT OR CINDER BLOCKS

18" MIN.   3" 8" 3"

CONCRETE FOOTING IS POURED IN WOODEN FORM, OR INTO EARTH TRENCH IF NEATLY CUT

CORD KEEPS BLOCKS IN STRAIGHT ROW

APPLY 1 1/2" MORTAR

BOTTOM COURSE IS MORTARED ON DAMP TOP OF FOOTING

4" TO 6"

14"OR 16"

FIG. 1 GUIDE LINES, CONCRETE FOOTING, AND LAYING UP CEMENT (OR CINDER) BLOCK FOUNDATION

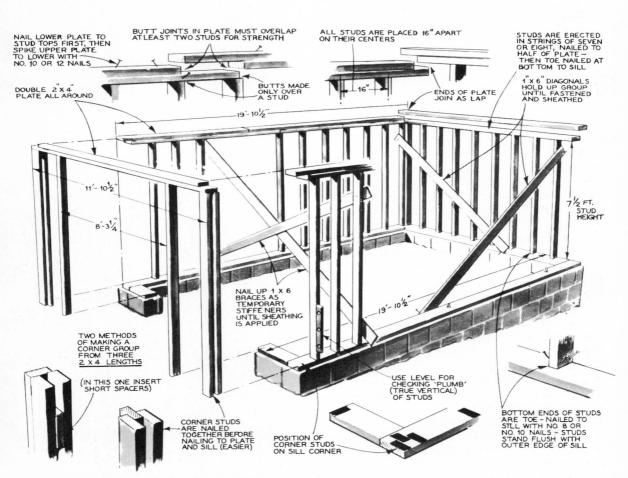

NAIL LOWER PLATE TO STUD TOPS FIRST, THEN SPIKE UPPER PLATE TO LOWER WITH NO. 10 OR 12 NAILS

BUTT JOINTS IN PLATE MUST OVERLAP AT LEAST TWO STUDS FOR STRENGTH

ALL STUDS ARE PLACED 16" APART ON THEIR CENTERS

STUDS ARE ERECTED IN STRINGS OF SEVEN OR EIGHT, NAILED TO HALF OF PLATE — THEN TOE NAILED AT BOTTOM TO SILL

DOUBLE 2"x 4" PLATE ALL AROUND

BUTTS MADE ONLY OVER A STUD

16"

ENDS OF PLATE JOIN AS LAP

1"x 6" DIAGONALS HOLD UP GROUP UNTIL FASTENED AND SHEATHED

19'-10½"

11'-10½"

8'-3¼"

7½ FT. STUD HEIGHT

TWO METHODS OF MAKING A CORNER GROUP FROM THREE 2 x 4 LENGTHS

NAIL UP 1 x 6 BRACES AS TEMPORARY STIFFENERS UNTIL SHEATHING IS APPLIED

19'-10½"

(IN THIS ONE INSERT SHORT SPACERS)

CORNER STUDS ARE NAILED TOGETHER BEFORE NAILING TO PLATE AND SILL (EASIER)

POSITION OF CORNER STUDS ON SILL CORNER

USE LEVEL FOR CHECKING 'PLUMB' (TRUE VERTICAL) OF STUDS

BOTTOM ENDS OF STUDS ARE TOE - NAILED TO SILL WITH NO. 8 OR NO. 10 NAILS - STUDS STAND FLUSH WITH OUTER EDGE OF SILL

FIG. 2 FRAMING WITH 2"x 4" STUDS AND PLATE

First course goes on mortar arranged on footing to cradle blocks. String serves as guide line.

Mortar is placed on block end and course. Excess is troweled away. Check blocks for level.

Completed foundation awaits wooden sill. Remove guide lines. Note considerable slope of land.

Securing 2x6 sill to bolt set in mortar. Spikes may be used instead, prevent garage "walking."

Gang cutting 2x4 studs to uniform 7½ ft. length. Power saw insures square joints, saves effort.

Studs erected in groups, held upright by diagonal temporary braces. Toenail studs to sill.

Doing it the easy way. Studs are assembled on ground, plate is nailed to tops, then doubled.

Bottom ends of studs are toenailed to sill with No. 8 or 10 nails, flush with sill outer edge.

Diagonal braces give extra frame rigidity, are a must if insulation boards used as sheathing.

Before sheathing, pull corners vertical with braces (see arrow). Check often with level.

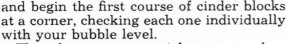

and begin the first course of cinder blocks at a corner, checking each one individually with your bubble level.

The other courses go right on top; when the last course has been laid, bolt or spike the sill planks to the foundation top. One word of caution—be sure you have allowed a ¾-in. ledge all the way around for the sheathing. Push the backfill dirt into the cavities all around the walls, wetting down to pack firm. You're all done with the first phase of your garage building project, ready to tackle the actual frame.

At this stage, when you think of filling all that thin air with a towering frame, your garage dimensions seem more like 120x200 ft. Fig. 2 will dispel that sinking feeling. Note that the entire frame is put up in sections, that is, studs are erected in strings of seven or eight, nailed to the lower plate. Your neighbors will be helping you long before this, out of sheer curiosity and admiration, so get one of them to help you push a string of studs, cut to

7½ ft., into vertical position, flush with the outer edge of the sill. Again, make liberal use of the level with each stud to insure that they're all standing "plumb"—then toenail each stud to the sill with No. 8 or No. 10 nails. You will have to use diagonals of, say, 1x6 lumber, nailed to the end studs to hold each group upright while you go on to each succeeding phase. Use other 1x6 diagonals as temporary braces until your sheating is applied. After all studs are up, add the upper 2x4 plates—making sure the butt joints for each length are made only over studs. Now, with all studs vertical and double plate fixed, add corner groups by nailing three 2x4 lengths together in clusters, and then nailing them to the plate and sill.

Framing is doubled all around each door and window opening, and it is wise to add short diagonal braces between each stud at corners. For the rollaway door, use 2x8 planks spiked together as a doorway header, and nailed to the jamb.

1x6 tongue and groove stock used for sheathing makes for a very strong box structure.

4x8 insulation panels may be used instead. But, only bevel, similar board siding may be nailed.

Nail 2x4 tie beam to joint of plate and rafter —ties walls against spread action of rafters.

Gable studs are short lengths of 2x4 beveled on top to fit slant of bottoms of all end rafters.

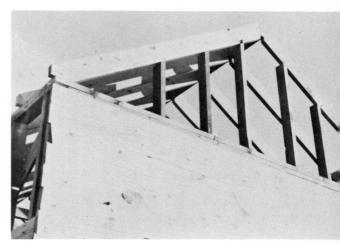

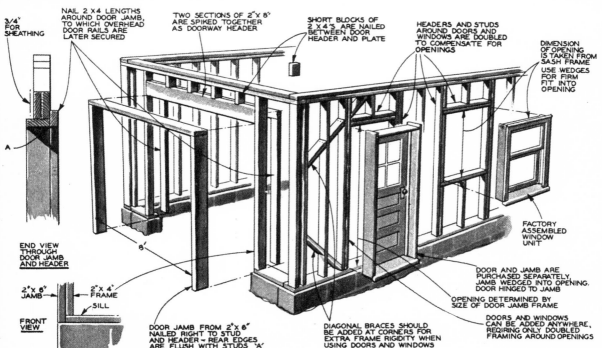

3/4" FOR SHEATHING

NAIL 2 x 4 LENGTHS AROUND DOOR JAMB, TO WHICH OVERHEAD DOOR RAILS ARE LATER SECURED

TWO SECTIONS OF 2"x 8" ARE SPIKED TOGETHER AS DOORWAY HEADER

SHORT BLOCKS OF 2 x 4'S ARE NAILED BETWEEN DOOR HEADER AND PLATE

HEADERS AND STUDS AROUND DOORS AND WINDOWS ARE DOUBLED TO COMPENSATE FOR OPENINGS

DIMENSION OF OPENING IS TAKEN FROM SASH FRAME

USE WEDGES FOR FIRM FIT INTO OPENING

A

END VIEW THROUGH DOOR JAMB AND HEADER

2"x 6" JAMB

2"x 4" FRAME

SILL

FRONT VIEW

DOOR JAMB FROM 2"x 6" NAILED RIGHT TO STUD AND HEADER — REAR EDGES ARE FLUSH WITH STUDS 'A'

DIAGONAL BRACES SHOULD BE ADDED AT CORNERS FOR EXTRA FRAME RIGIDITY WHEN USING DOORS AND WINDOWS

FACTORY ASSEMBLED WINDOW UNIT

DOOR AND JAMB ARE PURCHASED SEPARATELY, JAMB WEDGED INTO OPENING, DOOR HINGED TO JAMB

OPENING DETERMINED BY SIZE OF DOOR JAMB FRAME

DOORS AND WINDOWS CAN BE ADDED ANYWHERE, REQIRING ONLY DOUBLED FRAMING AROUND OPENINGS

FIG. 3 PLACING DOOR JAMBS AND WINDOWS

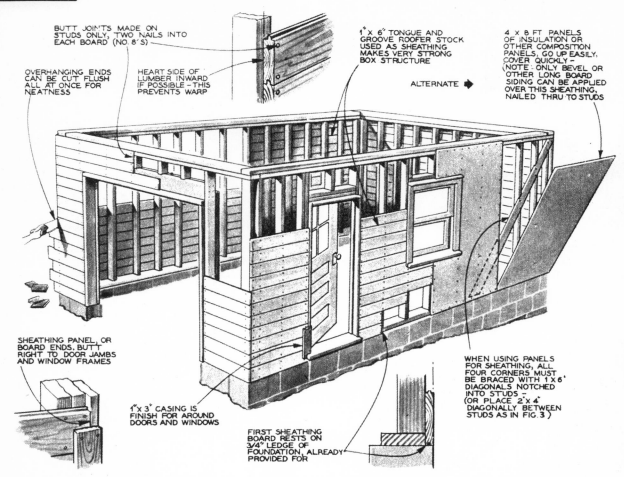

BUTT JOINTS MADE ON STUDS ONLY, TWO NAILS INTO EACH BOARD (NO. 8'S)

OVERHANGING ENDS CAN BE CUT FLUSH ALL AT ONCE FOR NEATNESS

HEART SIDE OF LUMBER INWARD IF POSSIBLE – THIS PREVENTS WARP

1" x 6" TONGUE AND GROOVE ROOFER STOCK USED AS SHEATHING MAKES VERY STRONG BOX STRUCTURE

ALTERNATE ➡

4 x 8 FT PANELS OF INSULATION OR OTHER COMPOSITION PANELS, GO UP EASILY, COVER QUICKLY – (NOTE : ONLY BEVEL OR OTHER LONG BOARD SIDING CAN BE APPLIED OVER THIS SHEATHING, NAILED THRU TO STUDS

SHEATHING PANEL, OR BOARD ENDS, BUTT RIGHT TO DOOR JAMBS AND WINDOW FRAMES

1" x 3" CASING IS FINISH FOR AROUND DOORS AND WINDOWS

FIRST SHEATHING BOARD RESTS ON 3/4" LEDGE OF FOUNDATION, ALREADY PROVIDED FOR

WHEN USING PANELS FOR SHEATHING, ALL FOUR CORNERS MUST BE BRACED WITH 1 x 6" DIAGONALS NOTCHED INTO STUDS – (OR PLACE 2" x 4" DIAGONALLY BETWEEN STUDS AS IN FIG. 3)

FIG 4   WOOD OR COMPOSITION SHEATHING OVER FRAMEWORK (BEFORE OR AFTER ROOF WORK)

**Pre-cut all roof rafters to shape before assembly.
Roof pitch is chosen first. Nail to ridge plate.**

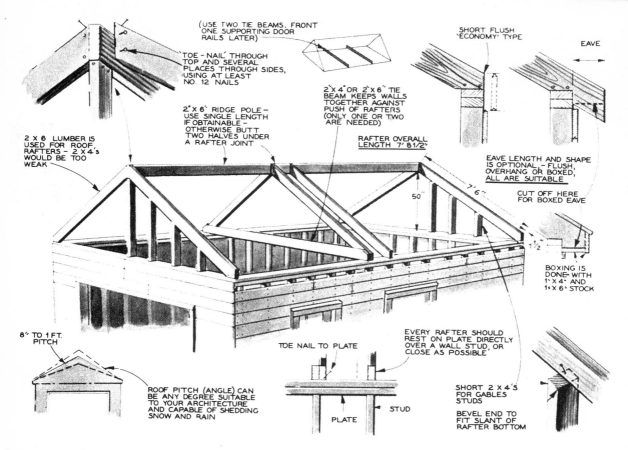

(USE TWO TIE BEAMS. FRONT ONE SUPPORTING DOOR RAILS LATER)

TOE - NAIL THROUGH TOP AND SEVERAL PLACES THROUGH SIDES, USING AT LEAST NO. 12 NAILS

2" X 6" RIDGE POLE - USE SINGLE LENGTH IF OBTAINABLE - OTHERWISE BUTT TWO HALVES UNDER A RAFTER JOINT

2" X 4" OR 2" X 6" TIE BEAM KEEPS WALLS TOGETHER AGAINST PUSH OF RAFTERS (ONLY ONE OR TWO ARE NEEDED)

2 X 6 LUMBER IS USED FOR ROOF, RAFTERS - 2 X 4's WOULD BE TOO WEAK

RAFTER OVERALL LENGTH 7' 8½"

SHORT FLUSH 'ECONOMY' TYPE

EAVE

EAVE LENGTH AND SHAPE IS OPTIONAL - FLUSH, OVERHANG OR BOXED, ALL ARE SUITABLE

50"

7' 6"

1½"

CUT OFF HERE FOR BOXED EAVE

BOXING IS DONE WITH 1" X 4" AND 1" X 6" STOCK

8" TO 1 FT. PITCH

ROOF PITCH (ANGLE) CAN BE ANY DEGREE SUITABLE TO YOUR ARCHITECTURE AND CAPABLE OF SHEDDING SNOW AND RAIN

TOE NAIL TO PLATE

PLATE

STUD

EVERY RAFTER SHOULD REST ON PLATE DIRECTLY OVER A WALL STUD, OR CLOSE AS POSSIBLE

SHORT 2 X 4's FOR GABLES STUDS

BEVEL END TO FIT SLANT OF RAFTER BOTTOM

FIG. 5 ERECTING RIDGE POLE, RAFTERS, AND GABLE STUDS

For sheathing, make up your mind whether you intend to use tongue and groove 1x6 stock or 4x8 panels of insulation board. If the latter, you can use only bevel or other long board siding over this sheathing. Also, all four corners must be braced with diagonals, as in Fig. 4. If you use 1x6 stock, make sure the heart side faces inward—to minimize warp.

Ready for the roof now? Decide the pitch you want, by laying out two lengths of 2x6 stock and penciling off measurements. Cut all the rafters and their bevels at the same time. The exact bevel will depend on how you like your eaves—flush, overhang or the more dressy boxed-type. See Fig. 5. Begin erection of the roof by stretching the 2x6 ridge pole between end rafters, and use a pair of rafters in the center for extra support. Now you need a few short studs of 2x4 stock, beveled and inserted at each end to support the rafters. Your roof is all ready for sheathing now, which is usually 1x6 or 1x8 tongue and groove stock. Put the first board on at the eave, allowing enough overhang for trim board.

Once the roof is sheathed, your garage is well on the way toward completion and the remaining details are far from imposing. When you can tear your eyes away from the "wonder" you have wrought but

not quite completed, get a couple of rolls of 15-lb. asphalt felt building paper over the entire structure. This is a sage precaution against rot, and well worth the very slight cost and few hours involved. One-inch galvanized nails are used every few feet to secure the paper.

For roofing, asphalt shingle is almost exclusively used. If you can afford the slight extra expense, use aluminum nails on shingles—for permanent protection against the possibility of streaks emanating from nail heads. The exact number of bundles of roof shingles for a 12x20-ft. roof will depend on the pitch, but should be five or six. The final courses along the top ridge are lapped over, and, for extra safety, capped over with short overlapped sections of cut up shingles. A few more details—like putting metal or asphalt felt strips over headers for rain sheds—and, presto, the garage is all finished except for the concrete floor and door installation. Check Fig. 6 for shingling and siding details.

Now for the final phase of construction. Tamp down the earth as firm as possible and, still better, provide a base of cinders about four inches deep. Call in Transit-Mix again, and have them pour in about 3½ yards of concrete. Level and trowel the fresh mix, pitching the surface slightly

1x6 tongue, groove stock used as roof sheathing. Start up from eave, saw off excess later.

Next, apply shingles. Tar roll should be used under asphalt shingles. Paper prevents rot in boards.

Shingle rows must be perfectly level to insure good-looking job. See sketch for nailing tips.

Bevel siding must be used over insulation board panels, nailed right through to studs beneath.

Transit-Mix pours in concrete for floor, apron. Skillful use of trowel (below), gives smooth floor, minimum of work later.

BILL OF MATERIALS

36 8" x 8" x 18" cement or cinder blocks (per row, rows depending on depth of foundation)

48 2" x 4" x 8' studs (cut to 7½')

128 lineal feet 2" x 4" for plate

52 lineal feet 2" x 4" (or 2" x 6") for sill

32 2" x 6" x 7'8" for rafters

20 lineal feet 2" x 6" for ridge pole

Assorted small 2" x 4"s for gable studs

2 2" x 8" x 9' for door header

420 sq. ft. 1" x 6" T. G. boards for sheathing (or about 12 ½" x 4' x 8' sheathing panels)

280 sq. ft. 1" x 6" T. G. board roofers

2 rolls 15-lb. asphalt felt paper

6 (approx.) bundles of roofing 3 in 1 tab shingles (12" x 36" single)

12½ (approx.) bundles of asbestos siding (12" x 24" size)

7' x 8' rollaway overhead roof

Several yards of Transit-Mix for foundation and floor (last)

½ yard sand (for mortar)

2 bags mortar cement (for mortar)

ROOF SHINGLES OVERHANG GABLE FACING ABOUT 1/2"

FIRST COURSE OF ROOF SHINGLE IS LAID WITH SLIT EDGES UP TO GIVE GOOD DRIP EDGE TO EAVES -- NEXT COURSE IS LAID DIRECTLY OVER THIS, WITH SLIT DOWN

ROOF RIDGE IS CAPPED OFF WITH SHORT OVERLAPPED SECTIONS OF CUT UP ROOF SHINGLE

FIRST ROOFER MUST OVERHANG ENOUGH TO COVER TRIM BOARD, ADDED LATER (ALSO ALLOW 1/4" FOR SHINGLE)

SUCCEEDING COURSES OVERLAP BY HALVES

1" x 6" TONGUE AND GROOVE ROOFER BOARDS WITH TWO NO. 8 NAILS INTO EACH RAFTER

15 LB. ASPHALT SATURATED FELT ROLL UNDER ROOF SHINGLE, PREVENTS ROT

BOX GABLE IF DESIRED

1" GALVANIZED NAILS OVER EACH SLIT, FOUR TO A SHINGLE

BUTT JOINTS ON RAFTERS ONLY

FACING BOARDS ARE 1"x 2" AND 1"x 4" PLAIN EDGE

1"x 6" PLAIN EDGE MOLD TRIM

MICA COATED ASPHALT STRIP USED BEHIND JOINT OF EACH SHINGLE BUTT

METAL OR ASPHALT FELT STRIP GOES OVER HEADER FOR RAIN SHED

SPECIAL METAL CORNER STRIP IS NAILED ON, AND SHINGLE ENDS BEGUN OR ENDED IN RECESSES

15 LB. ASPHALT FELT UNDER SIDING SHINGLES PREVENTS ROT

SHINGLE ROWS SHOULD RUN LEVEL RIGHT PAST DOORS AND WINDOWS FOR GOOD LOOKS AS WELL AS PRACTICAL NAILING

ASBESTOS OR OTHER DURABLE SHINGLES OF VARIOUS DESIGNS FOR FINISH SIDING (NOTE : CANNOT BE USED OVER 4 x 8 INSULATION BOARD)

COATED NAILS ARE FLUSH WITH OVERLAP, HOLES PRE-DRILLED IN SHINGLE

FIG. 6 ROOFER BOARDS, ASPHALT SHINGLES, AND ASBESTOS SIDING

toward the front entrance. When hard, this will shed water and slush away from your car. Or, if you are more ambitious and mighty sure of yourself with a garage under your belt, try sloping all four sides to a center drain leading to a pipe underneath your floor.

Once the floor and approach apron are set, you might do well to have the dealer install your overhead door. The installation charge the dealer makes may not be worth a full day's work by a helper and yourself. Moreover, the door will be subjected to many years of use (and, perhaps, abuse)— and it might be well to have a dealer's guarantee for at least the first year.

One last word of caution—before you even start working on your bill of materials, check the local building codes for your area. For instance, in some cities, a garage of this type must not be built right on your neighbor's property line, but three feet away from it. However, an all-concrete block garage might be built right up to the line.

Again, some local regulations stipulate that concrete or cinder blocks may be used over—but not as part of—the foundation. Some cities insist on the foundation being 3 or 4 feet of solid concrete for a garage floor. A telephone call before you start may save you lots of trouble. •

Installation of overhead door. Save time by having dealer install door for little extra cost.

It's Easy to Grow Fine Flowers

You don't have to be a budding genius. Timely observance of a few basic principles will tinge any thumb with green—even yours.

THE purpose of this chapter is to help grow flowers well. Neither the fact that you have had previous failures nor the fact that you are an absolute beginner need interfere with that. Growing good flowers is easy—once you understand a few simple, underlying principles.

To succeed, you must know what to do and you must do what needs doing at the right time. Procrastination and gardening do not mix well. Poor results can often be traced to delay. I cannot emphasize too much the importance of timeliness.

The Soil

As a flower grower you will deal with soil. You must learn to understand it. Not that you require a deep scientific knowledge of chemistry, physics and the like, but merely a simple basic appreciation of what soil is and how you can improve it and maintain its fertility.

Soil consists of mineral particles of varying degrees of fineness, dead organic matter (humus) and a living population, fantastically numerous, of bacteria and other micro-organisms, as well as earthworms and some other larger living things. It also contains air and moisture.

The sizes of the mineral particles give character to soil. When all are extremely small it is clay. Particles of silt are somewhat larger. Sand particles are bigger still, and gravel consists of the largest rock fragments commonly classed with soil. Above that are pebbles or stones.

Garden soils are neither pure clay nor pure sand. They are intermediates that contain some or all of the various sized fragments. Such intermediates are called loams. A clay-loam (or heavy loam) contains an unduly large proportion of clay, a sandy loam an excess of sand. All manner of inbetweens occur.

Soils may be acid, neutral or alkaline. The degree of acidity is measured on a pH scale with pH 7 neutral. Higher readings indicate alkalinity, lower, acidity. The vast majority of garden plants thrive in a neutral, slightly acid or slightly alkaline soil —those that range say from pH 6 to pH 8. Some few, such as heathers, must have acid conditions. Still fewer, such as carnations, decidedly prefer alkaline soils. Alkalinity is increased by using lime or crushed oyster shells, acidity by adding peat moss, oak leaf mold, cotton seed meal, sulphur, or aluminum sulphate.

Because clay soils consist largely of fine particles that lie closely together, neither air nor water normally pass freely through them. The gardener's effort is to keep them permeable. He does this by loosening them mechanically with spade, fork or other implements, by adding coarser particles such as sand, grit, and fine cinders (but not dust-like ashes), by adding coarse humus such as strawy manure, partly decayed compost, leafmold, peat moss and the like, by turning under green cover crops, and by periodic liming (except for plants known to need acid soils). Lime encourages the clay particles to cling together and form a crumb-like structure that permits air and water to pass. He further avoids as much as possible treading upon or working with clay soils when they are wet. To do so makes them pasty and impermeable.

Sandy soils that consist mostly of large coarse particles admit so much air that the organic matter soon decays and disappears. Water travels so rapidly through them that it is difficult to keep them moist enough for the plants' well being and nutrients leach away astonishingly quickly. The gardener seeks to prevent or compensate for these faults.

Sandy soils are improved by adding clay, by incorporating with them large amounts of well rotted cow manure, compost, leafmold, or other organic materials that are well decayed, and by turning under cover crops or green manures. Loosening them

Good soil saves toil. Here the surface is turned with a spade and mixed with manure or compost. In this way underside is exposed to organic matter.

Learn to understand and appreciate soil and find out how you can improve its fertility. After the soil is turned, use spading fork to loosen it up.

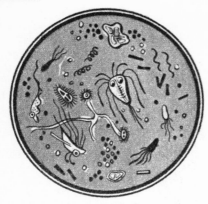

What is the living soil? Under a microscope, a bit of soil would look like this—teeming with myriads of highly beneficial organisms in each particle.

Most soils consist principally of rock and clayey particles. The rocks, as delineated above, take up more room, proportionately, than does clay or sand.

too frequently can be rather harmful.

A good depth of soil is essential for the best results. In flower beds and borders and even in the rock garden, make every effort to provide at least a foot of good soil. More is desirable. Always prepare the soil especially well where perennials are to go. Once they are planted you cannot do much to improve the soil until they are taken up again, which probably will not be for three or four years at the soonest, and likely longer.

Plants other than bog plants will not grow in poorly drained soils. Their roots do not get the air they need. In wet areas plant only wet-land plants or drain the soil before planting. A sloping surface does not necessarily guarantee good underdrainage. Sub-surface layers of clay may hold water and prevent the admission of air. If you suspect poor drainage, investigate. Few plants like wet feet.

You can improve soil tremendously by taking the appropriate steps indicated above to insure its good physical condition and to maintain its humus supply (the humus content of the soil is constantly being depleted). Because humus provides food for needed micro-organisms as well as improves the soil texture it must be replaced. But the improvement established by these means may not be sufficient. Not only must the physical condition of the soil be maintained, nutrients must be added. That is why we use fertilizers.

Nutrients commonly lacking in adequate quantities in garden soils are nitrogen, phosphorus and potassium. These are the important elements that fertilizers supply. A complete fertilizer contains all three. Incomplete fertilizers supply one or two only. Fertilizers used within reason do not harm the soil, do not reduce the earthworm population, do not predispose plants to diseases and pests.

They are great aids to good gardening. They do not take the place of bulk organic matter but they do supplement it to good purpose.

Fertilizers are of two types, organic, (derived from plant or animal remains) and inorganic, derived from minerals or synthesised from the air. The organics, such as bone meal, cottonseed meal, tankage and fish meal, usually act more slowly and so are effective over a longer period than are the inorganics, such as nitrate of soda, sulphate of ammonia and sulphate of potash. The nutrient elements they contain are identical. Use the former for the "long pull" as when preparing soil before planting, the latter for giving a quick "lift" during the growing season, when a rapid response is desired.

The Plants

Only in very large gardens is there room for second-rate plants. If your garden is small or of medium size, grow only the best. The space occupied by inferior kinds and the care they require are usually not less than for better ones. True, their initial

A rotary tiller will churn up the soil to depth of 8 or 10 inches and mix it with compost, manure and other fertilizer in the very same operation.

Fertile soils contain ten per cent or more humus or organic matter. Earthworms are active in conveying organic matter from the surface to below.

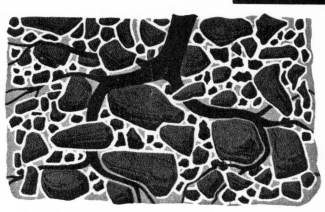

Ordinary soils for gardening contain air as well as water. In above enlargement, spaces between particles are air. Too much water produces a bog.

cost may not be as great, but the additional expenditure is soon forgotten. If it is a critical matter you may be able to have desired plants and still keep within your budget by starting with *smaller* specimens than you would normally get, or by starting with fewer of each kind and propagating them by division or other appropriate means. It will take a little more time before you attain your objective, but as a gardener you must acquire the patience of those who deal with nature and the soil—besides it's fun to sit back and watch things grow.

Beware of unknown plants given you by well meaning friends who assure you that "this what-do-you-call-it is *wonderful* for the rock garden. It's so pretty and it grows so easily and without care." (It's probably the variegated goutweed that in two or three years will take over vast areas of your rock garden and against which you will wage a long stiff battle before you finally eradicate it—if you ever do.) And don't accept at face value all that catalogs say. (Often it is what they *don't* say that is most significant.) Whenever possible, become familiar with plants by studying

them in other gardens before introducing them to your own. Visit public, private, and commercial gardens whenever you can. See the plants "on the hoof," as it were.

Remember, too, that whether a plant is "good" depends not only upon the plant but upon the conditions under which you want it to serve. That same variegated goutweed that is such a pest in the rock garden may be perfectly satisfactory confined to a bank between a stream and a bordering path. The variety of rose that thrives beautifully in your friend's clayey-soil garden may not give best results on your sandy soil. The finest chrysanthemums for garden decoration are not necessarily most suitable as cut flowers, or for exhibiting at flower shows. And so on.

Consider your situation. Decide for what purpose you want particular flowers. Seek the very best kinds to suit your purposes.

The cheapest seeds and plants are rarely the best, but neither are the most expensive necessarily better. Standard and well-proved varieties are usually less costly than the newer kinds and are often as good, or better.

Lime is particularly beneficial on clay soils and on acid soils. Never use it, however, where acid-loving plants like azaleas are expected to grow.

If you don't have a compost pile, black humus or peat moss may be purchased by the bushel from a dealer. Both are good sources of organic matter.

Only a thoughtless gardener burns leaves in fall, as above. The provident flower-grower saves them for the compost pile, except for diseased leaves.

Keep the surface soil between growing plants in a state of loose cultivation or covered with a mulch. A prong-cultivator is good for this.

Pests and Diseases

You will hear and read a great deal about pests and diseases. The number of bugs and sicknesses that *may* afflict your garden is tremendous. But not all of them *will*. In fact, a very small proportion will. Some that do will work havoc unless checked. Fortunately, the majority are easily controlled if timely action is taken.

Destructive insects are sometimes called "Nature's Censors," since they generally attack the weaker plants first.

Train yourself to observe. Walk through your garden frequently. Look closely at your plants. Be inquisitive. Lift up leaves and examine their undersides. Notice changes of color and other variations that may indicate trouble. If your plants are not thriving, find out *why*. Correct diagnosis is essential to effective control. It is obviously useless to spray with a fungicide if an insect is the cause of the trouble or to use an insecticide if the plants are merely

suffering from drought. If you are unable to make a satisfactory diagnosis obtain expert advice. This you may get from a more experienced local gardener, from your County Agent, from your State Agricultural Experiment Station, from a garden center or from a botanical garden. Many agencies are ready to serve you.

Both preventions and cures are used in combating pests and diseases. Most often, *prevention* is all-important with diseases. Most often, remedies applied at the very first sign of attack are successful against insects. These are generalizations. Use the best available control for whatever affects your plants. Follow instructions carefully and make a good job of applying sprays and dusts.

General Care

Give timely attention to routine matters. Keep the surface soil free of weeds and shallowly stirred with the hoe or cultivator,

DRAINING

 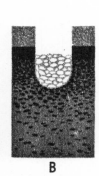 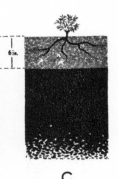 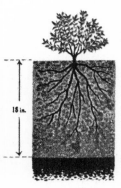

A   B   C   D

Dark areas in drawings at left show soil underlayer. Don't plant where this is waterlogged and impervious as in A. Dig hole deeper, fill with stones to reach porous underlayer as in B. Poor roots (C) is result of only 6 inches between level of water table and the ground. Soil should drain to 18 inches, as in D. At right is a piping plan to drain a 100 x 75 ft. plot.

Water freely during periods of drought. A board beneath the end of the hose is used to spread the water and keep soil from being washed away.

Both preventions and cures are used in combatting pests, blights and diseases. Police your plants frequently, looking for weeds and trouble-spots.

or keep it mulched (covered with a two or three inch layer of peat moss, leaf-mold, compost or other suitable material) throughout the growing season.

Stake and tie or in other suitable ways support plants that are in danger of falling over or of being harmed by winds or storms. Do this well before they suffer damage. Pick off all faded blooms unless it is your intention to save seeds.

During dry periods attend to watering. When you water, saturate the soil thoroughly. Give enough to sink in to a depth of six or eight inches. Then give no more for several days—until the soil is dry again. Avoid daily sprinklings that merely wet the top inch or so of soil. Cultivate shallowly a few hours after each watering.

Watering in sunshine does no harm. It is, however, a little more economical of water to apply it early in the morning or in late afternoon and evening. But if your plants are in need of it, give water at any time. ●

Keep the edges of paths and flower beds neatly trimmed. This edging tool, a semi-circular blade, is used for cutting the edges of grassy plots.

If grass is allowed to grow unchecked it will spill over onto paths and beds. Below, special edging shears are used to keep borders trimmed.

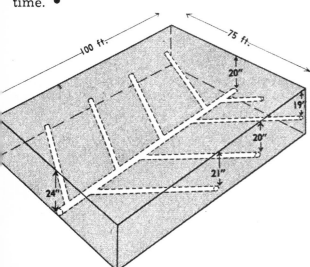

Flower Beds for Spring

**Keep your date with Spring
—and make the most of it.**

ONE of the simplest and most satisfactory kinds of gardening is that known as spring bedding. It consists of planting beds, for temporary effect only, with flowers that bloom gaily in spring. After the spring display has passed, the beds are ordinarily re-planted to provide summer color.

Spring bedding may be practiced in one or more small flower beds set in the lawn, in borders along the driveway or about the house, or in more elaborate formal gardens. It gives great opportunity to exercise one's taste and skill in plant arrangement and decorates the garden at a most lovely season of the year.

.The plants used in spring bedding consist of bulbs such as tulips, hyacinths and narcissi, biennials such as English daisies, forget-me-nots, and pansies and such perennials as evergreen candytuft, basket-of-gold, and dwarf polemonium.

If you have a reserve or nursery plot where you can grow your own biennials and perennials you are fortunate, otherwise you must secure these from a commercial nursery. After blooming, discard the biennials and divide and plant the perennials in the reserve garden, there to grow into usable plants for the following year.

If the bulbs are set deeply and if the summer plants you use are shallow-rooted kinds, such as portulaca, sweet alyssum and annual poppies, the bulbs may be left in the ground and the summer bedding plants planted over them. But even though this *can* be done, I strongly recommend, wherever summer bedding is to follow, to lift the bulbs and store them through the summer.

You may find it necessary to dig the bulbs *before* their foliage has turned completely brown. If you do this, do not store them right away. Instead, plant them temporarily closely together in a vacant piece of ground where they are shaded from strong sunshine. Only after their foliage has completely died should they be lifted, cleaned, sorted and stored. Store in a cellar or other cool, dry shaded place. Shallow wooden trays, preferably with bottoms of wire netting, are the best storage receptacles. Spread the bulbs in single layers.

Plant bulbs for spring bedding in fall. Usually, perennials and biennials are not set in the beds until spring, although in mild sections and in the case of particularly hardy kinds, these can be fall-planted too.

Set such plants, out *early*. Fully developed pansies, polyanthus, aubretia and the like, planted after spring is well advanced and the sun is warm and the winds drying, do not thrive nearly as well as those set when their spring growth is just beginning and before the majority of their flower buds have opened.

Take care that plants wintered in coldframes are properly hardened and have been without the protection of glass sash for a week or so before they are moved. If you buy your plants, see that they have large balls of roots. If you transplant your

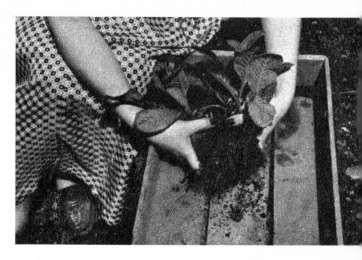

After the spring blooming season is over, lift polyanthus primroses (above) from beds. Divide.

See that these divisions, as with other plants you lift, have good root-masses, strong leaves.

Plant divisions in a nursery bed or a cold frame and grow them for use in next year's spring beds.

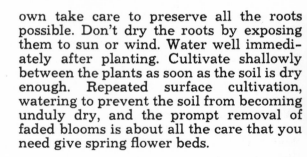

In late May, carefully lift plants from their bed as soon as they have bloomed. Place in flat box.

own take care to preserve all the roots possible. Don't dry the roots by exposing them to sun or wind. Water well immediately after planting. Cultivate shallowly between the plants as soon as the soil is dry enough. Repeated surface cultivation, watering to prevent the soil from becoming unduly dry, and the prompt removal of faded blooms is about all the care that you need give spring flower beds.

The Plants To Use

Bulbs: narcissi (including daffodils) tulips, hyacinths, grape hyacinths, Spanish, Dutch, and English irises.

Biennials: pansies, violas, Siberian wallflowers, English wallflowers, English daisies, forget-me-nots, sweet Williams.

Perennials: rock-cress, basket-of-gold, leopards-bane, evergreen candytuft, aubretia, Virginia bluebell, moss-pink, dwarf polemonium, polyanthus, English primrose, Phlox divaricata, forget-me-not anchusa, thrift.

Many of the above, tulips, hyacinths, pansies, and sweet Williams, for instance, may be had in a variety of colors. By using different plants and different colors of the same plant in the one bed or a series of beds, a nearly endless variety of lovely combinations may be had. Consider the charm of either soft pink or lavender flowered Darwin tulips planted among blue Phlox divaricata, or of yellow tulips above a carpet of blue forget-me-nots. Cream or pale yellow polyanthuses interplanted with deep red tulips are stunning, so too is the nearly black La Tulipe Noire above a sea of white rock-cress. A daring

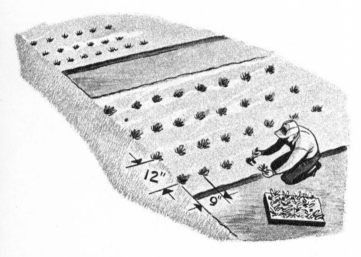

After dividing perennials, re-plant them in reserve garden for next year, observing above dimensions.

Come June and July, sow biennial seeds in a high-backed cold frame. Raise up sash for ventilation.

Seeds may also be sown in a well-sheltered plot. The shallow drills should be about 6 inches apart.

SPRING BEDS

but effective combination is a rose pink tulip such as Clara Butt underplanted with the thrift, Armeria laucheana. Daffodils and other narcissi may be effectively used either with pansies, violas, or forget-me-nots. Spanish, Dutch, or English irises associate well with English daisies. Sweet Williams, wallflowers, and hyacinths are each magnificent when planted alone. A bed of the deep yellow and the lemon yellow varieties of basket-of-gold intermixed is stunning. In beds of fairly large size a spectacular effect is obtained by planting a mixture of many kinds of spring bedding plants together, thus producing a true floral medley.

Work out your own combinations of spring bedding plants in colors that especially appeal to you. Do this in spring when the plants themselves are in bloom. At this time, too, make a plan on paper of what you intend to use the following year.

Observe carefully the space needed by each plant as it grows in the garden and in your planning allow for this when you estimate the number of each kind that you will need for next year's beds. Don't entirely depend upon the plantings in your own garden. Seek inspiration in the gardens of friends, as well as in public parks and botanic gardens.

These spring pilgrimages to other gardens will enable you to evaluate your own gardening achievements. In some places you will find some plants in much finer condition than those in your own garden, but almost always you will experience the satisfaction of discovering that some of your own plants are better than those you find elsewhere. •

October and November is bulb-planting time. Put a variety of corms in the ground, 15 inches apart.

After the ground freezes, cover the plot with a three-inch layer of straw, hay or equivalent mulch.

As soon as the seedlings have two pairs of good leaves (July-August) transfer to nursery bedding.

In March and April, carefully remove mulch from new shoots. Biennials may be set in their beds.

Flower Beds for Summer

Simplicity in arrangement and conformity to the lines of your general landscape are good bets for good beds.

SUMMER bedding, the massing in special beds of gaily colored flowering or foliage plants to produce temporary displays, can be a highly artistic achievement or an absolute horticultural horror. Too often it falls somewhere between. The mounded circular bed with cannas in the center and salvias around the rim has been ridiculed to practical oblivion, but modern counterparts of equally questionable taste are not uncommon. So much bad bedding has been done that the practice as a whole has been questioned and, by some, condemned.

This view is extreme. Properly carried out, summer bedding adds interest and pleasing color to the garden. It is particularly appropriate in home grounds where limited space prevents one from arranging for satisfactory summer color by having one area gay at one time and another at

When transplanting summer bedding plants from a flat, be sure that each has a good-sized ball of earth attached to its roots. These are asters.

another. If you want color all summer from the same area, fill it with summer bedding plants. You cannot do better. But give thought to the kinds you use, to their arrangement and to color combinations.

The placement of beds is important. In a designed formal garden, surrounded perhaps by a hedge, fence, or wall, they will follow a set pattern. Let this be simple.

If the beds are on a lawn, place them at its fringes rather than toward its center. Beds bordering paths are usually well located. Avoid over-elaboration. Intricate patterns or extremely fanciful shapes are out. Stars, suns, crescents, and comets belong in the firmament rather than on the grass plot. In shape and size, flower beds should conform to the scale and lines of the general landscape.

The topsoil in flower beds need not be over-rich, but it should be mellow and of good texture and should be a foot or eighteen inches deep. A soil that would produce fair vegetables is ideal.

There is a great variety of plants that can be used in summer beds. For practical purposes we confine ourselves to those that bloom or provide colorful foliage over a long period—from early summer, shortly after they are set out, until frost. These are of two kinds, tender perennials such as geraniums, lantanas and fuchsias—which are not ordinarily raised from seeds but which are carried over indoors from year to year—and plants such as Mexican tulip poppies, petunias, and marigolds which are normally raised from seeds each year. The line between these groups is not always clear. Some plants such as salvias and begonias (and petunias too, for that matter)

can be handled well in either fashion.

When spring bedding occupies beds that are later devoted to summer bedding, it is generally necessary to have the summer plants sizable and well advanced at setting-out time. This is always necessary with such tender kinds as geraniums, heliotropes and coleus. Such plants can be raised at home in greenhouse, sunroom or window garden or, in the case of more hardy kinds such as asters, snapdragons and stocks, in hotbeds or cold frames. Or they can be purchased ready to plant from your local nursery.

See that they are hardened and are accustomed to outdoor conditions before you plant them. Avoid setting out tender kinds before the soil has warmed and the weather has settled. Water them well immediately after planting. Keep the surface soil stirred. Throughout the summer give needed attention to watering, cultivating, pest control, picking dead flowers, etc.

The Plants To Use

Among the best summer bedding plants are geraniums, lantanas, fuchsias, heliotropes, wax begonias, tuberous begonias, ageratums, annual vincas, petunias, verbenas, snapdragons, stocks, impatiens, torenias, balsams, calendulas, globe amaranthus, dwarf marigolds, tagetes, sanvitalia, browallias, ice plant, sweet alyssum, zinnias and the sometimes despised red salvia. Coleus, perilla, amaranthus, alternantheras, and dusty millers are good foliage subjects. Of the above, only fuchsias, begonias, impatiens and torenias withstand shade tolerably.

To insure such a root-ball, slice through soil between plants with a sharp knife. Do this about a week before the plants are ready for removal.

Annuals that are separated from flats in such a way have a good block of soil attached to roots. They are now ready for planting in summer beds.

To have colorful summer beds dig tender plants, such as this geranium, in September and October, before frost. Cut back and plant in pots indoors.

The pot should be filled with sandy soil. Use potting stick about the size and thickness of foot rule. Note cut ends where flower is pruned

In January, February and March, sow indoors seeds of tender annual bedding plants such as petunias, snapdragons, verbenas and stocks. Label clearly.

Around this time, too, the cuttings planted in the previous fall will be ready for transplanting to larger pots. Use the same type of sandy soil

In March and April, start tubers of begonias and cannas to produce plants for setting out later. Use pots 4 inches in diameter at top, humusy soil.

March and April is also a good time to transplant the seedlings sown earlier. With ordinary pencil, mark holes in flat, set in without damage to roots.

When May and June arrive, toughen plants raised indoors by putting them in cold frames for a week or ten days before planting in beds. Plant as soon as weather is warm.

Summer beds can be effective when planted with one kind of plant to provide solid color or when two or more varieties of the same kind (such as white and red geranium) are planted together. It is also possible to combine two or three different kinds of plants in the same bed, such as geraniums and heliotropes, or geraniums, verbenas and sweet alyssum. Rare skill is needed to use more than three kinds together. A solid center of one plant bordered by another is sometimes effective, but in general do not set your plants in concentric bands. Instead, intermix them. A few taller plants scattered as "dots" among lower ones relieve uninteresting flatness. These taller plants may be kinds that naturally grow bigger than their associates, as geraniums among dwarf ageratum. They may be just bigger plants of the same kind as two or three year old plants of fuchsias among first year fuchsias, or they may be older plants of geraniums, heliotropes, lantanas or fuchsias specially trained as standards (small trees).

Among many interesting combinations of summer bedding plants are salmon pink geraniums among clear lavender verbenas, soft yellow lantanas interplanted with rich purple heliotropes, creamy white lantanas and pink verbenas or pink petunias, and scarlet geraniums, or scarlet salvia together with grey-foliaged dusty miller. Blue ageratum and soft pink petunias go well together. So too do yellow snapdragons and lavender stocks. The rather harsh pink of annual vinca associates well with white sweet alyssum and with white petunias. The red leaved varieties of the wax begonia are effective with white sweet alyssum. Lavender flowered sweet alyssum associates pleasingly with torenia and with ageratum.

Summer bedding affords great scope for the artistic and color conscious to express themselves—in a word, to say it with flowers. •

After the petunias have been planted in the bed they will look like the photo at right. They will provide a gay show of bloom through summer.

With the bed prepared and the weather just right, transfer plants from cold frames or flats. Above, petunias are being set out in regular rows.

If the ground is too wet to walk on the bed, keep its texture by placing a plank on bricks or blocks as shown above, and set in young plants from it.

Water in Your Garden

Whether a pool or stream is natural or on purpose, you needn't water flowers when you flower water.

Tropical water-lilies received from dealer are carefully unpacked. Don't let foliage dry, but cover plants with wet burlap before setting out.

WATER adds great charm to a garden. Arrange, if you can, to have a pool or stream in yours. If you are *very* fortunate a natural pond or brook may already be there. More probably you will have to build one. This is not difficult.

Water features are of two main kinds—those that are strictly formal and obviously constructed and those that are natural or at least appear so. Intermediates occur. These are, or seem to be, native ponds or streams purposely more or less formalized.

The geometrical pool—circular, elliptical, square or oblong—fits best in strict surroundings—in the formal garden, on the terrace or near the house.

The informal pool belongs where the landscape is freer. It may be part of the rock garden, be set toward the boundaries of a lawn or at the front of a casually arranged shrub or evergreen planting.

Streams, whether native or artificial, should appear to be natural, their surroundings informal or semi-formal.

Natural water occurs in low places. Seek these as locations for irregular pools and naturalistic streams. Or arrange for them in your grading operations. Formal water features can be frankly at artificial levels.

Quiet water provides reflection-pools that mirror garden and sky. It gives opportunity to grow a great variety of aquatics including water-lilies, water-hyacinths and other floating-leafed plants. Moving water —streams, cascades and waterfalls—is not adapted for the cultivation of such plants but along its margins a wealth of flowers that like their roots in wet earth can be made happy. Some, such as the water-forget-me-not, will reach out into the water. Moving water adds "life" to the garden and attracts birds.

A made pool may be anything from half a tub sunk in the ground to a miniature lake formed by damming a stream. Even in the former you can accommodate a pygmy water-lily, a water-hyacinth, a water-poppy and one or two other aquatics.

Whatever the size of your pool, arrange for convenient means of filling and emptying. You may use a hose for filling and, in some locations, you can remove the water by siphoning. In all but the smallest pools, however, it is better to install a drain and overflow. An inlet pipe fitted with a valve is a great convenience.

Do not permit any considerable inflow of water from fountains or other sources. A slow inflow is not harmful.

Streams, cascades and waterfalls may be supplied from natural sources, by piped water, or by re-circulating pumps.

Most formal pools are built of concrete. A good mixture to use is one part cement, two parts sand, and three parts one inch or three quarter inch gravel or crushed stone. Pour or place the concrete for the floor and walls in one operation. This avoids joints and so prevents leaks. If water-lilies are to be grown, the pool should be deep enough to allow the soil in which they are planted to be covered with eight to twelve inches of water. If the plants are in tubs this means that the pool should be two to two-and-a-half feet deep.

Make the excavation one foot deeper and one foot wider all around than the pool. Tamp six inches of cinders on the bottom.

In loose or crumbly soils both inner and outer forms are needed to shape the concrete walls. In solid soils the earth itself, clean-cut with a spade, may support the outsides of the walls; wooden forms are then needed for the insides only. Make sure that drainage pipes, water pipes and all reinforcings are in position before the concrete is mixed.

Remove the forms after forty-eight hours. Polish the inside of the pool with a carborundum brick dipped in water. Wet the exposed concrete two or three times a day for ten days after the forms are removed.

Section through a typical garden pool of reinforced concrete. Note shelves for shallow plants. One square equals half foot.

The flowers of hardy water-lilies float on the surface of the water.

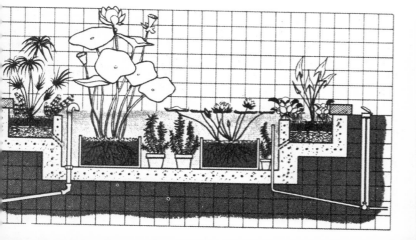

Fill a tub approximately 18 inches tall with rich soil and top with an inch of sand or gravel. Put tub in water-filled pool, then gently scoop a hole in the soil and set tropical water-lily in place.

Newly planted in the wooden tub, the tuber is a the surface of the soil, just covered with sand Leaves may not reach surface at planting but in few days their stems lengthen and leaves emerge

Fill the pool once or twice with water, allow it to stand for a few hours each time and then empty before setting your plants. This is to remove alkali from the cement.

Informal pools are also usually built of concrete. If their sides do not rise more steeply than one foot in each two feet of run you can construct them without forms. See that the concrete is reinforced.

If you are constructing an informal pool surrounded by naturalistic rockwork, take care that after the job is finished no concrete shows above the level of the water. If it does, the illusion that all is Nature's handiwork is destroyed. For the same reason concrete that is part of the construction of a cascade or stream should not be seen.

When installing the concrete bring it well up *behind* rocks that fringe the pool or stream. Take care that the arrangement of the rocks is convincingly natural.

The outlines of pools not rock rimmed should consist of sweeping, graceful curves. Short, uneasy wiggles of the shore line are not natural.

Plants To Use

It is not necessary and rarely is desirable to have trees or shrubbery near formal pools, but those designed to imitate nature look strangely naked without. Use planting of this kind somewhat sparingly, however, for above all water plants must have plenty of sunlight.

Aquatic plants suitable for growing in the water itself include water-lilies, both hardy kinds and tender tropicals (day bloomers and night bloomers), lotuses, water-lettuce, water-fern, water-snow-flake, water-hyacinth, floating-heart, papyrus, parrot-feather, pickerel-rush, primrose-creeper, primrose-willow, umbrella-palm, velvet-leaf, water-clover,

water-poppy, bogbean, sweet flag flowering-rush, and water-canna.

Wet-soil plants appropriate for planting in boggy areas at pool side or stream side include cardinal flower, Lobelia syphilitica marsh marigold, Japanese primrose, yellow flag iris, Japanese iris, taro, water forget-me-not, arrowheads, astilbes, wild calla and swamp-pink.

Caring For The Pool

A pool needs care. Not as much as an equivalent land area, but some. See that the plants do not crowd each other unduly Areas of clear water give best effects.

Congestion is easiest avoided by exercis ing restraint at planting time. If crowding occurs it can be relieved by taking off the outer leaves of water-lilies (even though still green) and by pulling out some of the excessive growth of such rapid spreaders as parrot-feather and primrose-creeper.

Remove faded leaves and bloom promptly. Destroy at once any infested with the leaf miner insect. Don't use insecticide on water plants.

Discoloration of pools by algae can usu ally be prevented by having in them suffi cient animal life of kinds that act a scavengers. Chief among these are fres water mussels or clams, tadpoles and vari ous water snails.

If, despite these, your water become cloudy with algae, mix thoroughly with one teaspoonful of a saturated solution permanganate of potash for each gallon water in the pool. To make the saturate solution, stir three teaspoonfuls of crysta of potassium permanganate into a gallon water. Pour off and use the liquid part onl

If not growing vigorously, fertilize water lilies and other aquatics in tubs by usin a 5-10-5 or similar fertilizer. Mix it to st

WOODEN TUB

After plant is set, soil is leveled and more sand is added. Tubs like this, or like the one at the right which accommodates several types of floating plants, can be very charming in a floral setting.

paste with water. Take pieces of the paste as big as a small walnut, wrap them in tissue paper and insert them into the soil at a depth of two or three inches. Space them a foot or so apart. Half-rotted cow manure squeezed into balls the size of an egg may be substituted.

In fall, before killing frost, take indoors aquatics that are tender. Hardy kinds may be left outdoors provided those that have tender roots, such as water-lilies, are deep enough under water to keep them from freezing or, if the pool is drained, are well protected by being covered with a thick layer of leaves or straw. As an alternative, the tubs in which they grow may be taken indoors over winter and safely stored.

The general attention needed by bog plants growing in wet soil areas does not differ materially from that of other perennials except that they need no watering or cultivating. In fall, take indoors any that are not winter-hardy. In spring, fertilize and lift and divide any that need this. •

Three excellent water plants are tropical water-lilies (above). Yellow floating heart (top, right) and arrow heads (shown right).

IF you possibly can, set aside a portion of your lot as a cut-flower and reserve (or nursery) garden. Grow in it young perennials, biennials and annuals for transfer to other parts of your garden as well as flowers for cutting. It is a practical and economical way of stocking your garden and of providing flowers for your home.

The area need not be large. A great many young delphiniums, foxgloves, and marigolds (for example) can be grown in one or two hundred square feet, and a hundred square feet measures only ten by ten.

To grow sufficient cut flowers will probably take somewhat more space—depending upon the lavishness with which you use them and the kinds you cultivate—but you can get a lot of cutting out of three, four, or five hundred square feet and a worth-while amount from less.

If you have a vegetable plot, your cut flower and reserve garden might well be part of it. Otherwise, set aside a separate area.

One great advantage of a cut flower garden is that you need not detract from decorative beds and borders by cutting from them. Another is that you can grow the flowers in straight rows and so cultural operations such as planting, cultivation, watering, staking, etc. are simplified. With the same expenditure of labor you can have more flowers.

It has always puzzled me why so many people go to so much trouble to plan, arrange and plant flower beds and borders for desired effects and then cheerfully cut most of the blooms as soon as they appear and carry them indoors to fill vases or to be used in flower arrangements.

Manage your cut flower and reserve

Raise Flowers for Cutting

Set aside a small preserve where flowers learn to grow—then transfer them to other parts or cut them off for show.

garden like a vegetable plot. Keep one portion for perennials and one for annuals and other temporary crops. If it is of such large dimensions that you use a wheel hoe, space the rows sufficiently to allow this implement to pass. Otherwise allow only sufficient room between rows for the full development of the plants with a wider space left every five or six feet to serve as a path. The plants are thus in five- or six-feet wide beds, each of which contains several rows running lengthwise. If the ground slopes, run the beds (and the rows) across the slope rather than up and down. Within the sections set aside for perennials and non-perennials, keep the taller plants together. Don't bury low growers between rows of taller plants. Rows should not be closer together than one foot (the minimum distance that permits the use of a hand hoe) and large plants such as delphiniums and peonies may be two-and-a-half to three feet apart. The distance between the plants that form the rows will ordinarily be less than the distance between the rows.

Snapdragons raised indoors in flats (shallow-type boxes) are planted outdoors in early spring. They are loosened by tapping edge of flat on the ground.

Succession is important. You probably don't want a flood of flowers at one time and none at others. You wish a continuous supply. Plan accordingly. Select perennials that bloom during different months. Make an early and one, or more, later sowings of many annuals, also successive plantings of gladioli, tuberoses and other tender bulbs. Plant early, mid-season and late flowering varieties of tulips, narcissi and other hardy bulbs as well as of irises, peonies, chrysanthemums, etc. Plant biennials too. Plan your garden on paper. Your first attempt will not be perfect, but if you keep records of sowing dates, flowering

Keep good balls of soil on the plants at setting-out time. Make holes with trowel using the grip as shown. This is less tiring than a scooping motion.

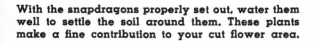

With the snapdragons properly set out, water them well to settle the soil around them. These plants make a fine contribution to your cut flower area.

To sow seeds of biennials and perennials, make a seed bed surrounded by a frame of sturdy boards.

After making the drills and watering them, as in top photo, sow the seeds in the drills, as above.

seasons, amount of cutting, etc., you can base changes upon these that will enable you to have a cutting garden that fills your own particular needs.

As a reserve garden the area should serve as a place in which to plant and grow perennials used temporarily in spring bedding such as rock cress, dwarf polemonium, Phlox divaricata and evergreen candytuft. It should serve as a nursery in which biennials such as wallflowers, canterbury bells, foxgloves and pansies are raised and grown on nearly to blooming size before they are planted where they are to flower.

Young perennials and rock garden plants may be grown in here too. All are grown strictly in rows, nursery fashion.

Late-sown annuals transplanted to four or five inch pots buried to their rims in the reserve garden soon grow on to sizable specimens that are mighty handy for summer replacements in annual and mixed borders.

Among the best flowers for cutting are: arctotis, Artemisia "Silver King," achilleas, anchusas (annual and perennial), Japanese anemones, asters (annual and perennial), babys-breath (annual and perennial), balloon flower, blanket flower, boltonia, browallia, calendulas, candytuft, canterbury bells, carnations, chrysanthemums (annual and perennial), columbines, cone-flowers, coral bells, coreopsis, cornflowers, cosmos, cup-and-saucer vine, cynoglossum, dahlias, day-lilies, delphiniums, everlasting flowers, false dragonhead, feverfew, forget-me-nots, foxgloves, gladioli, godetias, heleniums, heliotropes, irises, larkspurs, liatris, lilies, love-in-a-mist, love-lies-bleeding, lupines, marigolds,

Next take a rake and cover the seeds with a layer of shallow soil. Water adequately in dry weather.

Shade the plants with a covering made of wooden laths. When seeds germinate covering is removed.

mignonette, mist flower, monkshoods, morning-glories, narcissi (including daffodils), nasturtiums, pansies, petunias, peonies, phlox (annual and perennial), pinks, poker plants, poppies, pryrethrums, salpiglossis, salvias, scabious (annual and perennial) sea-lavender, shasta daisies, snapdragons, statice, stocks, strawflowers, sunflowers, sweet peas, sweet sultans, sweet Williams, tithonia, tuberoses, tulips, verbenas, veronicas and zinnias. •

By pulling out (thinning) cosmos plants, remaining flowers will have chance to develop more fully.

PLAN FOR SMALL CUT FLOWER AND RESERVE GARDEN

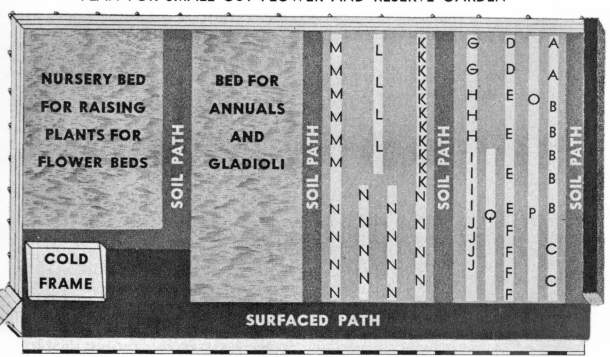

SCALE IN FEET

A Artemisia Silver King
B Japanese Anemones
C Coreopsis
D Feverfew
E Peonies
F Blanket Flower
G Perennial Babys-Breath
H Sea-Lavender
I Coral Bells
J Balloon Flower
K Irises
L Delphiniums
M Chrysanthemums
N Roses
O Lilies
P Narcissi
Q Tulips

Using a scuffle or Dutch hoe, operator walks backward, keeps surface loose without stepping on soil.

Borders
of
Bloom

Size and shape, content and color may vary from formal to "quite contrary"—but borders must fit the landscape.

BORDERS are flower beds that are considerably longer than they are wide. Those in which many different kinds of plants are set in neighborly groups or patches are extremely popular. If all the plants used are kinds that persist from year to year, you have what is correctly termed a perennial border. If they all nor-mally are sown, bloom, and die in one season the result is an annual border. If, as more often happens, annuals, biennials, hardy, and sometimes tender, perennials are used together, you have a mixed border. The latter is the most popular.

Borders may be of any desired length. For best effects they should be between

Neat staking and tying keeps a border tidy. Left, a soft, hooked wire is a good support for tulips.

Wire can be twisted to support carnations (arrows). Twine holds peony stems erect, using four stakes.

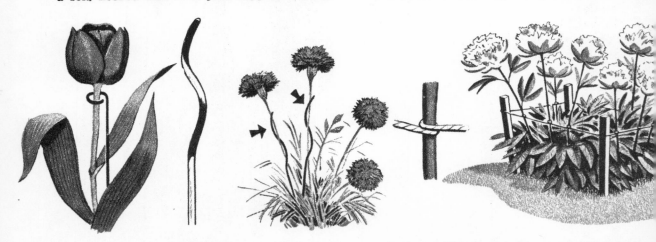

Every three years most perennials should be dug up, divided and replanted. Above, betony is being divided with a spade. Each division should have a good amount of roots and sturdy crowns, as below.

six and twelve feet wide. The width should bear some reasonable relation to the length, but a short, fairly wide area is preferable to one that is long and excessively narrow. The narrower the border the more difficult it is to have bold groupings of larger and more important plants. Such emphatic points of interest are the very soul of good border arrangement.

A width of at least six feet is desirable, but it is not impossible to design narrower borders that are pretty and effective. If you undertake one of these, confine your-

An attractive use of a narrow border is in setting off a path leading to the front door. A shrub planting backs up the border to support it.

self to plants of small or moderate growth. You should then be able to attain commendable results in a strip three or four feet wide.

Borders may be straight or curved. They may be uniform or variable in width. They may be with or without a background but are usually much more effective when set

Hollow bamboo cane with a piece of wire inserted as shown is recommended support for tall flowers.

Brushwood pushed well into the ground tepee-like is an excellent way to hold annual vines erect.

Outline a new border with hose or rope, then make cuts in sod with edging tool (above) or with spade.

Annuals for setting out should be plump and sturdy (flat on left) not tall and leggy like those right.

against a wall, fence, hedge or an informal planting of shrubs or evergreens. Logical endings are important. Don't let the border just finish—straggle off into nothingness, as it were. Walls, fences, hedges or groups of shrubs or evergreens can be used effectively to define the extremities of a border.

Locate the border so that it is important in the garden plan. Fit it pleasingly into the landscape. Place it where it will be seen —from an important window, from a terrace, from a main path. Or make it part of a formal garden.

A reasonable depth of good soil is necessary. Less than a foot of fertile topsoil is limiting. More is desirable. Prepare it thoroughly, particularly for perennials. Once planted, you will have no opportunity to improve the soil beneath them for several years. Annual borders are, of course, made anew each year.

Unless you are content to grow only bog and wet land plants, the border must have good subsurface drainage.

Full sunlight for more than half of each day is best. Failing this, use only plants known to withstand shade. Big trees close to a border root into it and extract moisture and nourishment needed by the flowering plants. Don't locate your border near them

if you can possibly avoid such big trees.

The arrangement of the plants calls for nice judgment. Too often the beginners' border is a hodge-podge. This need not be. A few simple rules carefully applied will prevent the worst mistakes. First, rely largely upon tested and true plants, kinds that with moderate care will reward you with a flower display year after year. Among perennials the best of these are columbines, hollyhocks, gas plant, gaillardias, oriental poppies, day-lilies, bearded and Siberian irises, peonies, phlox, balloon flower, heleniums, campanulas, shasta daisies, perennial babys-breath, rose-mallow, sedum spectabile, grass pink, coreopsis, evergreen candytuft, rock-cress, basket-of-gold, moss-pinks, veronicas, nepetas, and chrysanthemums.

Repeat the same kinds at intervals along the border. Such repetition gives character and strength to the planting.

The repetition need not be of precisely the same *varieties*. In July, different varieties of day-lilies will do. Phlox in groups of various colors are effective in August. Earlier in the season bold clumps of peonies of various hues spaced along the length of the border are good. At the front, clumps of lower kinds, such as evergreen candy-

When strong-growing plants are small, triangularly wired stakes may be placed in position as shown.

Never tie plant stems to stakes tightly, as at the left. Always allow for thickening of stem (right).

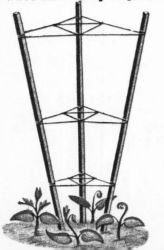

After annuals have been planted they must be well watered. Soil around them should be firmly settled.

tuft, basket-of-gold, flax and nepeta repeated at intervals give a good effect. Use enough of these basic plants to assure color and interest throughout the summer. Fill in with others to give diversity.

Set most plants in groups of three, five, or more of the same kind. Too many single specimens gives a spotty effect that lacks restfulness. Let the size of the individual groups vary. Use, however, a few individual plants. Solitary specimens of peonies, perennial babys-breath and other kinds of rounded outline are effective when used sparingly.

Don't plant all tall-growing kinds at the back of the border and all the low ones at the front. A planting carefully graded in this way is uninteresting. Instead, let bays of lower growing kinds recede to the rear and promontories of taller ones extend forward. Here and there let solitary plants or small groups tower somewhat above their neighbors, but avoid hiding low kinds behind tall groups.

Give attention to the color scheme. This is highly personal. So long as the result pleases you that is all that matters. Some like nothing but pastels; others appreciate brighter hues. Some like contrasts such as orange and deep blue planted together;

others respond to subtle harmonies. Avoid such horrible combinations as magenta and scarlet and strong pink and bright yellow planted near each other.

White flowers and gray foliage such as that of Artemisia Silver King and dusty miller make grand breaks between patches of color that otherwise would clash. Use them freely.

Don't expect too much from a border. Even with the most careful planning one devoted entirely to perennials (and here I include hardy bulbs) will not be a riot of color all spring and summer, but at all times some of it will be colorful if a careful succession is planned.

A mixed border consisting of groups of perennials with areas of annuals, biennials and perhaps tender perennials such as geraniums, fuchsias, and lantanas is very much more colorful through the summer than is a border of perennials alone. Summer bulbs such as gladioli, dahlias, tiger flowers, montbretias, Peruvian-daffodils, summer hyacinths, tuberoses, tuberous begonias, acidantheras, and cannas can be used too.

Leave ample spaces in your mixed border between the perennials to accommodate the summer plantings. Each group of annuals, biennials, summer bulbs or tender perennials will usually need at least a square yard. You must not expect satisfaction if you jam them among crowded perennials. Spade and fertilize the spaces in which the summer plants are set shortly before planting.

Borders devoted entirely to annuals provide brilliant displays. They are not colorful early in the year, however, and some kinds such as babys-breath, candytuft, calliopsis, cornflowers, gaillardias, larkspurs, leptosynes, linarias, love-in-a-mist, mignonette, poppies, rudbeckias, salpiglossis, strawflowers, and chrysanthemums bloom for a comparatively short season. When these cease flowering, pull them out and set

Don't tie plants like a sheaf of wheat to a center stake. Link stems separately for a natural effect.

Wires forming a half-circle are virtually invisible when used for peonies and such, as shown at right.

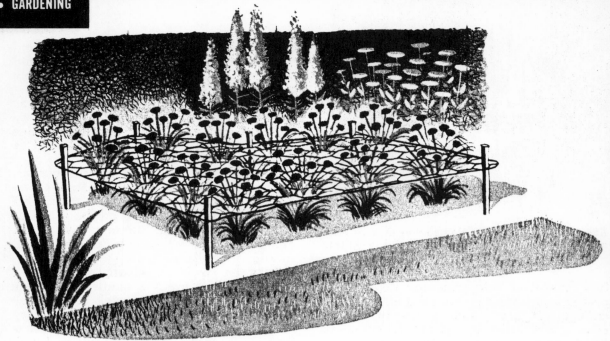

Carnations will grow up through ¾-inch chicken wire stretched a foot or so above the ground.

in their places plants of balsams, browallias, calendulas, candytuft, globe amaranths, marigolds (both African and French), flowering tobacco phlox, statice, sunflowers, and zinnias, raised in the reserve or nursery garden from late sowings. If you do not want to go to this trouble then use only annuals that have a long blooming season such as ageratums, browallia, calendulas, carnations, celosias, cosmos, four o'clocks, globe amaranths, ice plants, lobelia, marigolds, Mexican tulip-poppy, nasturtiums, flowering tobacco, petunias, portulaca, salvias, sanvitalia, snapdragons, snow-on-the-mountain, spider flower, star of Texas, statice, sweet alyssum, sunflowers, tithonia, torenia, verbenas, vincas, wax begonias, and zinnias.

Plant annuals in spring or early summer. Some can be sown directly where the plants are to bloom; others must be, or may be, raised indoors and later transplanted.

Perennials may be planted in early fall or in early spring, hardy bulbs such as daffodils and narcissi, tulips, hyacinths, grape hyacinths, squills, snowdrops, crocuses, glory-of-the-snows, summer snowflakes, camassias, English and Spanish bluebells and lilies in fall.

Biennials are raised in the nursery or reserve garden. They are usually planted in their flowering places in spring. Here belong foxgloves, honesty, pansies, violas, wallflowers, canterbury bells, English daisies, forget-me-nots, mulleins, rose-campion and sweet Williams.

Borders containing perennials should be remade every three or four years. When the time arrives, dig up all the plants (except possibly specimens of gas plant and a few others known to resent disturbance) in early fall. Plant them temporarily closely together in rows in another part of the garden and improve the soil by spading it deeply, by adding compost, manure or other humus material, and by fertilizing and liming as deemed desirable.

When the plants are re-set, divide those that are too large. Replant only strong, vigorous pieces. See that they do not dry before they are installed in the ground. The considerable work of remaking a perennial border may be spread by undertaking one third or one fourth of it every year rather than doing the whole every three or four years.

Care of Perennials

Once planted, the care of perennials consists of, in colder climates, covering them lightly with salt hay, evergreen branches, dry leaves, or similar loose material after the ground is well frozen, of pushing back into the soil in spring any that have heaved by frost, of removing the winter covering gradually when spring growth begins, of fertilizing and shallowly forking over the surface soil in spring, and of keeping it shallowly cultivated or mulched throughout the summer. Also stake and tie to give support, water thoroughly every few days during dry periods, remove promptly all faded blooms and spray or dust to control pests and diseases.

In addition to the plants already men-

Twiggy brushwood, placed among young chrysanthemums and similar border plants, offer good support.

tioned, the following are good for border plantings:

Perennials:

Achillea, aconite, coral bells, amsonia, anthemis, aster, astilbe, aubretia, bee-balm, betony, blackberry-lily, blazing star, bleeding heart, bluebeard, buttercups, butterfly weed, catchfly, centaurea, centranthus, Christmas rose, cimicifuga, clematis, cynoglossum, delphinium, dropwort, eupatorium, evening primrose, false-indigo, Solomons seal, false Solomons seal, fleabane, flowering onion, foxtail-lily, garden heliotrope, geranium, germander, geum, globe flower, globe thistle, sunflower, Jacob's ladder, Japanese anemones, leopard's bane, lily-of-the-valley, lobelia, lupine, lysimachia, lythrum, May-apple, meadow rue, miscanthus, penstemon, false dragon head, plantain-lily, plumbago, plume-poppy, potentilla, primrose, saponaria, saxifraga, scabious, sea-holly, sea-lavender, senecio, snow-in-summer, spurge, stonecrop, Stokes aster, swamp-pink, sweet rocket, thermopsis, thrift, toad-lily, turtlehead, yucca.

Annuals:

Annual poinsettia, anoda, asters, blue lace flower, California-poppies, castor bean, clarkias, cockscomb, convolvulus, cynglossum, dimorphotheca, everlasting flowers, gilias, godetias, Joseph's coat, lavatera, lupine, love-lies-bleeding, lychnis, matricaria, monkey flower, night scented stock, ornamental grasses, prickly-poppy, Virginia stocks. •

A suggested plan for a mixed border. Shaded areas are perennials, other areas are replanted each year.

SCALE: ONE SQUARE EQUALS ONE FOOT.

Flowers for Window and Porch Boxes

Window and porch boxes should be made with holes in bottoms for drainage. Screw wedges.

Side view of box shows it in its position, bolted into the side of the window. Wedges overlap.

Instead of wedges, metal or wood "ears" may be used on the bottom, screwed or nailed.

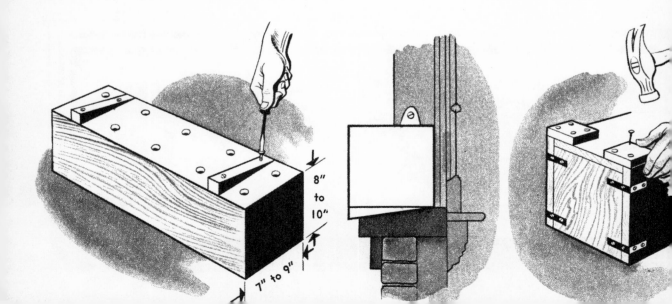

8" to 10"

7" to 9"

Proud of your home? You'll be prouder still, with boxes of flowers on porch and on sill.

WINDOW and porch boxes can be very gay. With them you can dress your house charmingly with a little effort. Well-filled boxes are a mark of proud home-makers. I never recall seeing an ill-cared for home sporting them.

Growing plants in boxes is an artificial method of cultivation. Such plants are under greater control than are those in the open garden. Because of this they suffer more quickly from neglect and respond more surely to care.

The difficulties that plants in boxes face are (1) their soil is strictly limited. (2) It dries comparatively rapidly. (3) Nutrients are washed away quickly. (4) Reflected heat from nearby walls may harm them and (5) The entire soil may be frozen solid for long periods in winter.

To help your plants in boxes thrive, make sure that the soil is suitable. Only rarely will unimproved topsoil do. Even though it grows good flowers and vegetables in the garden it needs modifying for window and porch boxes. If it is light (sandy) or medium-heavy (loamy) mix with it half its

An entrance takes on charm through decorative urns filled with white "balcony" type petunias.

Where it is not convenient to use the window sill, boxes may rest on brackets attached to frames.

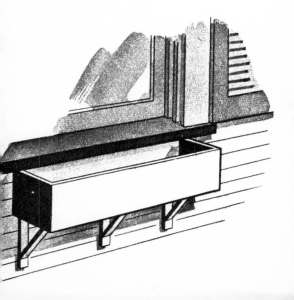

bulk of humus, leafmold, peat moss, old rotted manure, or good compost. If it is heavy (clayey) add as much coarse sand or gritty cinders as well. Mix with each bushel of the mixture a pint of bone meal, half a pint of a complete fertilizer such as 5-10-5 and, a pint of lime.

Use new soil each year if you can. If this is not possible turn the old soil from the boxes, loosen it, let it "air out" for a few days. Then add the bone meal, fertilizer and humus material.

Never let plant boxes get really dry. Avoid, too, keeping them constantly saturated. The soil should always be moist, but

No, it's not a basket—it's an earthenware pot full of newly planted geraniums and variegated vincas.

never so wet that if a handful is squeezed water oozes from it. To maintain this state, water must be applied more and more frequently as the season advances. Beware of overwatering before the box is well filled with roots, and of underwatering afterward. Saturate the soil, then give no more until it is obviously needed. No additional fertilizer is required until the box is filled with roots. Then supplementary feedings are in order. Use an ounce of a complete fertilizer (a 5-10-5 or equivalent) in a gallon of water every two weeks or a teaspoonful of nitrate of soda and a teaspoonful of sulphate of potash to each gallon once a week.

To avoid harm from reflected heat, choose summer blooming plants according to the exposure. In locations that do not receive long hours of direct sunshine you can have tuberous begonias, fuchsias, patience plant and wishbone flower. Here also, as well as in sunnier spots, you can grow wax begonias and annual vincas. For sunny places choose lantanas, petunias, geraniums, dwarf marigolds, zinnias, nasturtiums, ageratums, sweet alyssum, balsam, and heliotropes. Such trailers as German ivy, variegated vinca, ivy leaf geraniums, Kenilworth ivy, English-ivy, and variegated ground-ivy are good. In some places morning-glories, moon vine, climbing nasturtiums, and others can be used.

The above occupy the boxes in summer only. If you plant bulbs—hyacinths, tulips, narcissi, crocuses, grape-hyacinth, Spanish bluebells, squills, etc., or such perennials as Sedum spectabile and plumbago the plants are in the boxes over winter. You must prevent them from being frozen for long periods. The best plan is, in the fall, to stand the boxes closely together on the ground in a sheltered spot and to pack straw, hay or dry leaves between and around them. After the ground has frozen hard throw a few inches of covering over the tops as well. In spring uncover and move the boxes to their regular positions. Set spring bedding plants such as English daisies, forget-me-nots, and pansies in the

Two flats of petunias are shown at extreme left. When buying plants, select short, not leggy ones.

At planting time flowers should have good balls of roots (left). Water an hour or so before planting.

Below, terra cotta window box is used to flank a house entrance. Geraniums are often used here.

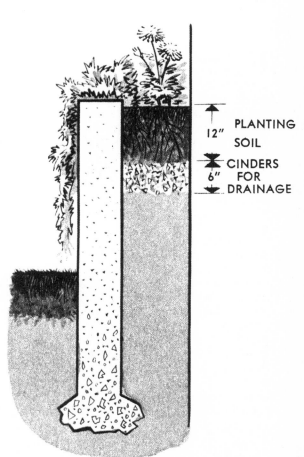

12" PLANTING SOIL

CINDERS

6" FOR

DRAINAGE

Sections above and below show how flowers are planted in so-called "planting boxes" that are part of the home frontage. Note proportions of drainage gravel to planting soil. Pack the soil in firmly and water well.

boxes in spring for the best results.

Fuss a little with your plants. Keep dead leaves picked. Prune straggly branches. Stake and tie. Keep the soil covered with an inch of peat moss or humus. Take steps against pests and diseases.

Boxes may be of wood, metal, terra cotta or concrete. In sunny locations metal ones heat badly. They must have holes in their bottoms to ensure drainage. Boxes should be at least eight and preferably ten inches deep, have a minimum width at the top of seven inches and be of lengths suitable to the space and to permit moving them with fair ease. Boxes may be bought ready made (some have a built-in self watering feature) or may be constructed. If of wood, use cypress, cedar or redwood. If you line the box with metal use zinc or galvanized steel, never copper. If unlined, paint the inside with cuprinol or with asphaltum paint. Never use creosote.

When filling boxes, place an inch or two of large pebbles or cinders in first, then a layer of moss or rough leaves, then the soil mixture. Always leave the soil sufficiently below the top to permit watering when planting is finished. •

12" PLANTING SOIL

CINDERS

6" FOR

DRAINAGE

Is Shade Your Problem?

Not all flowers are lovers of sun. Some, in fact, are shady characters.

FLOWER gardening in shade presents problems. Most flowers love sunshine; a minority only prefer subdued light and some few others tolerate it. Yet in all but the densest shade at least some flowers may be grown. Make a wise selection.

Among taller growers that thrive in more or less shade are foxgloves, monkshoods, cimicifugas, day-lilies, Japanese anemones, goatsbeard, certain bellflowers, cow-parsnips, climbing hydrangeas, silver lace vine, clematises, beebalms, summer phloxes, meadow-rues and camassias.

Medium-tall plants for shade or partial shade are columbines, jack-in-the-pulpit, astilbes, begonias, forget-me-not anchusa, marsh-marigold, certain bellflowers, turtle-head, clintonias, lady-slippers, bleeding heart, gas plant, shooting stars, leopard's bane, white snakeroot, fuchsias, coral bells, plantain-lilies, Senecio clivorum, some lobelias, Virginia-bluebell, false dragon-head, balloon flowers, May-apple, Jacob's ladder, Solomons seal, false Solomons seal, spiderworts, globe flowers, lilies, narcissi (including daffodils) and Spanish and English bluebells as well as others.

Low-growers for shaded or semi-shaded places are sweet woodruff, chrysogonum, Dutchmans breeches, dwarf bleeding heart, barrenwort, galax, wintergreen, Christmas-rose, hepaticas, bluets, evergreen candytuft, some lobelias, creeping Jenny, mazus, forget-me-nots, gill-over-the-ground, Phlox divaricata, dwarf Jacob's ladder, primroses, lungworts, bloodroot, shortia, foam flower, flowering tobacco, petunias, torenias, pansies, bog-bean, glory-of-the-snows, autumn-crocuses, lily-of-the-valley, dogtooth-violets, snowdrops, certain irises, snowflakes, lilies, grape-hyacinths and squills.

Not all the above are suitable for every shaded location. Factors other than light must be taken into account. Soil moisture, for example. Where the ground is dryish it is useless to try to establish such plants as astilbes, marsh marigolds and lobelias. In decidedly dry soil you may have difficulty getting most plants to thrive. To surmount this difficulty make adequate provision for watering. Also improve the soil before you plant by mixing with it to a depth of eight inches or more generous amounts of organic matter—peat moss, compost, humus or rotted manure. A three or four inch layer spread over the surface and dug in is none too much.

The amount of watering necessary depends not only upon the plants you use and the soil but also upon the location. Areas adjacent to walls and beneath overhanging roofs often get less than their share of rain. In other places the roots of trees (particularly those of beeches, maples and sycamores) and shrubs absorb great quantities of moisture from the soil leaving little for other plants. Under such conditions soaking the soil with hose or sprinkler from time to time is necessary. Do this whenever it approaches dryness. See that the moisture goes down to a depth of at least eight inches whenever you water. Under extreme conditions, as for example, beneath an old maple, beech or other surface-rooting tree, it may be impossible to grow flowers at all. Then groundcovers must be tried. If these fail, stone flagging or similar treatment is the answer.

Lack of soil water is no worse than too much. Only bog plants can survive in waterlogged soil. If your shaded place is constantly wet, plant only wet-land plants or drain the soil by installing sub-surface drains before you plant. Moss on the soil surface is often thought to indicate wet soil or acid conditions but this is not necessarily true. Lack of fertility often encourages a healthy growth of moss.

Other soil conditions can cause trouble. Some shade-loving flowers, shortia and wintergreen, for example, will grow in acid soils only. Check for such preferences before you plant.

Don't crowd the plants you set in shaded places. Space them a little further apart than you do when planting in sunny places. This permits them to spread their leaves widely and to take advantage of all available light. It also admits a certain amount of side, reflected and top light.

It is better to keep the surface of the ground beneath trees mulched with a layer of compost, leafmold, peat moss or other organic material than it is to stir it frequently with a cultivator. Such a loose covering absorbs the rain drip without being compacted. A great many shade-loving and shade-tolerant plants are by nature woodlanders and are accustomed to and especially appreciate such a mulch over their roots. This supplies nourishment which is especially important in shaded places. Not that the plants should be over-fertilized but they must never suffer from lack of nourishment. In fact, they should never be permitted to suffer from any cause at all. The shade itself is enough for them to contend with. Strive to make other conditions as perfect as possible. •

Foxgloves, tall and stately, thrive in semi-shade. They need a fairly good soil that is not too dry, and bloom in white and in delicate shades of pink.

Daffodils are good for colorful effects in lightly shaded places. If soil and growing conditions are favorable they bloom for years with little care.

Few plants excel the plantain-lily for ability to grow in shade and to thrive under fairly adverse conditions. This variety has delicate white flowers.

Plant Your Flowers as Nature Does

The well-tailored landscape is always in good taste,

but for a change in appearance try that natural look

FLOWER beds and borders are obviously man-made. Their occupants, placed with studied care, are neatly staked and tied. The soil is cultivated or trimly mulched and weed free. They have that manicured look.

Such beds and borders represent a good, but not the only, type of flower gardening. Naturalized plantings are excellent, too.

When naturalizing flowers, aim to simulate Nature. Give the impression that they are growing without having been planted. This calls for study, knowledge, and taste. Merely littering your garden with various kinds of flowers arranged casually and without reason will not do. The effect is messy and unconvincing.

First, consider the places suitable for naturalized plantings. Such plantings do not fit in formal surroundings. They belong in less tailored landscapes.

A patch of woodland, a meadow, an informal pond or a brookside give splendid opportunities. But these are not necessary. You can naturalize daffodils and narcissi, for example, in a grassy orchard or under a single apple tree or clump of birches. Crocuses or snowdrops planted casually in the lawn beneath a shade tree are examples of simple naturalistic plantings. So too are grape-hyacinths, glory-of-the-snows and winter aconites beneath shrubbery.

A few Japanese primroses, yellow flag irises or water forget-me-nots can be naturalized by pond or stream as successfully as greater numbers. Such plants as foxgloves and summer phlox can be used with good effect in lightly shaded places beneath trees. The possibilities are endless.

Consider the flowers. It is not necessary to use natives only. But those used should appear as if they *might* be indigenous. Don't use varieties that have double flowers or highly variegated foliage. Stick to simple types, kinds that fit into the landscape without doing violence to one's sense of what is right.

Naturalized plants get little care. They may be annuals you can sow and leave, biennials which, if set out, will develop practically untended, or perennials that live from year to year without fuss. They must compete with grasses of lawn, orchard or meadow, or among the wildings of streamside or woodland. Do just enough weeding to prevent them being crowded out. If they become too thick or overgrown, thin them or lift, divide and replant. When bulbous kinds are grown in grass always let their foliage die down before you cut the grass. Beyond this do little.

Thirdly, consider arrangement. This calls for an appreciation of how plants grow in nature. Look to the fields, woodlands and streamsides for inspiration.

Obviously, wildlings are not evenly spaced—they do not form rows or set patterns. In places they cluster and crowd each other; elsewhere they are spaced more widely. Outlines of groups are rarely well defined. Individuals well away from the main colony proclaim where chance seeds fell and grew.

Plants within a natural colony are usually of different sizes and heights. Those smaller and lower represent younger plants or specimens growing in less favorable spots.

Consider how wild plants get where they do. Often their seeds are windborne. If light or fine, as are those of aster and poppy, they are apt to besprinkle favored sites in patterns reminiscent of a starry sky. Heavier seeded plants such as narcissi and Spanish bluebells are likely to form denser groupings within the areas they colonize.

Each denser patch represents the progeny of a single mother plant. In the main, the youngsters will be to leeward of their parent. They will be thicker close to the mother than from her. The groups naturally thin out in the direction of prevailing breezes.

Not all seeds are dispersed by wind. On sloping ground they wash downward, so greater concentrations of many plants occur toward the lower parts of slopes. Plants growing on the brinks of cliffs often self-sow freely below. Seeds and bits of waterside plants float downstream and in likely places give rise to new individuals. Seedlings often arise beneath places where birds perch. Take these matters into account when you naturalize plants.

Observe too that wild plants ordinarily keep to locations suited to their kind. Those on higher and drier places are different from those growing where it is lower and more moist. The flora in full sun is not the same as that in the shade, and so on. Arrange your naturalized plantings to simulate these patterns of Nature.

When naturalizing bulbs such as crocuses and narcissi, throw handfuls of them on the ground with long sweeping motions. Then plant them where they fall. Throw all handfuls in the same general direction to form sweeps or drifts that look as though they had sprung naturally from windborne seeds. An Englishman suggested that naturalistic planting should be done on a day that is sunny, with patches of cloud. Plant, he said, where the cloud shadows fall and not in the sunny places between. The idea has merit.

The list of flowers suitable for naturalizing is very great. Some in addition to those already mentioned are: squills, English bluebells, Autumn-crocuses, camassias, summer snowflakes, lilies, trilliums, bloodroot, May-apple, hepaticas, Dicentra eximea, bluets, honesty, sweet rocket, Lobelia syphilitica, cardinal flower, polyanthus primroses, violas, Virginia-bluebell, bellworts, rue-anemone, spring beauty, trout-lilies, Johnny-jump-ups, butterfly weed, shasta daisies, blazing star, yucca, sedums, white snakeroot, lily-of-the-valley, day-lilies, California-poppies, larkspurs, cornflowers, lupines, and ferns. •

When you naturalize bulbs, throw them down group-fashion and plant them where they fall so effect, when blooming, will be wind-borne.

Gardens in the City

"Underprivileged" urban flowers need careful plannin

and special attention to thrive in a citified settin

GARDENING under city conditions is a real challenge. Yet lovely effects can be obtained and oases of greenery and flowers, no matter how small, are such welcome reliefs from masonry, sidewalks, noise and bustle that all who have the opportunity should create and maintain them.

First and foremost, the city garden must be well designed. Good lines and pleasing groupings of plants mean even more here than in suburban and country gardens. The plot is usually small. Surrounding buildings make it look smaller. Poor design can wreck the whole effort.

Almost always the garden will be formal or semi-formal. The informality of a naturalistic landscape is impossible to achieve in the city. Most often it will be a garden to live in—an extension of the house itself. Because of this, an area for sitting is needed

and this should be paved, gravelled o otherwise suitably surfaced. Grass lawn i a city garden is usually too precious to d more than look at.

Take care that the garden has unity. It details should make a congruous whol Paths that lead to nowhere-in-particula are out; so too are gates that obviously ar without purpose.

Avoid excessive ornamentation. In small plot a sundial, bench, birdbath, foun tain or statue may be used as a focal poir —some such point of interest, indeed, i ordinarily needed. But don't overdo it. On such is usually enough.

Be sparing with trellises, arbors and per golas. If used they must have substanti: purpose, and should fit into the over-a pattern. Choose garden furniture wit these same ideas in mind.

A well located pool or fountain is delightful. Interesting effects can be achieved by having varied levels and steps.

Walls or fences will surround your city garden. Work them skillfully into the design. Mask them in places with shrubbery and vines.

The Soil

After the pattern of your garden has been decided, or perhaps before, give attention to the soil. Plants in cities are up against too many other difficulties to expect them to thrive in uncongenial earth. When you begin it will probably be poor. Do everything possible to improve it.

Dig to ascertain its depth and character. If it is reasonably free of chunks of concrete, rocks, and other builder's debris, is recognizable as topsoil (rather than pure clay, hardpan or impossible subsoil) and is at least ten inches deep, make it fertile. Under less promising circumstances bring in new topsoil.

Soil in city yards is almost invariably acid. The pollution of the atmosphere makes it so. Therefore, except for plants that definitely need acid conditions such as rhododendrons and mountain laurel, lime it generously. At the beginning, use four pounds to each hundred square feet. Subsequently, two pounds to each hundred square feet applied every other year will probably be sufficient. If in doubt have the soil tested.

Add organic matter liberally. The kind you use will depend upon availability. Peat moss is convenient but not quite as satisfactory as leaf-mold or black humus. Good compost is excellent. Dehydrated cow manure can be used. Best of all is rotted manure. The important point is to use plenty. A layer three inches thick over the entire surface is not too much if the ground is lacking in organic matter and is hard and compact. Mix it thoroughly with the top ten inches of soil.

Lime and organic matter work wonders in improving soil texture. Add nutrients too. A complete fertilizer provides these.

Use one having an analysis of 5-10-5 (or thereabouts) at the rate of four pounds to each hundred square feet. Incorporate it into the upper three or four inches a week or ten days before you plant.

I have described the minimum preparation where underdrainage is good. In waterlogged soil lay land drains eighteen to twenty-four inches below the surface to carry surplus water to a drain or dry well. If you can possibly provide more than ten inches of improved top soil, do so. Twice that depth is not too much.

Plants

What plants are best for a city garden? Fortunately, a wealth of experience about this has been assembled. Trees and shrubs that lose their leaves in winter thrive better than most evergreens. Yet evergreens are needed to give winter cheer, backgrounds for flower plantings, and mass and weight to the garden picture. Most adaptable are yews, Japanese hollies, mountain-laurel, rhododendrons, leucothoe, euonymus, and pieris (andromeda).

Flowering trees that succeed include magnolias, dogwood, hawthorn, laburnum,

At right above, geraniums and hydrangeas are used to border a pleasant paved area. Fountain is flanked by rhododendrons and vine-clad fence.

At right, an effect of distance is created by the long side path in this garden. Petunias, flowering tobacco, castor-bean, morning-glories are grown.

crab-apples, Japanese cherries, Cornelian-cherry, plums, almonds and peaches.

Among the best flowering shrubs are: abelia, cotoneasters, Japanese quinces, deutzias, forsythias, rose-of-sharon, hydrangeas, bush honeysuckles, mock-oranges, privets, barberries, sweet pepper bush, jet-bead, tamarix, bridal wreath, lilacs, butterfly bush, viburnums, weigelias, and kerria.

Vines to use are English-ivy, Boston-ivy, actinidia, akebia, clematis, mignonette vine, cinnamon vine, climbing hydrangea, Virginia creeper, silver lace vine, kudzu vine, grape vines, wistarias, morning glories, hyacinth bean, Japanese hop vine, cypress vine, cardinal climber, nasturtium, and perennial pea.

Trees and shrubs generally, and plants ordinarily grown for foliage or fruits rather than flowers (such as English-ivy and pachysandra) are beyond the scope of this book. I have included them here as a guide for the city gardener whose choice is more restricted than that of his suburban and country cousins.

The surest flowering plants for city gardens are spring bulbs. You can scarcely fail with tulips, hyacinths, narcissi (including daffodils), crocuses, Spanish bluebells, grape-hyacinths, squills, snowdrops and snowflakes. The flowers are in the bulbs when you buy them. Plant them in the fall; spring brings forth the flowers. It is best to plant new bulbs each year but some, such as Spanish bluebells, grape hyacinths and narcissi, bloom more than one season if you can let the foliage die down completely before removing them.

Bulbous plants suitable for summer are gladioli, lilies, tuberoses, tuberous begonias, elephants-ears, caladiums, dahlias (especially the dwarf kinds) and calla lilies. All are easy.

In addition, during the summer you can set out geraniums, heliotropes, fuchsias, wax begonias, petunias, snapdragons, marigolds, torenias, and a variety of other annuals such as alyssum, and zinnias.

Choose perennials carefully. It is true that they flower year after year without replacement, but it is also true that most bloom for a fairly short season only and for longer periods are without bloom. This is all right if their foliage is attractive but not if they become straggly and untidy. Not all perennials that thrive in the country take well to city residence. Delphiniums and summer phlox do not, for example.

Among perennials that do withstand urban conditions well and that are of desirable habit are: ajuga, barrenworts, basket-of-gold, columbines, rock-cress, thrift, astilbes, asters, bellflowers, shasta daisies, coreopsis, dwarf bleeding-heart, gas plant, blanket flowers, heleniums, day-lilies, coral bells, plantain-lilies, irises, peonies, Phlox divaricata, moss-pink, balloon flower, plumbago, coneflower, sedums, houseleeks, spiderworts, violets, Stokes aster, lily-of-the-valley, Solomons seal, vinca, rose mallow, cimicifuga, Christmas-rose, Japanese anemone, Nepeta mussini, helianthus, and chrysanthemums. In addition, you may use foxgloves, sweet Williams, forget-me-nots, pansies, and English

Extreme left, tulips are a feature of a shaded city garden, making gay spring display. English ivy and plantain-lilies are prominent.

Left, a miniature flower bed is surrounded by a graveled area., A paved terrace and shrub-lined walls make an attractive boundary.

daisies, all of which are biennials. Set out plants in early spring and discard them after they finish blooming.

Because shade is often a problem in the city, choose plants with special reference to light conditions. It's useless trying to grow sun lovers such as marigolds and chrysanthemums where there is little sunshine. You can grow most plants listed here if they get direct sunlight for at least half a day, although some will thrive better with more. If you get less than this you had better stick to spring bulbs and to plants known to tolerate shade well such as begonias, fuchsias, torenias, flowering tobacco, caladiums, patience plant, ajuga, Christmas-rose, dwarf bleeding-heart, barrenworts, Solomons seal, false Solomons seal, cimicifuga, plantain-lilies, lily-of-the-valley, Phlox divaricata, violets and vinca. You may also be able to grow bloodroot, trilliums, and Virginia bluebell.

Maintenance

Keep your city garden neatly manicured, lawns cut, grass edges trimmed, plants staked and tied, faded blooms removed, and so on. Such care makes all the difference in the world. In a small garden a little neglect looms large. In a big garden you can get away with more without spoiling its appearance. So be meticulous about housekeeping if you garden in town.

This roof garden depends on plants grown in tubs and boxes for foliage and floral effects.

Varying levels add interest to the above garden. A small, well-kept central lawn is surrounded by narrow borders of flowers and trees and shrubs.

At right, creeping plants set between widely spaced paving stones give an unusual pattern to terrace. Summer flowers will succeed the tulips

Mulching is one of the greatest aids. to tidiness. It conserves soil moisture and protects the roots from blazing sun. Mulching consists of covering the soil between growing plants with an inch or two of peat moss, buckwheat hulls, compost, leafmold or other suitable material Loosen the surface to a depth of an inch before applying.

If not mulched, stir the ground with a cultivator or hoe frequently enough to keep it always loose. But don't disturb the soil to a greater depth than one inch. If you do you will harm tender roots. Cultivate within twenty-four hours after every heavy rain or watering. Never cultivate near rhododendrons, azaleas, or related plants.

Mulching and cultivating destroy weeds and conserve ground water. Despite these aids you will find it necessary to water. Do this whenever your plants show signs of needing this attention. When you water, give enough to soak to eight or ten inches deep then no more until needed. Avoid frequent sprinklings that wet the top inch or two only.

Daily spraying, not intended to water the roots but rather to refresh foliage and flowers, is in order in warm weather. Do this in early morning or in the evening Use a forceful spray and reach the unde as well as the upper leaf surfaces. Thi removes grime and discourages red spide mites and some other pests.

Every spring your garden will nee fertilizing. Additional light applications o fertilizer should be made two or thre times during the summer.

Keep your plants within bounds by appropriate pruning, trimming, staking an tying. Stake inconspicuously. Keep th humus supply in your soil up by spreadin peat moss, rotted manure or compost eac fall and forking it into the ground eac spring.

Where ground space is unavailable, roo gardens find favor. Not all are costly. in stallations by professional landscapers Many are the work of amateurs.

Before you attempt such a garden chec that the roof is strong enough to bear th increased weight and that its surface wil stand walking upon. If you are a tenan obtain the owner's written permission be fore you begin such an undertaking.

Roof garden plants may be contained in tubs and boxes or in permanent beds formed of brick or comparable material. Let such containers be fifteen inches or more deep. Make sure that they will not hold water. Place three inches of cinders in their bottoms for drainage then fill to within an inch or two of their tops with a mixture of two parts rich topsoil and one part peat moss, with one tenth part of cow manure by bulk and a pint of bonemeal for each bushel added.

High winds and bright sunshine are common on roofs. Walls, tight fences and hedges of privet or other tough shrubbery form good windbreaks.

When choosing flowers for the roof garden, avoid tall-growing kinds such as sunflowers and cosmos, and don't select those that have frail blooms. All such are likely to be damaged by wind.

Use low-growing sturdy plants such as petunias, dwarf marigolds, wax begonias, torenias, sweet alyssum, low zinnias, geraniums, heliotropes, fuchsias, calendulas, verbenas, impatiens, tagetes, globe ama-

ranths, coleus, portulaca, lantanas, ageratums, ice plants, and salvias. Such vines as morning-glories, cypress vine, and cardinal climber may be used on walls, trellises and fences.

All these are temporary summer plants. Plants of a perennial nature, including trees, shrubs and vines, can be grown on the roof provided their roots are protected from being solidly frozen for long periods. This can be done by keeping them covered with a thick layer of leaves, straw or hay during the winter. Among perennial plants adapted to roof garden culture are roses, wistaria, silver lace vine, coreopsis, evergreen candytuft, Nepeta mussini, coral bells, thrift, bellflowers, and day-lilies.

The care of the roof garden does not differ much from that of the city garden at ground level. The chief difference is that more frequent watering is needed. In hot, dry weather a daily soaking is usually not too much. More frequent fertilizing is also in order. Make a very light application of a complete plant food once every two to four weeks. Keep all beds, boxes and tubs mulched with a few inches of peat moss. •

Seaside Gardens

The unique problems in combatting wind, wave, sun and spray can be overcome by the shore gardener with rewarding results.

TO make a garden by the sea calls for a little special know-how. Not all plants that thrive inland will grow by the ocean; to encourage those that will demands particular tricks and attentions.

The unusual conditions that face the maker of a seaside garden are (1) The possibility of exposure to salt spray. (2) Exposure to strong, more or less continuous, wind. (3) Intense light. (4) Lack of topsoil.

Extremely few plants will withstand repeated wetting by spray. Certainly, no flower garden plants will. If you want to garden as close to the sea as that, then fences or other barriers must be erected to ward off salt water.

Wind, more than any other factor perhaps, controls where you may or may not have a good garden near the sea. Quite apart from the damage it may cause by breaking plants down it has a serious drying effect. Without protection from wind, drought resistant plants only will thrive because from others the wind removes moisture faster than it can be replaced by the roots even though there be plenty of water in the soil. Walls, fences and hedges and trees may be used to give protection from wind. It is surprising how well plants thrive on the lee side of such barriers that would not grow at all to windward. Among the best plant for windbreaks are: Japanese black pine (it will grow in practically pure sand), dragon spruce (Picea asperata), privet, arborvitae, tamarisk, rugosa roses and beach plum. These stand the toughest conditions. For slightly better conditions a wider variety of trees and shrubs is available and includes other pines and spruces, honey-locust, red maple, birches, poplars, junipers, Japanese barberry, rose of Sharon, sweet pepperbrush, tatarian honeysuckle, inkberry, Scotch broom, hydrangeas, sea-buckthorn, and Russian olive.

Brilliant sunshine characterizes coastal areas. Much light is reflected from water and sand. The ultra-violet rays are intense. Because of this for your main plantings select sun-loving plants. In inland gardens you may succed in sunny locations with kinds that in nature favor partially shade, but not by the sea. If you want to grow shade-loving species there provide ample shade.

Soils by the sea vary. Where they are reasonably deep, loamy, and of fair quality their treatment does not differ from that of soils elsewhere, but more often they are extremely shallow, are very sandy or are even all sand. Where the latter extreme prevails it is practically essential to bring

Shelter from wind is all-important in good seaside gardens. A board fence here protects this border of gladioli, sedums, coreopsis and other flowers.

An ordinary glass cold-frame sash set on its edge will act as an efficient wind-breaker in this seaside garden. Rhododendrons and hydrangea are shown.

Sometimes a wet wind will whip around the corner of a house with cutting effect. A low fence with glass fitted between the pickets saves flowers.

in six inches (more is better) of topsoil before serious flower gardening can be done. The addition of manure, humus, peat moss, compost or other forms of organic matter improves sandy soils tremendously. Dig under as much of these as you possibly can. Topsoil and clayey material added to sandy soils improves them. More fertilizing is needed than on heavier soils. Nutrients soon wash out of sandy soil. Let little and often be the rule for applying fertilizers.

Seaside soils are usually light in color. They reflect heat and light to an extent that may be harmful. Keep the surface soil between plants mulched with peat moss, compost, buckwheat hulls or similar material to minimize this effect, to keep the roots cool, and to conserve moisture. Sandy soils dry fast. Plenty of watering must be done during spells of dry weather to keep plants coming along as they should.

If you live beside the sea all year you can begin your gardening operations in spring as gardeners normally do. Just allow for the fact that spring growth begins a little later at the coast than it does inland.

Should you not go to the seaside until late, the season may be too far advanced to sow annuals that require a fairly long period of growth and to lift, divide and plant perennials. The answer is to attend to the perennials in the fall and to rely upon quick maturing annuals such as sweet alyssum, calendulas and portulacas, or to purchase plants of slower growing kinds, ready started, from a nurseryman. As a matter of experiment you might like to try sowing some annuals such as poppies, larkspurs and cornflowers outdoors in late fall. On sandy soils they sometimes do quite well.

If you leave your seaside garden early, before winter is really upon it and the ground has frozen hard, it is too soon to do much about protecting perennials. Particularly it is too early to cover those that retain green leaves through the winter such as evergreen candytuft. No matter. Temperatures near the sea do not ordinarily go as low as those inland during the winter, the water acts as a moderator. In any case it is much better to leave perennials completely without winter protection than it is to cover too early. Their chances of survival are then much greater.

Plants to Use

Perennial plants specially suitable for seaside gardens are: thrift, dusty miller, yucca, loosestrife, rock-cress, coreopsis, irises, flax, evergreen candytuft, basket-of-gold, day-lilies, butterfly weed, hollyhocks, columbines, pinks, Silene maritima, sea-lavender, rose-mallow, sea-holly, sedums, globe-thistles, fleabane, coral bells, veronicas, blanket flower, anchusa, lavender-cotton, leopards-bane, artemisia, Nepeta mussini, babys-breath, peonies, and chrysanthemums.

Among the best annuals are: ageratums; calendulas, California poppy, poppies, coreopsis, candytuft, cornflowers, cosmos, gaillardias, globe amaranth, ice plant, larkspurs, lupines, marigolds, petunias, phlox, pinks, sand-verbena, salvias, love-in-a-mist, mignonette, strawflowers, portulacas, spider flower, sweet alyssum, verbenas, scabious, zinnias, snow-on-the-mountain, nasturtiums, geraniums, and lantanas.

Sweet Williams, pansies, gladioli and dahlias are also successful. •

Low fences with glass panels can be set out in the most effective pattern to overcome a mischief-making wind.

Grow Your Favorite Flowers

Detailed instructions on how to raise 15 popular varieties.

A formal bed of hyacinths.

Roses

A rose is a rose, but certain types won't bloom in certain localities. Find out what varieties are best for your garden, then give them the best care.

HYBRID TEA ROSE

THERE are many hundreds of varieties of roses grouped into a few distinct types, such as hybrid teas, hybrid perpetuals, dwarf polyanthas, floribundas, large flowered climbers and small flowered climbers. Except for pruning and minor cultural details all require the same care. They need full sunshine, good air circulation and deep. rich soil. Don't plant them in stuffy, damp corners, or crowd them where breezes rarely reach. If you do they will surely fall prey to disease.

Don't plant close to south-facing walls. In such situations reflected heat harms the foliage and produces hot, dry conditions which encourage red spider mites which suck the juices from the underleaf surfaces and cause a sickly yellowing.

Prepare the soil well before you plant. Spade it eighteen inches or two feet deep. Incorporate with it a three or four inch layer of half-rotted cow manure or, if this is not available, other animal (but not bird) manure, compost, leafmold or humus. Add bone meal at the rate of half a pound to a square yard and mix it thoroughly with the top foot. Roses like moderately heavy soil. Sandy soils are improved by adding loamy top soil. Do not add raw clay or heavy subsoil.

Sub-surface drainage must be satisfactory. Stones placed in the bottoms of the planting holes assure this in wet land only if the under layer is fairly porous, otherwise drain tiles must be installed.

Plant dormant roses in early spring or early fall. Started plants obtained in containers may be set in late spring even up to flowering time.

Make the holes big enough to allow for the full spread of the roots and for the plants to be placed so that the point of budding or grafting is just under the surface. Don't break the ball of soil that con-

When planting a started rose bush, make a large hole and put manure in.

Before setting bush in, carefully remove wrapper from around the soil-packed roots.

Place roses in so that graft-union on the stem is 2 inches below the ground level.

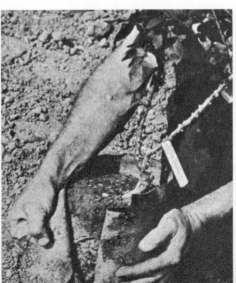

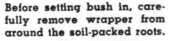

tains the roots of started plants. Pack good soil firmly around it and water well. Spread the roots of dormant plants more or less horizontal by packing good soil between them and firm well. No watering is ordinarily needed. Prune spring-planted dormant roses severely at planting time, those planted in fall lightly, and then severely the following spring. Started plants need no pruning.

Don't let roses lack moisture. During dry weather soak the ground to a depth of eight inches or more weekly. Apply a complete fertilizer each spring. Repeat this about midsummer if your soil is retentive and fertile; if it is sandy or gravelly fertilize every month up to and including August.

To keep roses free of pests and diseases, spray or dust repeatedly. Black spot marks the leaves with dark spots, turns them yellow and causes them to fall. Mildew forms a whitish film over the leaves and buds. Both are controlled by spraying with dormant strength lime-sulphur just before the buds burst in spring and by dusting or spraying with sulphur or fermate at weekly intervals, spring through fall. Sucking pests such as red spider, aphids and leaf hoppers are controlled by spraying with a nicotine insecticide, Japanese beetles and some other chewing insects by using DDT. All-purpose sprays and dusts are available and are effective if used weekly.

Hybrid teas bear large flowers throughout summer and fall. Prune out dead and thin shoots and shorten stronger ones to six or eight inches before buds burst in spring. For cut flowers disbud by removing all but the terminal flower bud from each shoot. Keep faded flowers removed. Protect against severe winters by hilling six or eight inches of soil about bases of plants just before ground freezes. Prune down to eighteen inches before hilling.

Hybrid perpetuals bear large flowers in June. They are mostly taller and hardier than hybrid teas. Prune and otherwise care for as for hybrid teas but leave the shoots retained about two feet long.

Dwarf polyanthas or baby ramblers produce small flowers in large clusters more or less all summer. Prune in early spring, removing only dead, thin, crowded and badly placed branches. Don't disbud. Otherwise care for as hybrid teas.

Floribundas flower in large clusters and are somewhat intermediate between dwarf polyanthas and hybrid teas. They bloom all summer. Treat like dwarf polyanthas.

Small-flowered climbers (ramblers) have large clusters of small flowers in June. Immediately after flowering prune out all flowering canes near their bases if enough new canes are developing to replace them. Otherwise, retain some old canes but trim them free of all side branches. In very cold climates remove canes from supports, pin to ground, cover with two inches of soil and with evergreen branches or straw, just before ground freezes. Replace in early spring.

Large flowered climbers are mostly one-time bloomers, although in the south climbing hybrid teas flower over a longer season and some few others tend to bloom more than once. Prune hybrid teas in spring, others immediately after blooming. Retain a framework of old stems, cut side branches back close to them. Occasionally remove old stems as young, vigorous ones become available to replace them. Otherwise treat like ramblers. •

With the bush in position, fill the hole with good soil around the rootball.

Next, take a tamper and pack the soil around the roots, filling air spaces.

Water well, then mulch surface with leafmold, compost or peat moss.

Irises

Care for bearded irises. In the autumn, pull off and burn all dead and loose foliage in order to reduce danger from diseases, blights and pests.

Friendly and faithful, these flowers respond to good care.

NEARLY all irises are easy to grow, although not all like the same soil and situation. For convenience, the numerous varieties are grouped according to types. Varieties of the same type require identical cultural conditions.

Bearded irises are the best known. They include dwarf, intermediate and tall varieties. The dwarfs bloom earliest (late April at New York) the talls latest (early June at New York). All thrive in any moderately good porous soil. Wet soil spells disaster. They need full sun.

Spade the ground and mix in a moderate amount of well rotted manure, compost or other organic matter, also bone meal at the rate of a third of a pound to each square yard. If distinctly acid, lime the soil.

Plant immediately after blooming, in early fall, or in early spring. Planting-size pieces are single fans of leaves (with the upper one third trimmed off) each with a husky section of fat, smooth rhizome (horizontal root-like stem from which the leaves sprout) attached. Plant so the tops of the rhizomes just show above the soil.

Allow nine to twelve inches between divisions. Every third or fourth year immediately after blooming lift, divide and reset. Fertilize each spring with bone meal and unleached wood ashes or with a complete fertilizer low in nitrogen. Lime whenever necessary to keep the soil neutral. Water during drought only. Keep well weeded but do not mulch. Pick faded blooms promptly. In fall, clean off and burn all brown and loose foliage.

Japanese irises bloom early in July at New York. They need full sun and deep, rather acid, soil well supplied with organic matter. They thrive beside pools and streams where their roots can reach moisture but where their crowns are well above water level. They grow well in borders and elsewhere provided they get plenty of moisture, spring through fall. They die in soils that are waterlogged in winter.

Spade the soil deeply and add at least a three or four inch layer of rotted manure, compost or peat moss. Cotton seed meal and bone meal or any complete garden fertilizer may be used too. Do not lime. Plant in early spring or early fall, spring preferred. Lift, divide and replant every three or four years. Let each division be of six or seven shoots taken from the outside of a clump. Set them two feet apart with their thin

To divide bearded iris, dig up plant and pull the large clumps of leaves and roots apart with hands.

Cut into smaller pieces with a sharp knife. Make sure that you discard any weak or diseased leaves.

Dwarf bearded irises bloom earlier than their tall relatives. They need full sun and a dryish, well-drained soil. These are excellent for rock gardens.

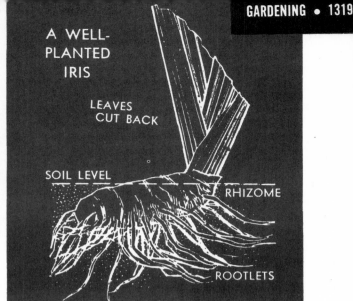

A WELL-PLANTED IRIS

LEAVES CUT BACK

SOIL LEVEL

RHIZOME

ROOTLETS

rhizomes two inches beneath the surface. Cut the upper third of the foliage off before planting. Japanese irises are gross feeders. Apply a complete fertilizer freely each spring; keep ground mulched always.

Siberian irises are May bloomers. They thrive under exactly the same conditions as Japanese but are better if not lifted and divided unless they are flowering poorly.

Louisiana irises are particularly valuable for warm sections of the country where bearded irises do not succeed. They respond to care accorded Japanese irises.

Dutch, Spanish and English irises, like tulips, have true bulbs and like tulips gradually die down after blooming and remain dormant through the summer. They bloom at New York in May and June and in the order named. They are fine for cutting. They need full sun, a light, warm, well-drained soil (except for the English which need a heavier and somewhat moister soil) and, in the north, shelter from north and northwest winds. Plant in late fall four or five inches apart, the tips of the bulbs four to five inches beneath the surface. In cold climates apply a heavy winter covering of leaves or salt hay after the ground has frozen. After foliage has died, lift, dry and store the bulbs in an airy, dry, shaded place until fall.

Other irises include iris cristata, iris gracilipes and iris tectorum which are dwarf species that thrive in light shade in moderately moist woodsy soil; they are well adapted for the rock garden. Iris pseudacorus (yellow flag) and iris versicolor (blue flag) are waterside species that thrive in bogs and wet soils. Iris reticulata is a tiny bulbous kind for a warm place and gritty soil in the rock garden.

All irises except bulbous kinds suffer from rhizome rot. Clean cultivation and good sanitation are preventatives. Dig affected plants. Cut out and burn all rotted parts, steep in a one to one thousand solution of bichloride of mercury (poison) for thirty minutes and replant in a new location. Leaf spot diseases affect Siberian and other irises. Control by removing and burning affected and all dead foliage and by spraying with fermate. Control iris borers (grubs that enter the leaves in spring, eat their way to the rhizomes and there feed until July) by spraying or dusting with DDT three or four times in April and May, and by destroying all grubs found when the plants are divided. Aphids sometimes appear. They are easily eliminated by spraying with a nicotine insecticide. Thrips, often particularly troublesome on Japanese iris are controlled with DDT. •

Cut back the foliage fully half way, as shown at right. These divisions are ready for re-planting.

Plant irises with rhizomes level with the ground. With foliage cut this way less moisture is lost.

Dahlias

The luxury-loving dahlia favors full sun, rich loam, plenty of air—and protection from frost.

YOU may grow dahlias on a wide variety of soils, if sub-surface drainage is good. A fertile medium loam suits them best. Heavy clay is unfavorable but can be made suitable by adding quantities of gritty cinders or sand, and rotted manure, compost, leafmold or other humus material. A four or five inch layer of sand or cinders, well mixed in, works wonders. A three or four inch layer of humus is not too much if the soil is lacking organic matter. The cinders and sand remain permanently; it is not necessary to add more each year. The humus gradually breaks down and disappears. It must be replenished.

Sandy soils grow better dahlias when improved by heavy dressings of rotted manure, compost, peat moss or other organic matter. Green manure crops turned under help greatly.

Whatever your soil is, spade it deeply and, in addition to organic material, mix in bonemeal at the rate of a third of a pound to each square yard and either unleached wood ashes (a pound to the square yard) or sulphate of potash (one and a half ounces to the square yard). As an alternative, use a complete fertilizer high in phosphate and potash but low in nitrogen. Add the organic matter in fall or, at latest, in early spring. Mix the fertilizers through the upper ten inches of soil a couple of weeks before you plant. Don't add them to the planting holes at planting time.

Dahlias thrive best on slightly sloping ground. They need protection from strong winds. They appreciate full sun but get along quite well with as little as five or six hours direct sunlight each day.

All except dwarf dahlias need staking.

Divide tuber clumps in spring, making sure that each division has a piece of stem attached to its upper, on which is an "eye." Don't divide till setting time.

Dig a hole six inches deep. A stake should then be driven in firmly. Put the division on its side, with the eye near stake. Then cover with soil and level.

When setting out young plants from a pot, make sure that they have a well developed system of roots. Don't break any off. Wet the rootball before planting

Drive the stakes before you plant. Wooden stakes one and a quarter inches square and of appropriate lengths are suitable. Space tall dahlias three to four feet, dwarfs one and a half to two and a half feet apart.

Set out "green plants" (young potted specimens raised from seeds or cuttings) or "tubers" (fat roots of last year's plants). The former are cheaper, the latter often easier for amateurs to obtain from home stocks. Dwarfs are often treated as annuals, raised from seeds and planted as green plants. Sow seeds indoors about twelve weeks before you expect to plant.

Plant tubers about the time common lilac passes out of bloom (late May or early June at New York). Before planting, divide clumps so that each division is a healthy, plump root with a small portion of last year's stem attached bearing an "eye" (growth bud).

Make planting holes six inches deep. Set each tuber horizontally with its eye near the stake and pointing up. Cover with two or three inches of soil.

Don't set green plants until the weather is warm and settled, usually about ten days after tubers are planted. Leave a three inch deep saucer-like depression around each plant. As the plants grow, fill soil around them until the surface is level.

Except with dwarfs, allow one or two shoots only to develop. When a foot high, pinch out their tips (except in northern gardens where the two-week delay in flowering caused by pinching prevents blooming before frost). If branches obviously crowd, prune out a few of the weaker ones. When large-flowered varieties form flower buds at their branch ends, remove all side growths from the stem for a distance of two or three pairs of leaves below the bud. Remove also the two smaller flower buds that appear beside each terminal one. Don't do this with small flowered types.

Tie the plants securely but not tightly with soft twine or narrow cloth strips. Keep the soil free of weeds and loose by cultivating shallowly once a week until mid-August. Then mulch with rotted manure, compost, peat moss or the like.

On fertile soils no fertilizing other than that done before planting is needed until mid-August. On poorer soils fertilize every month from the time the plants are a foot tall. Use a complete fertilizer high in potash and phosphate but low in nitrogen. In dry weather water often enough to prevent dahlias wilting. They like plenty of water after flowering begins.

After killing frost dig the root clumps without breaking. Shorten the stems to about an inch. Turn the clumps upside down. Let them dry in the sun for a few hours. Dust the cut stems with sulphur, wrap in newspaper and store where the temperature is between thirty-five and fifty degrees. In heated cellars store in a cool part and cover with peat moss or dry sand to prevent shrinkage through drying.

Common diseases include: *Stunt* (plants short, excessively branching, with pale mottling, blotching or crinkling of the leaves). Dig and destroy all affected plants promptly. *Wilt* (stems rot, leaves droop). Destroy affected plants and remove soil immediately surrounding them. *Mildew* (whitish coating on leaves). Dust with sulphur. •

With plant in place, pack good soil firmly about the rootball. Leave a saucer-like depression around the plant when finished. Water dahlia well immediately.

Put a stake in to support the plant, then remove superfluous side-shoots from the flowering stems by pinching them off at a point well below the new bud.

Tall dahlias need help to stand erect. Tie loosely so that the cord will not cut into growing stem. Use a square knot rather than a less secure granny knot.

Lilies

Lilies like to root in cool, shaded soil but show their blooms in sun.

NOT all plants commonly known as lilies are true lilies. Day-lilies are not, neither are plantain-lilies, foxtail-lilies, water-lilies, or lilies-of-the-valley. True lilies bear the botanical name Lilium. There are many kinds. All have bulbs. Not all are easy to grow. We shall consider those that are reasonably easy.

Lilies like cool soil. They don't thrive if the sun beats on it. Shade over their roots is highly desirable. To assure this, plant them among well-spaced peonies or other plants that provide shade without their roots interfering with the lilies.

Such plants are: columbines, meadow rues, germander, bleeding hearts, veronicas and lavender.

Suitable too are many low shrubs if not planted too thickly. Although lilies like their roots shaded, their upper stems and flowers should be in the sun or at most lightly shaded.

Lilies thrive in any deep, mellow soil that contains an abundance of humus, has good under drainage, yet is reasonably retentive of moisture. If your soil will grow potatoes it will grow lilies. Improve light, sandy soils by mixing with them considerable amounts of peat moss, leafmold or compost. One fourth or one third part (by bulk) of organic matter in the soil is not too much. Lighten heavy soils by adding gritty cinders, coarse sand and organic material. Never use manure unless it has decayed to a soft, spongy, amorphous state. Bone meal is a safe fertilizer to mix with the soil. Most lilies prefer acid soil, some such as the Madonna and henryi like neutral or even alkaline conditions. For these lime may be needed.

Fall is the best time to plant. Early spring is satisfactory provided the bulbs have not dried in storage. If bulbs do not arrive before the ground freezes prepare planting sites in advance and cover them with a thick layer of straw or leaves to prevent freezing. You may plant up to January provided you mulch the ground heavily afterward. Never transplant established lilies unless bulbs become so crowded that the quality of the flowers is threatened or unless you are forced to. When transplanting don't cut off roots or let them dry.

Set lily bulbs with their bases three times as far below the soil surface as the bulb is high. Exceptions are the Madonna and the Nankeen lilies. Plant them with their tips two inches beneath the surface.

Make your soil fertile to at least twice

planting depth. Large-flowered lilies and those known to multiply rapidly, such as henryi and umbellatum, may be spaced a foot or more apart. A little over half this distance is suitable for small flowered kinds such as pumilum. Plant in groups (in the cutting garden in rows) rather than singly. Place an inch or two of sand beneath each bulb and fill sand around and over it before you cover with soil. This aids in locating the bulbs and encourages rapid rooting.

Seasonal care is simple. Keep the soil always mulched with a two or three inch layer of peat moss, leafmold, pine needles, buckwheat hulls, rotted manure or other loose, organic material. Hand pull all weeds. Never use a hoe or cultivator near lilies. Water copiously in very dry weather. Fertilize in early spring with rotted manure and bone meal or with a complete fertilizer used at half the usual rate (use a quarter of a pound of 5-10-5 to each square yard) and repeat a month later. When staking, take care not to push the stake through the bulbs. When cutting flowers, be sure to leave one and a half or two feet of stem. Otherwise you may get no blooms the following year. Do not allow seed pods to form unless you wish to collect seed.

Here are the best Liliums, by name, color and blooming time: amabile, orange-red, June-July; candidum (Madonna lily) white, June-July; canadense, yellow to red, July; cernuum, pink, July; concolor, scarlet, June-July; elegans, yellow to red, June-July; formosanum, white, Aug.-Sept.; hansoni, orange-yellow, brown speckled, June-July; henryi, yellow-orange, Aug.-Sept.; longiflorum (Easter lily) white, not reliably hardy north, Aug.; pardalinum, red-orange, brown-spotted, July; pumilum (tenuifolum) red, June-July; sargentiae, cream, outside of petals brownish, Aug.; speciosum, white, pink and crimson, Aug.-Sept.; testaceum (Nankeen lily), apricot, July; tigrinum (tiger lily) orange-red spotted black, Aug.; umbella-

PLANTING LILY BULBS

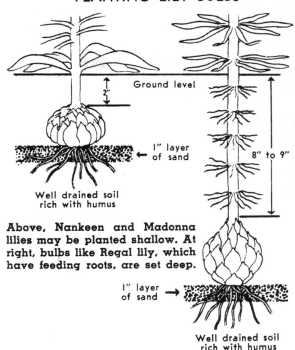

Above, Nankeen and Madonna lilies may be planted shallow. At right, bulbs like Regal lily, which have feeding roots, are set deep.

tum, yellow to red, July-Aug.; Green Mountain hybrids, white, darker on outside of flower, July; regale, white, outside of petals wine colored July; T. A. Havemeyer, buff, Aug.

Lilies are not difficult to raise from seeds but some kinds take several years before they bloom. Regale, pumilum, cernuum, amabile and concolor flower in about two years from seed.

Mosaic disease (pale mottling of foliage, stunting) caused by virus transmitted by aphids. Some lilies (candidum, speciosum, T. A. Havemeyer, elegans and tigrinum) show little ill effects but may be sources of infection. Grow them well away from other lilies. Destroy affected plants. Control aphids promptly by spraying with nicotine insecticide. Botrytis (spotting, blighting or rotting of leaves, stems and flowers). Pick and burn affected parts. •

If you grow regal lilies for cutting, pick off the anthers (left) before the yellow pollen discolors the petals. Anthers are at the ends of the stamens.

Potted Easter lilies (center) may be planted outdoors after danger of frost is past. Set rootballs six inches under surface, fill with good topsoil.

Tulips

Quality bulbs plus mellow soil plus good drainage equals tip-top tulips.

ANYONE can have grand tulips the spring following planting. All that is necessary is to buy quality bulbs and set them in fall in any fairly good soil that is not water-logged. To have the same bulbs flower for several successive years calls for a little more care. Here's how.

Buy the best bulbs. Don't fall for "special bargain offers" which bring you bulbs of sub-standard size at what (quite mistakenly) appear to be attractive prices.

Satisfactory tulip bulbs (except those of species —"botanical tulips") should measure 11 to 12 centimeters in circumference; at least 1½ inches in diameter. They should be solid and heavy; plump, not shriveled.

Get your bulbs as early as possible (early purchasers have the best choice) but don't plant until the end of October or the first days of November unless your ground is apt to freeze hard before then.

Unpack bulbs upon arrival. Notify the supplier at once if they are not in good condition. Store until planting time in open topped bags in a cool, dry place safe from mice and other rodents.

Tulips need deep, mellow soil, not enriched with fresh manure or containing excessive nitrogen. Sandy rather than clayey soils are best. Lighten clayey earth by mixing with it coarse sand or gritty cinders, compost, peat moss or leafmold.

Sharp drainage is imperative. You will not succeed if water lies around the bulbs.

The topsoil must be deep. Remember, roots strike downward from the bases of the bulbs which are at least six inches beneath the surface. These roots seek nutrients to provide strength for flowering the following year. They should have at

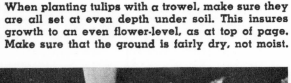

When planting tulips with a trowel, make sure they are all set at even depth under soil. This insures growth to an even flower-level, as at top of page. Make sure that the ground is fairly dry, not moist.

Don't let tulips form seed pods. At petal-fall, cut the young pod away. Seed production takes up energy that would be better used in fattening the bulb for a lovelier flowering when spring comes again.

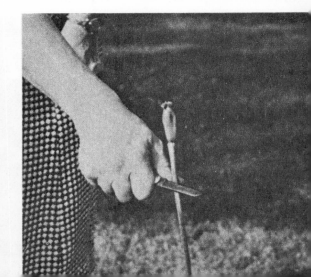

least six inches of fertile soil in which to ramify. The quality of the soil *beneath* bulbs is more vital than that *above* them.

Sometimes it pays to prepare for planting by digging out a foot of soil and putting the topsoil back in the bottom and the under soil on top. If the subsoil is very poor it is better to remove it and replace it with better material. Bone meal used at the rate of a pound to every two or three square yards is an excellent fertilizer. You may use, too, any complete fertilizer not high in nitrogen. Mix these with the soil to a depth of six inches or more.

Tulips thrive best in full sun. New bulbs bloom well in partial shade but are less likely to flower in succeeding years.

Plant when the soil is fairly dry. Minimum spacing between bulbs is six inches, nine to twelve inches if spring bedding plants are to go among them. Some planters remove the soil from the entire area to a depth of six inches, set the bulbs in position, then replace the soil. Planting each bulb individually with a trowel is just as good and less laborious. Be sure to set all at the same depth.

After planting, rake level. When the ground freezes hard apply a light covering of salt hay, leaves, or evergreen branches. Remove this gradually when the shoots show in spring. Then apply a complete fertilizer. Scratch it in lightly.

Tulips need plenty of moisture in spring. Water freely if dry weather occurs before their foliage dies naturally. To have good flowers in following years do not cut more than the uppermost leaf when gathering flowers. If you don't cut the flowers, don't let seed pods develop. Remove faded flowers promptly but not foliage until completely withered. If the bulbs must be taken up before this happens, dig them carefully and replant temporarily closely together elsewhere. As long as leaves are green they are working to fatten and strengthen the bulbs. Don't hasten their withering.

After the foliage is dead you may dig the bulbs, clean off old skins and soil, dust them with sulphur and store them in a cool, dry shaded place until fall. Don't expose them to strong sun for long periods. Spread them in shallow layers in trays with wire-mesh bottoms.

If you prefer, you can leave the bulbs in the ground. This is much less work and is as satisfactory. Only thing is, you must be content with setting easy-to-plant annuals over them. Nothing that involves digging more than four inches deep will do, otherwise you may injure the bulbs. Sweet alyssum, portulaca and California poppies are a few of the many annuals that can be used.

Varieties of tulips are numerous. The earliest to bloom belong to the Single Early and Double Early classes. Immediately following are varieties of the Mendel and Triumph classes. Most important are varieties of the May-flowering classes which include Darwins, Breeders, Parrots, Rembrandts, Cottage, and Lily-flowering tulips. Species ("Botanical") tulips bloom at various times in spring.

Mice eat tulip bulbs. They follow tunnels made by moles. Discourage moles by trapping, by using mole-nots, by any other means. Trap and poison mice but do not put such devices where birds, pets or children may be harmed. In extremely bad locations plant tulip bulbs in wire-net baskets. Botrytis or "Fire" disease causes spotting and rotting of leaves and flowers. Dig out and burn affected plants. •

For storage of the bulb over summer, wait until the foliage has completely died down, then remove bulb to cool, dry spot.

If you must move the tulips before their foliage is entirely dead, dig them up carefully so that soil is attached to roots.

After digging them up, heel in. This means laying them more or less horizontally in a shallow trench with tops above ground.

Gladioli

Glads will brighten beds and borders, are quick to grow and make the ideal bloom for summer cutting.

FEW flowers give as much satisfaction for as little trouble as do gladioli, or "glads" as they are called. They may be grown anywhere in the United States. They tolerate much neglect but repay good treatment. Individually they take little room so that a large number can be grown in a small space. They are tops for cutting and are good for setting among other plants to brighten beds and borders.

Glads grow from corms, (solid bulbs which, unlike true bulbs, renew themselves annually). The corms harvested are not the ones planted. Each is an entirely new growth developed on top of the original corm which, by harvesting time, has almost shrivelled away. It is important to understand this, for then you realize that the quality of the corms you dig, as well as of the flowers, depends upon your care. And upon the quality of the corms depends next year's flowers.

The best corms for planting are one-and-a-half inches or more in diameter, have small basal scars and are deep and high-crowned rather than thin and flat. Smaller corms bloom well under good conditions.

Make your first planting about the time the trees leaf out and successive plantings every two or three weeks until the latest date you can plant with expectation of bloom before killing frost. This depends upon your location and upon the variety. Some varieties of gladioli bloom in sixty days, others take a hundred and forty days, most need between seventy-five and a hundred days. In the South, use corms from cold storage for late plantings.

Glads will stand a little shade for part of each day but are much better in full sun. Any fairly good garden soil suits them. They do not like "wet feet" so drainage must be good. Do not use fresh manure when preparing the soil. Any well decayed organic matter such as compost and leaf-mold may be used advantageously. Bone meal and wood ashes are good fertilizers. Use the former a pound to three square yards, the latter a pound to one square yard. Alternately use commercial fer-

Gladioli corms are solid, bulb-like bodies. The best have high centers and are 1½ inches across.

tilizers at the same rates as in the vegetable garden (about 6 ounces of a 5-10-5 to a square yard). Apply all fertilizers a week or two before planting and mix them thoroughly through the soil.

In beds and borders, space glads six to nine inches apart. For cut flowers, plant in rows two and a half feet apart. If a single line of corms is planted in each row, allow four inches between individuals, if a double row, six inches. Plant four to six inches deep, the lesser depth if the corms are smallish or the soil heavy, the greater when reverse conditions hold. When planting in rows, open trenches or furrows, lay the corms in the bottom and fill back soil to surface level. When planting in beds and borders use a trowel and make large holes. Never use a dibble.

Clean cultivation is important. Stir the surface soil repeatedly but shallowly with the cultivator or mulch it. When the shoots of glads grown in rows are six inches high, hill three or four inches of soil against them. This supports them against storms. Provide additional support by stretching strings or wires between stout stakes driven at intervals along both sides of each row. Glads in beds and borders may be supported by other plants among which they grow, or by being tied to slender stakes. When their second leaves have fully developed apply liquid fertilizer and repeat twice monthly until the flowers show color.

When you cut glad flowers do not take more than two leaves. Leave the others to manufacture the food necessary to build good corms for blooming next year.

After gladioli have finished blooming, continue to cultivate and encourage the plants to keep growing. Eventually they will begin to die back. When the foliage has turned brown, dig the corms, cut off the foliage and spread the corms to dry in a shaded place where they will not be frosted. After about ten days, clean them off, dust them with DDT powder and store over winter in a dark or shaded place in a temperature of 40 to 50 degrees.

Glads are propagated by cormels (young corms) that form at the bottoms of the old corms. Often large numbers are produced. They have very hard outer coatings; therefore, before planting, soak them in water for several hours to soften them. Plant cormels in the same manner as regular corms but only about an inch deep and about half an inch apart. Harvest and store them in the fall as with ordinary corms. In from one to three years they attain flowering size.

Three common diseases are: *scab* (spots on lower parts of leaves, stems topple, varnish-like exudation from corms), *hard rot* (spotting at bases of leaves mummifying of corms) and *dry rot* (reddish brown corm lesions). Clean and soak corms in a one to one thousand solution of bichloride of mercury (poison) for one hour.

The commonest insect pest is *thrips* (foliage silvery, flowers streaked and deformed, plants stunted). Spray weekly throughout growing season with DDT. Dust corms with DDT powder before storing them for winter. *Aphids* (plant lice), sometimes are troublesome. Spray with nicotine insecticide. •

Glads need support against wind and storm. Interval stakes on both sides, stretch cord between.

Using a trowel, set the corms 4 to 6 inches deep, then cover them with fertile soil to ground level.

Groups of corms will make an attractive border. Be sure that the holes you make have space to spare.

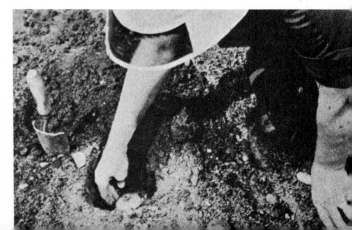

Peonies

Varied in form and color, these durable, decorative plants enjoy cold winters and live to be twenty-five.

PEONIES are of two main types, herbaceous, that die to the ground each winter, and tree, which have permanent woody stems and are actually low shrubs. The former are more common; tree peonies are very choice.

Herbaceous peonies are among the most hardy and decorative of garden plants. They are easy to grow wherever winters are fairly cold. They do not thrive in Southern gardens. They come in a great variety of forms and colors. If kept free of pests and diseases they may, without transplanting, bloom annually for a quarter of a century or more. Should they begin to deteriorate, transplanting may be desirable earlier.

Peonies grow best in full sun but get along with as little as six hours direct sunlight daily. They need rich soil, but not excessive amounts of nitrogen. One medium heavy and moderately moist is best but they thrive in a wide variety

The gaps in the peony stems below indicate where the small side buds of plant should be disbudded.

Botrytis disease is one of the commonest blights of peonies, causing the buds to wither unopened.

from clays to sands provided under-drainage is good and they get ample moisture. They will not thrive in soil that is invaded by tree roots. Dig deeply and mix through the soil humus-forming material such as old rotted manure, compost and leafmold. Don't use fresh manure and make sure that none not completely rotted comes in contact with the roots. If the manure is only partly decayed, spade it into the under soil at least six inches beneath the surface. Use bone meal and wood ashes. Half a pound of the former and twice as much of the latter to a square yard sprinkled over the surface and well mixed in is none too much. You may substitute one and a half ounces of sulphate of potash for each pound of wood ashes. Slightly acid soil is best. If decidedly acid, apply lime. Don't plant peonies where peonies have been before unless absolutely necessary. A change of location is good. Use the old ground for something else for four or five years.

Late summer or early fall is the best time to plant but you can do so later in the fall or early in spring. Planting divisions should each have three to five growth bud or "eyes". Make big holes and set the divisions so that when planted their eyes will be one to two inches beneath the surface. Deep planting is very harmful. Work good soil carefully among the roots and pack it firmly. Allow three to four feet between plants.

As routine care of herbaceous peonies, cultivate in around them a mixture of bone meal and a complete fertilizer when the shoots appear in spring. Four ounces bone meal and a 5-10-5 or comparable fertilizer to each square yard is satisfactory if the plants are moderately vigorous; if they are very robust omit fertilization. If growing in poor soil, increase the amount of fertilizer to six ounces to each square yard. Water during periods of drought, giving thorough soakings at weekly intervals rather than daily sprinklings. Keep weeds down, but be careful not to cultivate deeply close to the plants. Stake to prevent flopping. Remove faded blooms promptly and cut the stems off just below ground level and burn them after the foliage is blackened by frost.

If you want the finest flowers, disbud. This means remove all flower buds but the terminal one from each stem. Do this while they are tiny. Don't cut foliage when picking faded blooms; don't take more than necessary when cutting flowers. The plant needs its leaves to build its strength for future years. If possible, leave two or three leaves below the cut; cut no more than half of the total number of blooms from any one plant.

Practical propagation of herbaceous peonies is by division. Do this in late August or in September. Carefully dig up a large plant. Cut its foliage off and with a hose wash the roots free of soil. With a sharp, heavy knife divide the clump into divisions of three or more eyes each.

Tree peonies bloom earlier than herbaceous kinds. They require the same care except that they are not cut down in fall. They are somewhat less hardy; where winters are severer than in Boston, Mass., protect their stems by wrapping them in late fall in straw or similar material. Prune when necessary to remove weak stems and to rejuvenate specimens that lack vigor by inducing new growth. Tree peonies are propagated by seeds, which take many months to germinate, and by grafting.

For *botrytis blight* (buds shrivel without opening, stems and leaves decay) pick off and burn affected parts promptly. Spray with Bordeaux mixture when shoots are nine inches tall and repeat at ten day intervals. *Leaf spot diseases* (various spotting of foliage) spray with Bordeaux mixture. *Root knot* (plants dwarfed, small galls on roots) discard and plant new stock in new or sterilized soil, or immerse roots in water at 115 degrees F. for thirty minutes and plant in new or sterilized soil. •

Appearance of a dormant peony root as it appears in the fall. This root is now ready for dividing.

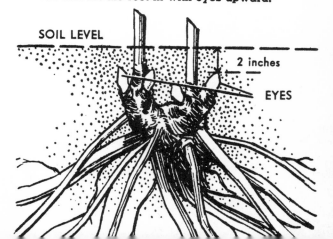

In planting peonies, fill in the hole with good loose soil and set the root in with eyes upward.

SOIL LEVEL

2 inches

EYES

Daffodils
and Narcissi

When spring is here can these garden guests be far behind?

DAFFODILS and narcissi are among the loveliest heralds of spring. Plant them plentifully and enjoy their flowers year after year. Pick the flowers freely, but if you want them to bloom year after year take little or no foliage. If you cut too many leaves the bulbs are robbed of the sustenance they need to grow fat and strong in readiness for next year's flowering. Mice and other rodents will not harm daffodil and narcissi bulbs as they do tulips, crocuses and some others. Without fear of these you can, at minimum expense, make a long-time investment that will yield floral dividends each spring for decades, with little care.

Plant daffodils and narcissi, I said. Just what is the difference between these? The truth is that daffodils are a type of narcissus. We call by this name those narcissi the flowers of which have large, bold

trumpets, trumpets that are as long as the petals. Sometimes daffodils are mistakenly called jonquils. True jonquils are narcissi that have slender rush-like leaves and a cluster of several small, very fragrant flowers at the top of each stem. In addition to daffodils and jonquils there are several other distinct types of narcissi.

A selection can be grown in every American garden. Some, such as the tazetta (polyanthus) group, are suitable for Southern states only; in the far north the poeticus varieties are more reliable than are daffodils. Under less extreme conditions a very wide variety can be grown. Yellow, varying to orange is the commonest color among narcissi; a few daffodils and many other narcissi have flowers that are white or predominately so; a few daffodils are of delightful pinkish hues.

Narcissi, unlike tulips and hyacinths, are

After blooming and before it dies, narcissus foliage tends to sprawl. To prevent such a condition, tie with a string.

Narcissi may be grown indoors for transplanting in gardens. Keep the pot watered till the leaves die, then remove plant.

Make sure that the plant has good system of roots before is set outdoors. Properly p out, it will bloom for year

not displayed at their best when planted formally in beds or borders. They are ideal for naturalizing in meadows, under scattered trees, at the fringes of shrubberies and woodlands and in orchards. They are excellent for grouping in perennial and mixed borders. Wherever located it is essential that their foliage ripens and dies completely before it is removed. If planted among grass it will be quite late before you can mow the grass. Consider this when selecting sites.

Obtain new bulbs as early in the fall as you can. Plant promptly on arrival. While success may be had from plantings made any time before the ground freezes, getting the bulbs into the earth in September is better than delaying until November.

Narcissi bulbs root downward from their bases. It is vitally important that the soil under them for a depth of six inches at least, be fertile. As the bottoms of the bulbs are set from six to eight inches deep, the soil must be good to twelve inches or more. It is useless to expect success if you merely dig holes into infertile subsoil and sink the bulbs in these.

Narcissi thrive in any ordinary soil; they will not do well in dry, barren earths or in those that remain wet for long periods. Spade deeply and add plenty of organic matter; compost is good—so is leafmold, humus and peat moss. Best of all is rotted manure, but it must be placed well below the bulbs; a two-inch layer of soil without manure should separate bulbs from manure. In addition, mix in five pounds of bone meal and three pounds of a complete fertilizer (analysis 5-10-5 or thereabouts) to each one hundred square feet. When planting, make holes big enough to let the bulbs go to their bottoms. Narrow-bottomed holes result in the bulbs jamming against the sides, leaving air pockets beneath, which is very bad. If planted in lawn or meadow no winter covering is needed but if in bare ground in colder sections of the country cover with straw, salt hay, leaves or evergreen branches after the ground freezes.

Care of established plantings of narcissi is simple. In early fall each year apply four or five pounds of a 5-10-5 or similar complete fertilizer to each one hundred square feet. In cold sections winter-protect those not growing in grass. If dry weather occurs in spring before the foliage dies, water copiously at weekly intervals. After the foliage dies remove it.

When narcissus plantings become crowded to the extent that bloom deteriorates in quantity or quality, lift the bulbs, rehabilitate the soil by spading, adding organic matter, and fertilizing and re-plant.

Lift as soon as the foliage has died (usually in early July). Sort to size. Plant the larger bulbs where flowers are wanted, the smaller in a nursery area or elsewhere where they can grow to flowering size.

You may re-plant immediately (the best plan) or store the bulbs in a dry, airy place, where they are not exposed to direct sun and plant them in fall.

In addition to the larger narcissi and daffodils there are a number of miniature kinds particularly suitable for the rock garden. Notable among these are the hoop-petticoats narcissus, the angel's tears narcissus, Narcissus cyclamineus, and narcissus minor.

Narcissi and daffodils are remarkably free of pests and diseases. There are some that affect commercial plantations but they are rarely troublesome in home gardens. If you suspect any, send samples to your State Agricultural Experiment Station for examination and diagnosis. Failure in home gardens is much more likely to be due to faults of soil or location than disease or insect. •

Sometimes bulbs are too small for the garden. After rubbing off loose skin and cleaning roots, sort them out for size.

When narcissi begin to crowd and the blooms deteriorate, dig up in summer after the foliage has withered and died.

Separate the bulbs, clean and replant them in deep, fertile soil. Smaller ones should be put in nursery beds to grow.

Poppies

These popular flowers are always dressed for a party, add gayety to any garden and behave well in mixed company.

MOST poppies are easy to grow if you give them plenty of sun and light, reasonably fertile soil. None like clayey earth or wet or shaded places.

Poppies are of two types, annuals and perennials. Sow seeds of annuals as early in spring as you can work the ground. In places where winters are not exceptionally severe sow in fall to have flowers in early summer. No elaborate preparation is needed. Annual poppies will grow in rather poor soil but repay reasonable efforts to improve it. Spade the ground. If deficient in organic matter add compost or other humus-forming material. Mix in a little bone meal or other fertilizer. Make the surface very fine. Sow broadcast or in rows a foot to a foot and a half apart and cover not more than a quarter of an inch deep. Most gardeners sow too thickly. Plants of the Shirley varieties should stand four to six inches, those of somniferum twelve to eighteen inches apart. Sow four or five times as thickly as these spacings and pull out surplus plants before they begin to crowd each other. Young plants of annual poppies cannot be transplanted with much prospect of success. Sow where you want the plants to bloom and discard surplus.

Don't let the flowers go to seed. This exhausts the plants and shortens their season of bloom. Use twiggy brushwood or other suitable stakes to give support.

Chief of perennial poppies are the gorgeous orientals with huge blooms of flaming reds, oranges, exquisite pinks and other attractive hues. Their ferny foliage is highly decorative, their seed pods handsome, their flowers dramatic in the garden landscape. They bloom in June.

Oriental poppies repay good cultivation. Even heavy soils can be made suitable for them if under-drainage is good. Mix with such soils a three to six inch layer of coarse

In this Western garden, Iceland poppies planted among Nemesia make a charming floral display.

sand or gritty cinders and great amounts of humus, leafmold or compost. Don't use manure unless it is completely rotted. On lighter soils omit the sand or cinders but not the organic matter. Planting in raised beds is a partial solution to the drainage problem if natural drainage is not too good.

When selecting sites for oriental poppies bear in mind their one bad habit: their foliage dies down completely about mid-summer. This leaves a conspicuous "hole" if the plant is in a mixed border. Such gaps may be masked by setting out from pots quick growing annuals such as petunias, marigolds and balsams. New poppy foliage appears in fall and remains green through the winter. Oriental poppies need at least two feet between plants; an additional six inches or a foot is advisable.

Plant in September if possible. Make each hole three inches deeper than the length of the thick roots. Set the roots upright with their tops two inches below the surface, pack good soil around them and water thoroughly. If dry weather follows, soak at weekly intervals.

Oriental poppies are best when undisturbed. Don't transplant unless quite necessary. Each fall before the ground freezes make sure there are no depressions around the plants that may hold water. After hard freezing mulch the soil with loose salt hay, straw or dried grass. Don't use peat moss, manure or anything else that holds water and prevents air circulation at the base of the plants.

Remove the mulch in spring. Immediately afterward apply a complete fertilizer and an inch deep mulch of leaf-mold, compost or humus. Don't hoe near oriental poppies. Hand weed. Careless hoeing is responsible for many failures.

Propagation may be done in August by careful division or by cuttings consisting of pieces of the thick roots trimmed cleanly across at top and bottom and planted in sandy soil.

Iceland poppies, although technically perennials, are best treated as annuals or biennials. They come in a great variety of colors and last longest of any poppies when cut. They are splendid cut flowers. A light, fertile, well drained soil suits them. Unlike annual poppies, seedlings of these may be transplanted fairly easily if you are careful not to break their roots.

Sow in a frame in mid-August or indoors in January. Transplant the seedlings to sandy well-drained soil outdoors, in a cold frame, or, in the case of those raised from a January sowing, to flats. Grow at all times under cool, airy conditions. In early spring, set the plants where they are to bloom. Allow about a foot between individuals. Iceland poppies succeed best where summer nights are cool.

The Alpine poppy is really a very dwarf edition of the Iceland poppy. It requires the same culture. It is a good rock plant.

Diseases and Pests

Diseases: *Mildew* (whitish patches on leaves, stems distorted, plants collapse). Spray with Bordeaux mixture. *Bacterial blight* (water soaked spots which turn black on leaves, stems and flowers). Destroy badly infected plants. Plant clean stock in new location or sterilize old soil. Pests: *Aphids* (plant lice). Spray with nicotine insecticide. *Four-lined plant bug, tarnished plant bug* (both puncture leaves and stems and suck juices causing distortion and spotting of buds, stems and leaves). Dust with rotenone. Spray with DDT. •

Shirley poppies, delicately petaled, are one of the loveliest of annuals. Do not transplant them.

Iceland poppies are very hardy and make excellent cut flowers. They thrive where summers are cool.

Hyacinths

High and scented, these blooms of military bearing will command your attention and capture your fancy.

HYACINTHS—Dutch hyacinths—the kinds that bear tall, stout, cylindrical spikes of sweet scented flowers in early spring are among the most noble of garden flowers. They carry themselves in soldierly fashion, erect and commanding in appearance. Because of this deportment they are adapted best for planting in beds and borders in precise ranks that emphasize the formality and gardenesque quality of both beds and flowers. For terrace and lawn beds near the house or other architectural features they are ideal. They may be used somewhat less primly along the fronts of mixed flower borders, planted in drifts or groups, mingled with early flowering ground-covers such as rock-cress, forget-me-nots, pansies, basket-of-gold and English daisies.

Spring bedding plants such as these interplanted with hyacinths are effective in formal beds too. Try a yellow hyacinth among blue forget-me-nots, blue dwarf polemonium or purple aubretia; or a clear soft porcelain blue one among a mixture of forget-me-nots and white rock-cress. Carmine and white hyacinths dotted among pale blue forget-me-nots are stunning; so too are pink hyacinths among a mixed planting of white and pink English daisies. Many other attractive combinations can be worked out.

Dutch hyacinths are not suited for naturalizing—at least not when you first obtain them from your dealer. It is a fact, however, that under garden conditions the character of the flowers borne changes. Even in their second season the flower spikes are less obese and regular than are those of first year bulbs and after two or three seasons in the garden they usually are much looser and informal in appearance and often each bulb carries more than one spike. When they reach this condition they resemble very heavy Spanish bluebells and are well suited for planting along the fringes of shrubbery or in other semiformal places; they are then less adaptable for formal bedding.

Hyacinths may be had in a great variety of colors. Catalogs usually list more than one size of bulbs. It is not necessary, indeed it is not wise, to buy the largest exhibition bulbs for outdoor planting. Reserve them for forcing indoors. For your outdoor effects buy the best grade of bedding size bulbs. These should measure 6 to 7 inches in circumference, about 2¼ inches in diameter, and be plump and heavy.

Plant your hyacinths early in fall, earlier than tulips. It is important that they have as much time as possible to develop roots before the ground freezes. Make sure that the soil is fertile and well drained and at least a foot deep. It's no use expecting success from bulbs planted in raw clay or other unsuitable subsoil; after all, they must send their roots into whatever is *under* the bulb; they do not root upward.

Lighten clay soils by adding coarse sand or gritty cinders. Add compost or other organic matter, except manure, and bone meal at the rate of one pound to every three square yards, to all soils except the most fertile.

Plant so that the tips of the bulbs are 4-5 inches beneath the surface and, if they are to be without other plants between them, space them 6-8 inches apart. If interplanted with other spring flowering plants space the hyacinths about a foot apart. Where cold winters occur, mulch the beds with straw, leaves or other covering during the winter but remove this in early spring. If really dry weather occurs

at any time while green foliage is above ground, water thoroughly every four or five days. If hyacinths are in locations where you want to replace them with summer flowers, dig them after their foliage dies naturally and store them through the summer one layer deep in trays with bottoms of wire mesh in a cool, dry, airy place. Handle carefully so that they are not bruised. If you *must* move them before the foliage is brown, keep as much soil to the roots as possible and re-plant them immediately, closely together, in some out of the way place where they get some shade and can be watered and kept healthy as long as they will grow. Finally, when the foliage turns brown, store them as already advised. The longer the foliage keeps green the stronger the bulbs will be for the following year. Hyacinth bulbs located where it is not essential to move them to make way for other plantings may be left in the ground over summer.

In addition to the ordinary Dutch hyacinths there are others that have merit, notably the Roman hyacinth. Unfortunately, this is not hardy North, but for Southern gardens it is charming. It is white flowered, slenderer and more graceful than its larger-flowered kin, and each bulb produces several flower stems. It is equally as fragrant and blooms earlier than the Dutch hyacinths and it needs the same general culture. In Southern gardens are found too, hyacinths that in general resemble Roman hyacinths but are lavender, light purple or, more rarely, pink. Because of their informal appearance they can be used advantageously for naturalizing and when happily located multiply freely and bloom profusely each spring.

The Little Hyacinths

In addition to the big hyacinths, the Dutch and Roman varieties, there are a few tiny ones that the casual observer would scarcely recognize as such. They are the species of Hyacinthus (botanical name of hyacinths) suitable for choice spots in rock gardens, at the fringes of shrubberies and similar places where one would ordinarily plant grape-hyacinths, squills and glories-of-the-snow. They need well drained fertile soil and full sun or very light shade. Once planted they may remain undisturbed for years and if conditions are at all favorable increase bountifully. Of these, try amethystinus (6 ins. tall, light blue), ciliatus or azureus (9-10 ins. tall, blue) and romanus (1 ft., blue and greenish white). Plant in fall 2-3 ins. apart and 3-4 ins. deep. •

Chrysanthemums

This younger generation of mums has left the oldsters far behind in size, variety, range of colors and length of blooming season.

NO flower has been more spectacularly improved than the chrysanthemum. Today it is undisputed queen of autumn. If you know only older varieties that bloom so late that frost often kills them before their flowers expand and that have smallish blooms in a limited variety of colors, you have a great surprise in store. Modern mums are numbered in hundreds, even thousands of varieties. They range in height from a few inches to four feet or more, in flower-form from tiny pom-poms to large dahlia-like decoratives, with singles, semi-doubles, anemones and other intermediates. Many are more winter hardy than the old timers. They have flowers of white, cream, yellow, apricot, bronze, crimson, pink, lavender, everything except blue. The blooming season has been extended so that the earliest bloom reliably, even where killing frost comes early. And the end is not yet. Breeders each year offer new and better kinds.

Growing quality mums is simple. All you need is good soil, healthy stock, plenty of sunshine and the application of a little easily acquired know-how. Mums will grow in any soil that is reasonably good so long as it has no tendency to hold stagnant water. Drainage must be sharp. I have seen chrysanthemums flourish in

Chrysanthemums need rich, deep soil for the best results. Dig in plenty of compost and manure and each year prepare the soil anew and then re-plant.

nearly pure sand by the sea and I have grown them on stiff clays.

Fortify sandy soils by adding considerable organic matter, by generous and frequent fertilizing, and by watering freely during dry weather. In summer, mulch with organic material. Improve clay soils by digging them in fall and leaving them exposed in rough lumps to winter weather, by liming and by mixing in gritty cinders, or coarse sand as well as humus-forming material. Do not walk about on clay soils when they are wet. Chrysanthemums grow best in slightly acid or neutral soils.

In early spring, a week or ten days before you plant, fork into the upper four inches of soil a complete fertilizer (a 5-10-5 say) at six ounces per square yard.

Set plants raised from cuttings or from well-rooted single shoot divisions. If the latter, be sure they are not taken from plants that suffered from leaf nematodes the previous year. If the ground is dryish, water well. A few hours later cultivate shallowly and repeat at ten day intervals and after every rain until the plants nearly touch and make further cultivation difficult. Mulching with peat moss, buckwheat hulls or similar material reduces the need for cultivation and helps prevent the spread of nematodes.

When mums are four inches tall pinch out their tips. Repeat this on all branches and sub-branches until the third week in July. Don't pinch later. Mums like moisture. Never let them wilt. Soak the soil deeply at about weekly intervals during dry weather. Don't sprinkle every day.

On sandy or poor soils, fertilize regularly through the summer. Two ounces of a 5-10-5 fertilizer (or equivalent) applied to each square yard every two weeks is not too much. On more retentive soils less frequent fertilizings are satisfactory. None at all may be needed after planting if the soil is heavy and rich. Be guided by the appearance of the plants.

Mums need supporting. For this use brushwood, stakes or bamboos. Secure the plants firmly but be sure their branches are disposed naturally. Don't bunch them.

You may improve the size and quality of large flowering varieties by disbudding. This consists of removing, while small, all the flower buds that surround each central terminal flower bud on each stem. This does not apply to the occasional buds that appear in July or August but to the later ones from which flowers are expected.

Chrysanthemums are easily propagated by division or by cuttings taken in spring. Use only the latter if the stock plants had nematodes. Let the shoots grow long in a cold frame or greenhouse and use their tips only for propagation. Be careful not to wet the foliage when watering.

Diseases and Pests

Leaf Spot (yellowish spots becoming dark brown or black). Spray with Bordeaux mixture. *Wilt* (stunting, yellow leaves, failure to bloom). Destroy affected plants. Plant clean stock in new soil or sterilized old soil. *Mildew* (whitish film on foliage). Avoid wetting leaves. Dust with sulphur. *Aphids* (plant lice). Spray with nicotine insecticide. *Tarnished Plant Bug* (stems crooked beneath flowers, blooms distorted). Destroy weeds nearby. Dust with rotenone. *Leaf nematode* (yellowish brown wedge-shaped spots enlarging until entire leaves are brown and dry). Plant clean stock in soil where mums have not been grown for a year or in sterilized soil. Keep ground mulched. Spray regularly with mixture of nicotine and Bordeaux mixture. •

Division is a satisfactory way of propagating chrysanthemums, providing old plants are good.

See to it that each division consists of a single shoot and a healthy root system attached.

To keep mums bushy, pinch out tips of shoots occasionally in the spring and in early summer.

Day-Lilies and Plantain-Lilies

Looking for something colorful and easy to grow? These blossoms will suit you down to the ground.

DAY-LILIES (Hemerocallis) and plantain-lilies (Hosta or Funkia) are grand plants if you seek something colorful, decorative and easy to grow. Neither demands much skill or care, both bloom freely during summer or fall. Plantain-lilies are among the finest plants for shaded locations; day-lilies grow well in full sun or partial shade. Day-lilies have flowers of lemon, yellow, orange, brown, maroon, tawny-red and pinkish tones; plantain-lilies are white, lavender and near-blue.

Day-lilies may be grown anywhere in the United States; for Southern gardens those that have evergreen foliage, such as aurantiaca, aurantiaca major, fulva, and Mikado are best. They are not particular about soil, any that is fairly good will do. They thrive with average moisture, in rather dry locations, and in moist places by streamside or pond. They will not take absolute bog conditions nor extreme dryness. If the soil is too rich they are likely to produce excessive foliage and too few flowers. Too much shade has a similar effect and may result in slender, weak

flower system needing special care.

Early spring and early fall are the best times to plant. Divide overgrown plants then, too. Both dividing and transplanting can, however, be successfully accomplished at any time. They are simple procedures. Merely dig up the plant and split it into pieces, each having three or four shoots and a goodly amount of roots.

If foliage is present, cut it back to about a foot long. Set the plants so that when finished their crowns are an inch under the surface. Spread the roots, work good soil among them and make quite firm. Water if soil is dry. Space from two to three feet apart according to the spread the particular kind attains. If planting is done in the fall mulch around, but not over, the plants after the ground freezes to prevent heaving by alternate freezing and thawing.

Day-lilies need scarcely any seasonal attention. Remove old stems after the flowers fade and cut off old foliage just before new shoots start in spring. In Northern gardens kinds that keep their foliage green through the winter may

suffer somewhat then; to prevent this, apply a protective covering of salt hay, straw or evergreen branches after the soil freezes.

Unless in extremely poor soil, day-lilies need little or no regular fertilizing. Do not use lime unless the soil is very acid, they prefer slight acidity. Bone meal or other fertilizer low in nitrogen is best for them. Apply a moderate amount each spring if foliage growth is not too lush. Watering is not needed unless soil becomes extremely dry as in droughts.

All withstand hot weather well; each day of their blooming season new perfect flowers open no matter what may have harmed those of the day before. Day-lilies bloom the first season after planting but are not at their best until their second or third season.

Day-lilies are useful not only for beds and borders but for naturalizing, holding banks and for cutting. Many bloom when other flowers are scarce.

Plantain-lilies come in fewer kinds than day-lilies, and those mostly natural species rather than products of the plant breeder. They are long-lived and easy. They form attractive specimens both in foliage and flower and are useful in beds, borders, and as ground covers. The larger leaved ones such as sieboldiana, fortunei gigantea and caerulea are magnificent as bold specimen clumps, others are wonderful for grouping.

Plantain-lilies appreciate deep, rich, fairly moist soil that contains plenty of organic matter. Before planting add compost, manure, leafmold or peat moss liberally; a three-or-four-inch layer turned under is not too much. Plant early spring or early fall, space according to kind to allow for full spread at maturity. Let each division consist of two to four shoots with

Hosta undulata, a popular plantain-lily, is pale lavender, with leaves that have a white center.

roots attached. Set them with their crowns an inch below the surface.

Once planted, plantain-lilies may remain undisturbed for many years. Keep the ground cleanly cultivated or, better still, mulched. Apply a complete fertilizer each spring. (Six ounces of a 5-10-5 to a square yard.) Among the best Hostas are: plantaginea, flowers white, fall; caerulea, dark lavender-purple, summer; japonica, lilac, summer; japonica albo-marginata, like japonica but white-margined leaves; sieboldiana, light lilac or white, summer; fortunei, lilac, summer; fortunei gigantea, like fortunei but larger; undulata, light lilac, summer, leaves white and green; decorata (Thomas Hogg), dark lilac, white-margined leaves, summer.

Neither day-lilies nor plantain-lilies suffer much from diseases or pests. *Thrips* feed on day-lilies (flowers die without opening, young foliage dies prematurely). Spray with DDT. *Slugs* attack plantain-lilies (leaves eaten in lacy pattern). Clean up debris and hiding places, use baits. •

Hosta caerulea has the darkest flowers among all plantain-lilies, being lavender-purple in color.

Day-lilies brighten the corner of this back yard. They are not choosy about soil, need little care.

J. Horace McFarland

Delphiniums

These flowerful blooms can well afford to be generous—and are.

DELPHINIUMS are technically perennials. However, in many gardens they are short-lived and must be propagated fairly frequently. Propagation by seeds is easy. Use the best only. Get a good "strain" from a specialist or from a seedsman who sells specialist's seeds in the originator's packets, or save seeds directly from exceptionally fine plants.

Old seeds often won't grow. Sow shortly after they are gathered or store in sealed packets where the temperature is about 50 degrees. Don't store beyond 60 days.

Preferred sowing times are late August or early September (in cold frames or in sheltered beds outdoors), January or February (in greenhouses or sun-rooms where temperatures between 50 and 60 degrees exist), March or April (outdoors or in cold frames)

Plants from March-April sowings won't bloom their first summer. August-September and January-February sown plants bloom their first summer between the first and second blooming of old established plants and again after their second flowering. Thus, by raising a few new plants each year you can have a continuous succession of blooms. In June, the first flowers from two-year and older plants appear. These are followed immediately by those of the new seedlings. By the time these have passed, the older plants are producing their crop which is followed in September by the second blooming of the seedlings.

Seed soil for delphiniums should be light but not woodsy. Mix equal parts good topsoil, peat moss or leafmold, and coarse sand. Add a sprinkling of lime. If the mixture seems not porous enough to drain freely, add more sand. Sow in well drained flats or beds. Don't cover the seeds with more than one eighth of an inch of soil and don't pack it. Firm slightly.

Keep the seed bed always moist but not constantly saturated. Shade until the seedlings break through. Delphiniums germinate rather slowly.

When four true leaves have developed, transplant the seedlings to beds, to flats or small pots. Don't do this later in fall than a full month before the ground freezes. Transplant into soil similar to the seed soil but coarser and with a little well rotted (or dried) manure and bone meal added. Space two to three inches apart. Protect fall-sown seedlings by covering them after the ground has frozen with cold-frame sashes or with a light layer of salt hay, leaves or evergreen branches. Don't use peat moss or other mulch that holds water and packs.

Set plants raised from August-September and January-February sowings in their flowering positions in April. In early fall, transplant those raised from March-April sowings to the places where they are to bloom.

Delphiniums need full sun. They grow well in a wide variety of soils but resent wetness and excessive acidity. They like best a deep, well drained fertile loam that is neutral or slightly acid and is fairly supplied with humus. When preparing the ground incorporate a two inch layer of rotted manure as well as bone meal at the rate of a pound to every three square yards, or a two or three inch layer of compost, leafmold or similar organic material and a complete fertilizer (a 5-10-5 at the rate of a pound to each three square yards is O.K.) Use lime to reduce acidity.

Established delphiniums need three to four feet between individuals. I like to space first-year plants about two feet apart and re-space them the second season.

Seasonal care is not arduous but calls for repeated attention. In early spring, remove winter covering (such covering is not necessary except for fall-planted delphiniums), apply a complete fertilizer and fork it shallowly into the soil. If too many shoots develop (a first-year plant can carry four or five, an older plant twice as, many) cut out the weakest while small. Stake and begin tying before the stems are two feet tall. Make additional ties as growth necessitates. Water copiously during dry weather. Keep the surface soil shallowly cultivated to admit air and destroy weeds.

Unless you want seeds, snip flower spikes as soon as the flowers fade. Don't cut them low. Let the plant retain as much foliage as possible.

After the first flowers go, delphiniums rest briefly then produce from their bases new shoots which bear a second crop. When these are a few inches tall apply a complete fertilizer high in potash.

Diseases and Pests

Crown and root rots (foliage wilts, crown and roots decay) are serious. Destroy affected plants and drench soil around them with a one to one thousand solution of bichloride of mercury (poison). *Bacterial blight* (irregular black spots on leaves) and *mildew* (white film on leaves) are not very serious. Dust with sulphur. *Virus stunt* (dwarfing of plant, pale mottling of foliage). Destroy affected plants. Microscopic mites cause "blacks" (dwarfing, distortion of leaves, blackening of flower buds). Destroy badly affected plants. Spray repeatedly with rotenone at double ordinary strength. *Snails and slugs.* Encircle plants with layer of gritty coal ashes sprinkled with lime. •

At right, stems should not be cut like this, for such low, unkind cuts serve to weaken the plant.

When cutting delphiniums (above) leave plenty of foliage on the plants. Also keep the stems long.

Hydrangeas

A little planning and foresight weeds out much trial and error.

THE failure of certain hydrangeas to bloom is a common trouble. The kinds that usually fail are varieties of the summer-flowering macrophylla group—those that have large globular heads of pink, blue or occasionally white flowers and are sometimes called French hydrangeas. Failure is nearly always because something has destroyed the terminal shoot buds which are the only buds of most macrophylla varieties that produce blooms. In northern gardens these fat buds may be killed by winter cold. If the cold is not excessive you can adequately protect them by wrapping their branches in straw or similar material in late fall after the ground has frozen. Remove this when leaf growth begins in spring.

Faulty pruning is another common reason for these hydrangeas not blooming. Any cutting in fall, winter or spring that removes the ends of stout shoots is likely to prevent flowering. This is not invariably the case; a few macrophylla varieties will bloom on side shoots that develop after the terminal bud is cut off—but don't bank on this unless you know for certain that your plant behaves in this way. Trial and error is the only way to find out.

The proper time to prune these hydrangeas is in late summer immediately after their flowers fade. At that time strong new shoots push from among the older stems. Leave these untouched. They are the ones that should bloom the following year. It is the terminal buds on these that must be preserved. Prune out the shoots that have flowered. Cut them as low as possible without taking any new shoots that arise from them that you want to retain. Cut out also any weak and spindly shoots that crowd the bush without giving promise of bloom.

This method of pruning applies also to the oak leaved hydrangea (Hydrangea quercifolia) and to Hydrangea sargentiana. It does not apply to the hills-of-snow (Hydrangea arborescens grandiflora) or to the pee-gee (Hydrangea paniculata grandiflora). These popular kinds flower on current season's shoots rather than on stems developed the previous year. You may prune them back in spring close to the bases of the shoots that developed the previous summer. The removal of terminal buds is of no moment.

Pink flowered macrophylla hydrangeas have pink flowers only if the soil is neutral or alkaline; in acid soils their flowers are blue. Lime added to the soil causes alkalinity; sulphur added causes acidity.

Perhaps the surest method of bringing about acidity and hence blue flowers is to water every two weeks during spring and early summer with a solution made by dissolving one pound of aluminum sulphate in five gallons of water. Apply about one gallon to each plant at each watering. To make penetration surer stab the soil deeply with a fork before applying the liquid. White flowered kinds can not be induced to change colors.

Hydrangeas when well located and flourishing are excellent shrubs for American gardens. They succeed splendidly in coastal areas and are often at their best quite close to the sea. This is particularly true of the macrophylla varieties and also of the climbing hydrangea (Hydrangea petiolaris). This plant, which normally clings to masonry or tree trunks like ivy and grows to a height of fifty feet or more may be trained to cover low walls as well as high ones. It is very effective in summer with its lacy heads of white flowers.

When considering hydrangeas for planting bear in mind several kinds that are not as frequently seen in gardens as are the French types, the pee-gee and hills-of-snow. Notable among others are the fertile flowered forms. These, like the climbing hydrangea, have heads composed of two distinct types of flowers, numerous tiny fuzzy ones and fewer large showy ones. The combination gives a lacy, daintier effect than when the heads are all of large flowers as is the case with the kinds commonly grown.

The fertile form of the pee-gee hydrangea (the kind called Hydrangea paniculata rather than Hydrangea paniculata grandiflora) is one well worth having. It is an excellent change if you are tired of pee-gee, and its blooms are elegant as cut flowers. There are also splendid fertile varieties of macrophylla and one of hills-of-snow, the latter is named Hydrangea arborescens (not arborescens grandiflora).

Most hydrangeas thrive best in a sunny situation although they will stand light shade. The oak-leaf kind, Hydrangea quercifolia, is good in shaded places. It is remarkable for its large lobed leaves and looks well when planted in bold masses. Sargentiana is another kind that prefers light shade. It is of distinctive appearance with its hairy stems, large leaves and large flat clusters of small bluish white fertile flowers and large white sterile ones. All hydrangeas thrive best in a fairly rich soil that is not too dry. They wilt badly when lacking moisture but soon recover if water is applied promptly and generously.

Hydrangeas are easy to increase. Some, such as macrophyllas, from clumps which can be dug in early spring and with an axe or sharp spade can be divided into sections, each consisting of a husky mass of roots and a few shoots. Re-plant the pieces promptly in fertile soil. All hydrangeas can be increased by cuttings of leafy shoots planted in sandy soil in a shaded location in July and covered with a Mason jar.

A vine related to Hydrangea and sometimes listed as "climbing hydrangea" is Schizophragma. Like the true climbing hydrangea it is a tall grower that clings to masonry or tree trunks by aerial roots. It blooms somewhat later than Hydrangea petiolaris and its sterile flowers have each only one large white sepal rather than four as in the true hydrangeas. It is an excellent vine and thrives under conditions suitable to hydrangeas. •

Pee-gee hydrangeas, such as shown in bloom on the opposite page, may be pruned in either winter or spring by cutting back old flowering shoots.

This unusual hydrangea has highly variegated patterns in its foliage. It is a variety of French hydrangea, a summer-flowering macrophylla group.

Wistarias

Sometimes it takes a wistaria twenty years to bloom. But when it does, you'll say it is worth the wait.

"MY wistaria grows well but doesn't bloom," is a common plaint. What can be done about it? you ask. Mature, suitably located wistarias that are making balanced growth, flower freely. Those that don't are immature, are planted where conditions are unsuitable or are making excessive vegetative growth.

Wistarias raised from seeds often don't bloom for many years, perhaps ten, twenty or more. Until they reach the flowering stage they are immature. Don't plant seedlings; use instead grafted plants, the grafts or scions of which have been taken from plants of known flowering ability. These should bloom after two to four years.

Lack of sufficient sunshine is a common environmental condition that prevents flowering. Wistarias grow well but will not bloom freely in shade.

Over-vigorous growth, the production of excessive leafage, commonly results from faulty pruning and from too much nitrogen in the soil. Even grafted plants that bloomed in the nursery may give way to this for a few years after they are set in rich soils where their roots can run without interruption.

Check this by pruning twice a year instead of once. Summer—prune as soon as the new shoots have formed eight or nine leaves. Cut off their tips so that only seven or eight leaves are left on each shoot. If side growths develop from these shortened shoots pinch out their tips promptly just above their first or second leaf. The only shoots that should not be shortened are the leading (terminal) shoots of each main branch that are needed to extend the plant.

Give the second pruning in spring immediately after flowering or, if flowers are not borne, when the new leaves begin to develop. Prune the shoots shortened to seven or eight leaves the previous summer to within half an inch of their bases. By repeating this treatment each year the most stubborn wistaria will be induced to bloom.

Root pruning is another way of inducing wistarias to bloom. It is more drastic and less sure than the pruning method outlined, but is sometimes very effective.

At a distance of two to three feet from the main stem or trunk dig a trench around the wistaria to a depth of three feet, then cut underneath to sever any tap roots. Fill the trench with lean, porous soil.

Wistarias that are blooming well may benefit from annual fertilization with a complete fertilizer. Give those making excessive vegetative growth superphosphate (three ounces) and sulphate of potash (1½ ounces) to each square yard. •